FACTORY-ORIGINAL
AUSTIN-HEALEY
100/6 & 3000

FACTORY-ORIGINAL
AUSTIN-HEALEY
100/6 & 3000

The originality guide to six-cylinder Austin-Healeys, 1956-1967

This book is dedicated to the memory of
Brian "Bic" Healey, 1925-2014

BY BILL PIGGOTT

PHOTOGRAPHY BY SIMON CLAY

Herridge & Sons

Published 2014 by
Herridge & Sons Ltd
Lower Forda, Shebbear
Beaworthy, Devon EX21 5SY

Photography by Simon Clay
Designed by Ray Leaning, MUSE Fine Art & Design

ISBN 978-1-906133-57-3
Printed in China

CONTENTS

INTRODUCTION AND ACKNOWLEDGMENTS 6
A LITTLE AUSTIN-HEALEY HISTORY 12
AUSTIN-HEALEY 100/6 – AN OVERVIEW 27
AUSTIN-HEALEY 3000 – AN OVERVIEW 32
ENGINE 40
CARBURETTORS AND FUEL SYSTEM 48
COOLING SYSTEM 55
EXHAUST SYSTEM 58
TRANSMISSION AND REAR AXLE 60
CHASSIS 65
STEERING 68
SUSPENSION 70
BRAKES 72
WHEELS AND TYRES 75
ELECTRICAL EQUIPMENT 78
LAMPS AND LIGHTING 84
DASHBOARD, INSTRUMENTS AND CONTROLS 89
INTERIOR TRIM AND BOOT INTERIOR 98
BODY AND BODY FITTINGS 112
WEATHER EQUIPMENT 125
TOOLS AND HANDBOOK 134
OPTIONS, EXTRAS AND ACCESSORIES 136
PAINT AND COLOUR SCHEMES 143
IDENTIFICATION AND DATING 150
THE NUMBERS BUILT 155
PRODUCTION CHANGES 161

INTRODUCTION AND ACKNOWLEDGMENTS

I was very pleased a year or so ago to be asked if I would undertake this present volume. Not only because it is always a pleasure to work for a family firm such as Herridge & Sons in this age of corporate mega-publishers but also because, having written a companion book on the earlier four-cylinder Austin-Healey 100 models back in 2005, it is gratifying to have the opportunity to "complete the set" by covering the later six-cylinder cars.

This book deals with the Austin-Healey sports cars assembled by the British Motor Corporation under their Austin aegis between the summer of 1956 and the start of 1968, initially at their Longbridge plant, but for most of this period at the MG works in Abingdon. I use the word "assembled" advisedly for in truth a very large proportion of the finished Austin-Healey was actually put together at the Jensen plant in West Bromwich, near Birmingham. Jensen's, as sub-contractors to Austin, not only built up the body/chassis units but painted them, fitted the dashboards, instruments and wiring and even partially trimmed the cars.

These six-cylinder Austin-Healeys are now usually referred to by the generic epithet of "Big Healey", a term which dates back

This lovely BN4 100/6 belonging to Sara and Nick Walker was once owned by the author back in the 1980s; in those days it was red with a white works hardtop. The car is one of the 50 100/6s originally fitted with Dunlop 4-wheel disc brakes.

Also unusual is an Austin-Healey 3000 Mark I in what appears to be factory black, belonging to Peter Hayward. In fact, this car is actually a very dark blue and is doubly unusual as it still has disc wheels and is fitted with a white works-style hardtop.

to the introduction of the diminutive Austin Healey Sprite in 1958, "Big Healey" being employed simply as shorthand to differentiate these cars from their little brothers. The term has now spread backwards to encompass also the 1953 to 1956 Austin-Healey 100 models. On the subject of nomenclature, where it is necessary to refer to the six-cylinder Austin-Healey's four-cylinder predecessor, I shall use its correct title of Austin-Healey 100 and not the retrospective and ugly "100/4". Similarly I will not describe the 1962/3 3000s as "Mark IIA" cars – this was not their designated title, which at the time was "Mark II Convertibles" to differentiate them from the earlier Mark II cars which had retained side screens and the old "kit of parts" soft-top. The factory type number of "BJ7" can also be used correctly as shorthand for this Mark II Convertible.

On a practical note I should point out that throughout this book, where I use the terms right- and left-hand side, I am writing from the standpoint, or rather sitting point, of the driver, rather than looking at the car from the front. The initials BMC, used throughout the book, are of course short-hand for the British Motor Corporation, the "umbrella" company that brought together former rivals Austin and Morris in 1952, along with MG, Wolseley and Riley. Fortu-nately I do not have to refer much to the subsequent disaster of British Leyland. Luckily the demise of the 3000 almost exactly coincided with the transformation of BMC into the ill-fated and unloved British Leyland conglomerate, thus ensuring that Donald Healey's masterpiece was never disfig-ured by the BL corporate "plug-hole" badge. Nor did the car have to suffer the indignity of emasculation by USA market

Quite by coincidence the other 100/6 photographed for this book also carries an original Warwick XNX registration number. This 100/6 in the rare Primrose Yellow has belonged to Mike and Mell Ward, stalwarts of the Austin-Healey Club, for many years.

emission-control equipment, which manifested itself at roughly the same time. The Big Healey remained a splendid, politically-incorrect and anachronistic dinosaur to the end!

In compiling this book I have been greatly assisted by three gentlemen in particular, two directly and one indirectly. Directly by photographer Simon Clay who has travelled very many miles to capture superb images of several lovely orig-inal or correctly restored cars and also directly by Roger Moment in the USA, a man who is one of the world's leading authorities on the Austin-Healey, having driven, studied and

Kindly made available while for sale at Rawles Motorsport is this low-mileage 3000 Mark I BN7 two-seater, fitted with the rare disc wheels.

This 3000 Mark II BN7 car has spent much of its sheltered life on the Isle of Wight. A rare and original car, it has covered just 26,000 miles from new in 1962 and was kindly made available by the owner Jo Harwood.

Lee Manley's attractive Mark II Convertible is finished in Colorado Red. The A-suffix on the registration number indicates that the car dates from 1963. Note the BMC "rosette" emblem showing in the top corner of the windscreen.

Another low mileage car is Peter Healey's Mark III 3000, Peter being Donald Healey's grandson. This car still has all its original paperwork, weather equipment and interior and has never been either restored or fully resprayed.

restored these cars for more years than he may care to remember. Roger has patiently dealt with my queries and even managed at short notice to produce photographs to illustrate points that were not otherwise covered.

Indirect assistance has come from the work of Anders Ditlev Clausager , a man to whom the British classic car movement as a whole owes a great and often underestimated debt. His pioneering and painstaking work in uncovering,

organising and collating the production and build records of so many British car marques during the time he held the post of Archivist at the British Motor Industry Heritage Trust at Gaydon is truly invaluable, and I have drawn heavily on his research for this present volume. Although it is nearly a quarter of a century since he produced his book *Original Austin-Healey*, little improvement on his work has proved possible, particularly in the area of production records,

Mike Huish's 3000 Mark I started life as a 100/6 and was used by the Abingdon Works as a development car and 3000 prototype. It looks particularly dramatic against a clear blue sky.

Gordon Bailey's 1966 Mark III 3000 represents the final development of the Big Healey, the "Phase III" version of the Mark III. This is confirmed in this head-on view by the presence of the separate indicators and side lights.

The Austin "corporate" crinkle-bar front grille of the period shows up well in this frontal view of the late 1957 100/6, one of the last of the Longbridge-built cars.

numbering and dating of the cars. There is after all no need to "reinvent the wheel", so where appropriate I have quoted Anders Clausager's figures and tables very much as he compiled them. Facts are facts and where better for these to have been drawn from than from the archives of BMIHT when Anders was Archivist there. Thank you all, gentlemen.

As to the cars themselves, my thanks are due to the following owners who kindly made their vehicles available for photography, sometimes in weather that was not too clement. They were: Sara and Nick Walker (Blue/White 100/6), Mike and Mell Ward (Primrose 100/6), Mike Huish (Red/White prototype 3000 Mark I), Peter Hayward (Dark Blue/White 3000 Mk I), Jo Harwood (Black/Red 3000 Mark II), Lee Manley (Red 3000 Mark II Convertible), Peter and Trudy Healey (Red 3000 Mark III) and Gordon Bailey (White/Black 3000 Mark III). In addition I received great help and courtesy

The Primrose Yellow hue of this Abingdon-built 100/6 stands out nicely on what was a dull Autumn day.

All it needs is a chromed bell on the front! This view of an almost black 3000 in your rear view mirror in 1960 might have meant that you were being followed by the police; several forces ran 3000s as pursuit cars, and a photo of one is on page 21.

Seen from this low angle, the Mark II 3000 looks particularly aggressive – almost as if it is baring its teeth! The Big Healey was one of the Kings of the Road in its day and is still a car to be respected 50 years later. Note the correct "Ace" type number plates.

from Andrew Cluett of Rawles Motorsport near Alton in Hampshire. This firm specialises in Big Healeys, both sales and restorations, and Andrew made their workshops and sales stock available to myself and the photographer. This included the Green/White 3000 Mark I car featured, and also enabled us to include shots of cars under restoration.

My thanks are also due to Charles and Ed Herridge of the publishers, for having the faith to commission this work and for their understanding when delivery of the manuscript was somewhat tardy; to Mell Ward for her answers to my many questions; to James Taylor for so ably editing my jumble of

A Phase II Mark III 3000 always looks good in red, particularly with the top down. The unusual rear indicator arrangement is original to this car.

The 1950s Lucas 7in auxiliary lights look smart in this view of a Mark I 3000, but they must have impeded the flow of cooling air to the radiator. This lovely car was provided by courtesy of Andrew Cluett of Rawles Motorsport Ltd.

words and pictures; to the late Brian Healey and to Bill Cummings both of the Healey Drivers Club for their help with archive photographs and also with the sourcing of the cars; to John Wheatley for granting me access to his collection of Austin-Healey pictures; to Bob Kemp for all his assistance with matters photographic and to Brian Wheeler for providing a gallery-head 100/6 engine to be photographed at a time when no other could be found. I must also thank the unknown enthusiast who parked his nicely original 100/6 at Silverstone just at the time when I needed some detailed photographs of this model that were otherwise missing. He may be surprised to see his car in this book.

Finally, a large thank-you and a metaphorical bouquet must go to my wife Stephanie, not only for her patience while this volume was in preparation and for putting up with a dining room strewn with Austin-Healey photographs, but also for so ably converting my poor handwriting into an electronic format that could be understood by those much better versed in the ways of computers than I am. Thank you all.

Bill Piggott
Herefordshire, May 2014

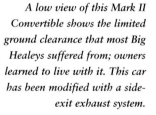

A low view of this Mark II Convertible shows the limited ground clearance that most Big Healeys suffered from; owners learned to live with it. This car has been modified with a side-exit exhaust system.

A side-on view of a late 3000 Mark III from 1966 shows clearly the extra ground clearance that this model had.

A LITTLE AUSTIN-HEALEY HISTORY

A delightful shot of Donald Healey in later life, looking relaxed and leaning against one of his most famous creations, the racing 100S. (By courtesy of the late Brian Healey)

January 1932 in Perranporth, Cornwall, and Donald Healey is about to leave for Sweden in a low-chassis, works-entered Invicta to start the Monte Carlo rally. He won the event outright in 1931, and in 1932 he came second. The man shaking his hand and wishing him and his crew well as he departs is none other than his own father. Cigarettes appear to have been essential! (By courtesy of Bill Cummings)

If ever a car was of its time, that car was the big Austin-Healey. In those carefree days of petrol at four gallons for a quid, minimal regulation and (allegedly) endless summer, the compact yet brutish and powerful Healey embodied all that was best in British sports cars – cars that you could go to work in from Monday to Friday and yet drive far and fast at the weekend. You could even race and rally them in standard form, should the fancy take you. With their large saloon-car and even truck-derived engines and transmissions, they were rugged and reliable.

The age-old formula of putting a relatively big engine into a relatively light car endowed the Healey with more than adequate performance, even for today's roads, let alone those of the 1950s. In 1959, the Austin-Healey 3000 was one of the fastest British production cars you could buy, giving more oomph per pound spent than almost anything else, though Triumph TR owners might beg to disagree... The car was simple mechanically, capable of home maintenance though demanding a fairly intensive schedule, and very tolerant of abuse. Luggage capacity was reasonable for a sports car and waterproofing was better than average, particularly if the attractive optional hardtop was specified. Should the buyer have opted for the 2/4-seater version, as most did, it was even

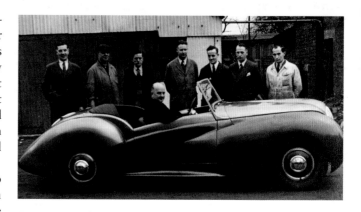

Donald Healey sits proudly in one of the earliest Healey cars, a Westland roadster, at the Warwick works where it was assembled. The date is circa 1947 and the men behind probably comprised the majority of his workforce at that early date. On the extreme right is Roger Menadue, a senior engineer on the project. (By courtesy of Bill Cummings)

possible to pack two children into the rear, thus postponing for some years the need for the rather sad "family forces sale" advert that used to appear regularly in the classified columns of *Motorsport* or *Exchange and Mart*.

Yes, maybe the six-cylinder Austin-Healey was a little thirsty, even for its day; yes, maybe it was prone to overheat both its engine and its passengers; and yes, maybe the ground clearance did leave something to be desired. But it looked both beautiful and purposeful – million-dollar looks that meant one could forgive the car's relatively few shortcomings. As someone memorably said, "It looks as if it is doing 100mph when standing still" – such was the beauty of line displayed by the Healey's sleek, Gerry Coker-designed bodywork, particularly in its original 1952 four-cylinder form. It was a car that one could forgive almost anything just for the pleasure of looking at it, but more than that, it went as well!

So, how did this combination of looks, speed and durability come into the world? To answer that, we must look back to the 1920s and the exploits of the car's eponymous creator, Donald Healey. Healey, born in Cornwall in 1898, grew up with a fascination for things mechanical; in his teens he took up an engineering apprenticeship with the Sopwith Engineering Company, one of the leading early aeroplane manufacturers. However, by 1916, when he was still not 18 and not really old enough to enlist, events had taken a hand in the form of the Great War and he found himself in the Royal Flying Corps, the predecessor of the Royal Air Force, his grade that of aircraft mechanic.

From this it was but a short step, in those pressing times, to becoming a pilot, which was what Healey had set his heart on. However, he had a number of near-misses flying early aircraft and was considered lucky to have survived a final crash which caused him to be invalided out of the RFC before the end of the war. He was transferred to the Air Ministry as an aeronautical inspector when he was barely 20 years of age!

Concurrently with his interest in aircraft, Donald Healey developed a passion both for wireless building and, more importantly for this story, for motoring, rapidly becoming a successful trials and rally driver with a series of Rileys and Triumphs. By the late 1920s, his was a well-known name in competition motoring and in 1931 he was awarded a works drive in a 4½-litre Invicta sports, one of the period's most rakish and rapid cars. He justified the company's faith in him by winning the Monte Carlo Rally outright that year, and almost repeated the feat in 1932, when he finished second. During the 1930s, Healey went on to become Riley's rally car engineer. This was followed by an appointment at Triumph as their experimental engineer, a post which allowed him to create the legendary straight-eight supercharged Dolomite sports racing car in 1934. Rising to become Triumph's technical director, his career was interrupted at the end of the 1930s by two events – Triumph's insolvency and the outbreak of war.

War work for Healey, by then aged 41, meant overseeing the production of aircraft carburettors at the requisitioned Triumph works, and it was while thus engaged that he mulled over ideas for a post-war sports car. When the time finally came in 1945-46 to translate his paper sketches into reality, there was a major problem – shortage of almost all raw materials. However, by a combination of his business acumen and his motor industry contacts built up in the 1930s during his time with Rileys and Triumphs, Healey was able to source a limited amount of steel and aluminium. Most importantly, he was also able to secure small supplies of a powerful, compact and well-proven engine – the 2443cc Riley "Big Four". This advanced design featured twin camshafts with a cross-flow cylinder head, and punched out almost 100bhp. Its only major disadvantage was a long stroke, which rather limited revs, although it did ensure large quantities of torque at low speed.

The new Healey chassis featured massive side- and cross-members and an unconventional trailing link design of independent front suspension. Further Riley components

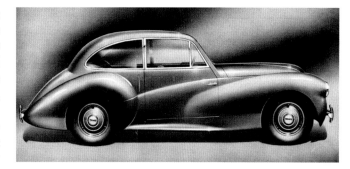

In addition to the open cars, a close-coupled saloon was devised, as shown in this catalogue illustration. The Healey chassis was bodied by Elliott's of Reading. This car was officially timed at 110mph in 1946-47 and was recognised as the fastest closed production car in the world.
(By courtesy of Bill Cummings)

This exceedingly rare and charming period colour photograph from around 1949-50 shows a Healey Westland at an unknown event and location. As the car is unregistered, it could be a Press or demonstration day or similar, and the driver looks as if it could be Roger Menadue. Note the rather home-built looking special in the background. (By courtesy of the late Brian Healey)

included the gearbox, the torque-tube transmission and the rear axle, the latter controlled by coil springs and a Panhard rod. Healey rented a small industrial premises in Warwick, where he assembled the chassis himself with his son Geoffrey and a handful of talented engineers recently released from war work. Such was progress that the first car, bodied as an open tourer by Westland Engineering in Hereford, was running and ready to be shown to the press in January 1946.

One of the very first British cars of post-war design, this prototype had proved easily capable of topping 100mph, then the benchmark of a really fast car, and it received very favourable press comment. Indeed, Healey could have sold hundreds in that first year had he been able to manufacture them, but lack of finance to expand and continuing materials shortages conspired against him. Just a handful of Healeys was built in 1946, including a four-seater sports saloon bodied by Elliot Coachworks of Reading which promptly claimed the title of the world's fastest saloon car.

By late 1947, production of the completed Healey chassis had reached two or three a week, all being bodied by various specialist coachbuilders in a variety of styles. The cars quickly gained a reputation for both speed and quality, but the time had now come to produce an out-and-out sports car. So the standard chassis was bodied with a stark, cigar-shaped two-seater with cycle wings, minimal weather protection and weight, and a windscreen that could be lowered to reduce frontal area. Enter the Healey Silverstone, named after the then newly opened racing circuit in Northamptonshire. Although only 105 examples were built in 1949-51, it proved capable of 110-115mph and was an excellent and safe circuit car, as well as a perfectly practical road vehicle.

Many later-to-be-famous racing drivers learned their craft driving a Silverstone, and the model did much to cement Donald Healey's reputation as a serious builder of serious sports cars. It was only the imposition of a huge Purchase Tax levy and continuing materials shortages that prevented many more Healeys being built. As it was, Donald's small Warwick concern, employing fewer than 30 people in total, managed to build and sell nearly 1300 Healeys of all styles in the 1946-1954 period – quite a feat for what was very much a motor industry "minnow".

However, Mr Healey had his mind set on bigger things and in 1951 his thoughts turned to how he could penetrate the lucrative export market for sporting cars, particularly that of the USA. The fabulous Jaguar XK120 at the top end and the basic but fun MG T-types at the bottom end had proved that there was a large market in North America for cars that were different to their home-grown products, and the UK government was prepared to back potential dollar exports with plenty of raw materials in what was still a strictly controlled post-war austerity market.

What was needed was a sports car that would inhabit the middle ground between the XK120 and the MG – something capable of 100mph, 25mpg, carrying two plus their luggage in reasonable comfort, being used as an everyday car and able to be built to sell at a basic price of well below £1000. It also had to incorporate well-tried, simple mechanicals from a major manufacturer, for Healey could not hope to finance the design and production of his own engines and transmissions. Healey was not alone in correctly identifying the gap in the

market, so there was time pressure to come up with a completed design as soon as possible; it was known for instance that Sir John Black at Standard-Triumph was also desperate to capture this potential market.

Thus, in mid-1951, Donald and his son Geoffrey began working on what became the Healey 100 in conditions of great secrecy, with only a handful of talented right-hand men to assist them. The car was designed and assembled in the experimental shop at the Warwick works behind closed doors; the majority of the small workforce had no idea what was afoot. For the mechanical components, Healey turned to another of his many motor industry contacts. This was Sir Leonard Lord, managing director at Austin, which had yet to be absorbed into the British Motor Corporation. Austin had tried to break into the US market with their Atlantic model in 1949, but without much success. As production was lower than anticipated, there was a stock-pile of Atlantic 2660cc engines, gearboxes and associated components for which Austin had no immediate use. Although quite heavy, this four-cylinder engine was proven, reliable, rugged, and produced 90bhp with plenty of torque at low revs. It was also cheap and available. Donald was therefore minded to base his prototype around this engine and transmission, and Lord was happy to oblige with the loan of components to ensure the prototype 100 chassis could be constructed.

This was running by spring 1952, but as yet neither Healey nor his body stylist Gerry Coker had settled on what the car should look like when clothed. Many mock-up bodies were tried over that summer, but eventually the sleek, sweeping two-seater body that we have come to know as the Austin-Healey was arrived at, although some small details of the front grille and the question of whether to add rear fins remained unresolved. Coker had a difficult job in that he had to fit the body around a number of immovable fixed points on the chassis and yet retain the purity of line that Donald wanted. That he succeeded brilliantly has never been doubted by those who have seen his work, for the (Austin) Healey 100 is frequently cited as one of the most beautiful cars ever designed.

As soon as the body style was agreed, Coker himself drove the unclothed chassis to Tickford Coachworks in Newport Pagnell, where he stayed while their craftsmen translated his ideas into reality. Thankfully, any suggestion of rear fins was deleted and a diamond-shaped grille was added – a lowered version of that used on the bigger Healey cars. A unique feature was added in the form of a folding windscreen which slid forwards into what was called a "racing" position for high-speed work.

At this stage, it was assumed that Tickford would be building the production bodies, a maximum of 10 per week being envisaged. In the event, however, the car's instant success saw production transferred to Jensen Motors, which

This is the more than somewhat eccentric Austin Atlantic, the car that gave its engine and other mechanical items to the Healey 100 in 1952. The Atlantic was the British idea of the car that the Americans wanted... they didn't!

proved capable of building them at 10 times that rate, such numbers being totally beyond Tickford's capability. In the few weeks between the prototype's completion and the opening of the 1952 London Motor Show on 21 October, the car was driven for several thousand miles with relatively few problems becoming manifest. Some of those miles were at top speed, for the car was taken not once, but twice, over to the Jabbeke-Ostend highway in Belgium. Its use here included a flat-out road test by Gregor Grant of *Autosport* magazine, surely a risky procedure as there existed just the one car! With the screen folded, the 100 more than lived up to its name, finally being timed at 111mph with its creator at the wheel. This was indeed a sports car.

Upon its return safely to the UK, the prototype was hurriedly touched up and duly appeared as a last-minute entry at the Motor Show – too late to be included in the catalogue. Healey was still unhappy about the front grille, but was reluctantly persuaded to allow the car to be exhibited. His concerns were unfounded; the Healey 100 was the star of the show and was continuously surrounded by admiring crowds. The basic price had been set at £850 plus tax, which in the UK took it to £1084, a figure still within the realms of middle-class affordability. The real problem was going to be how to finance production and make enough to satisfy demand.

Luckily, these difficulties did not have to exercise Donald's mind for long, for at the show's press day were Sir Leonard Lord and Lord Nuffield, perhaps better known as William Morris. Both were impressed with the car and saw that it could fill a gap in the range of their newly created British Motor Corporation. Lord was particularly enthusiastic, as the car would utilise those redundant Austin Atlantic components, so he arranged to meet Healey that evening where the bones of a deal were agreed. Austin would take over production of the 100 at its Longbridge plant, paying Healey a royalty on each vehicle. Donald and his team would be responsible for development of the car at Warwick and would run a competition department to be financed by Austin. As it would be six months before a production line could be readied at Longbridge, it was agreed that the first 20 cars, to be used as demonstrators and competition cars, would be assembled by Healey's workforce at Warwick, who were still at that time also building chassis for the Riley-engined Healeys.

THE 100 (BN1)

The deal with BMC suited both parties admirably. Literally overnight, the prototype car at the show was re-badged as an Austin-Healey and a further £100 was cut from the price at Lord's behest. It is not exaggerating to say that the new Austin-Healey was an overnight sensation and huge numbers of orders were taken for the car, especially from the USA. All that remained to do was to develop the model for series

A recently unearthed 1953 Austin publicity shot of the 100 emphasises the car's sporting credentials. Although the transparency has faded it is worthy of inclusion here as a photograph of a very early 100. (By courtesy of John Wheatley)

production and build it in quantity. Those ordering accepted that they would have to wait for delivery and it was June 1953 before the first production cars rolled off Austin's line.

By that autumn, the first customer cars were starting to appear in competition, following the works team cars that

This is one of a series of well-known photographs taken at Austin's Longbridge plant in September 1953. Production of the 100 was then reaching full capacity. This is the finishing shop, and an inspection party of some sort appears to be making a visit. (By courtesy of John Wheatley)

had competed successfully in the June 1953 Le Mans race. Press road-test reports were glowing and the Austin-Healey 100 was an undoubted hit, both on the race tracks and in the showroom. The basic concept was so "right" that few modifications were needed as production increased through 1954 and into 1955. Gearboxes gave trouble when worked hard and lack of ground clearance caused many complaints, but overall, as a value-for-money 100mph car, it was hard to fault.

The rival Triumph sports car, by then renamed the TR2, had had many more problems reaching its series production stage, its development being some six to nine months behind the Healey. It was £150 cheaper than the 100, but was much more basic and once it was equipped with options to bring it to the same level as the Healey, it cost almost the same. Nor did it look anything like as beautiful, as even its most ardent fans would have to admit.

With the 100 becoming so successful so quickly, the other Healey models became increasingly sidetracked and although small-scale production did continue into 1954, the Riley and American Nash engined cars simply faded away, with all efforts at Warwick being concentrated on the Austin-Healey. That first series of 100s was given the Austin designation of BN1, a shorthand which is still in use today to differentiate the first three-speed and overdrive gearbox cars from the second series of 100s, type BN2, which emerged in late summer 1955.

The racing Austin-Healey was the 100S model, and this one is finished in White over Lobelia Blue, as were most of the 50 production examples. This car, RLF 500, is one of only seven originally sold new on the UK home market. (Author)

100 (BN2) AND 100 S

Although looking virtually identical, the BN2 series featured a much stronger four-speed gearbox with overdrive as well as a more robust hypoid rear axle and other detailed mechanical improvements. It was also available with the option of a somewhat tuned engine producing 110bhp, a 22% increase, and this derivative became known as the 100M. A clamour from existing owners of BN1 cars soon ensured that this "Le Mans" tuning kit was made available separately from Warwick, and over the years very many BN1s and standard BN2 cars have been, and still are being, upgraded to this specification. Sadly, the much sought-after BN2 series cars were only built from August 1955 to July 1956, a total of 4604 being constructed, compared with 10,030 BN1 variants.

Part of that 1952 agreement between Donald Healey and Leonard Lord had been that Austin would finance a competition programme for the 100. Four "special test" works cars were built at Warwick in 1953, three for circuit racing and one designed to break speed records, which it duly did. Two of the three cars were developed over the next 18 months into what became a limited-production "off the peg" sports racing car called the 100 S. This proved very successful, both in the hands of Healey works drivers (including Donald himself) and also keen amateurs, and 50 "production" examples found buyers during 1955, mainly overseas. Three more special works 100 S cars were also built in 1954. The model was equipped with a cross-flow cylinder head which helped the 2660cc engine produce 132bhp, performance being assisted by extensive use of aluminium panels which made the car considerably lighter than the BN1 or BN2 models.

The author's Austin-Healey 100 shows off its stylish rear view during a tour of Mid-Wales. Well wrapped-up in the passenger seat is the author's wife, who typed up much of this book. The car is finished in the classic and enduring Healey blue, a colour available throughout Big Healey production from 1953 to 1967. Donald Healey himself selected this colour for use on the prototype 100; it had originally been devised for use by Alvis on their post-war TA21 saloon. (Author)

Probably the most famous Austin-Healey of all is NOJ 393, seen here in 2013 at the Knockhill circuit in Scotland following its meticulous rebuild. This car was one of the original Healey Works "Special test" cars built in 1953 for racing, and became a forerunner of the production 100S model. It was involved in the disastrous accident at the 1955 Le Mans 24-hour race that killed more than 80 people, although its driver, Lance Macklin, was absolved of all blame. Following more than 40 years of storage up to 2011, it is now once again doing the job it was created for. (Author)

The tuned version of the 100 was the 100M model, roughly half-way in terms of power output between the standard car and the 100S.

Austin-Healey "royalty" seen in 2013. On the left is a low-mileage 100M, fitted with the stylish louvred bonnet and leather strap. Although not finished in a standard colour, the car looks extremely smart in this deep shade of blue. Next is the wonderful Austin Healey 100 fixed-head coupe ONX 113 that Donald Healey had made for himself in 1955. It was fitted with a 100S racing engine, was by all accounts both comfortable and rapid, and was used by Healey for many years. Consideration was given to putting this car into limited production, a plan that was curtailed by the arrival of the 100/6 model in 1956. Beyond can be seen the 100S racer NOJ 393 and then one of the Abingdon Works rally Healey 3000s. (Author)

100/6 (BN4 AND BN6)

The Healey factory continued to race the 100 S in a limited way into 1956, by which time the works cars were giving nearly 150bhp with reliability. Early that year, however, a major change was thrust upon the reluctant Healey family when senior management at BMC insisted that the Austin-Healey should use the Morris Engines-developed six-cylinder 2639cc engine in place of the old Austin Atlantic "four". This caused curtailment of the competition programme of the four-cylinder 100 S and indeed indirectly the demise of 100 S production. It also caused some consternation at Warwick

One of the rarest of Healeys is the factory-built 100M version of the short-lived 100 BN2 model. One such, SLR 7, is seen here at Healey's Warwick works in 1956. The lady is Angela Lane, a fashion model of the day who is believed to have owned the car. The gent sitting in the vehicle is Brian "Bic" Healey, one of Donald's sons, who at the time was the company's sales manager. Sadly Brian Healey passed away at the age of 88 while this book was in preparation. (By courtesy of the late Brian Healey)

This recent shot of a 100M engine shows the larger 1¾in H6 SU carburettors and the associated cold-air box air intake and trunking. The medallion on the cold air box was a normal feature of the 100M, although the polished rocker cover is a later addition. (Author)

A dramatic shot of a new BN2 car taken in 1956. The windscreen is in the folded position and the car is finished in the then newly introduced colour of Florida Green. This was available right through to the Mark III 3000 cars in the mid-1960s, although the author has never actually seen a Florida Green Mark III! Haute Couture was still the order of the day, the picture being taken at the Donald Healey Motor Co's sadly long-gone London showroom at 64 Grosvenor St, Mayfair. (By courtesy of John Wheatley)

when a BN1 car, fitted retrospectively with the six-cylinder motor, proved both slightly slower and more cumbersome to handle than the four-cylinder car.

The reasons for imposing the change were said to be a management decision to use the C-series six-cylinder engine in as many models as possible, coupled with a desire to end production of the four-cylinder engine at once. In the event, production of the four-cylinder motor continued for different applications for at least a further 10 years, so the change need never have happened! Nevertheless, BMC moguls insisted and overrode Healey's objections. Eventually all turned out well, for, as we shall see, the C-series engine proved capable of considerable development with reliability right up to 150bhp and the handling problems caused by its extra weight proved possible to resolve. However the two cars did, and still do, feel quite different to drive – the BN1 and BN2 models appear lighter and more nimble than the six-cylinder cars, which have heavier steering and a tendency to understeer. The later cars are more rugged and eventually proved faster, albeit with a considerably increased fuel consumption. Few of the six-cylinders can better 22mpg, whereas a well tuned BN1 or BN2 will get near to 30mpg on a long run. Both types have their own faults and advantages; you pays your money and you takes your choice, as they say.

This first model of six-cylinder Healey was designated type BN4 and was called, logically, the 100/6. Next to the new

An early 100/6 catalogue which emphasises the luxury aspect of the car...well, all things are relative, aren't they? (Author)

All instruments are easily readable, being closely grouped in a panel in front of the driver. On the opposite side of the covered fascia is a grab-handle for the convenience of the passenger.

Each of the adjustable bucket seats in the neatly designed interior is upholstered in latex foam rubber, with hide facings. The backs tilt forward to give access to the rear seats.

Gears are selected by a short central gear lever and for driving comfort the 17-inch diameter wheel has spring spokes.

As well as a parcel shelf beneath the fascia, each door has an open pocket for personal items, and a hard wearing carpet over the entire floor completes the stylish interior trim.

The spare wheel and battery with master switch are stowed in the rear compartment and there is a surprising amount of space available for family luggage. A master switch operates from inside the compartment which has a lockable lid enabling the car to be safely left unattended.

'100 Six' with De Luxe Equipment

In this view of the finishing shop at BMC's Abingdon sports car factory, 100/6s are to the fore. As both Mark 1 Sprites and a Twin-Cam MGA are in view, the shot must date from mid-1958 or later. (By courtesy of John Wheatley)

engine, the other major change was the addition of two small bucket seats in the rear. These were capable of seating children of maybe 8 or 9 years old maximum, but not suitable for even the smallest adult, at least when the top was erected. Austin felt that these extra seats would broaden the appeal of the car, which to some extent they did. However, even though an extra two inches were added to the car's wheelbase, their incorporation still meant that both the battery and spare wheel had to be repositioned into the boot, and this made serious inroads into what had earlier been good luggage capacity for a sports car. Certainly, the extra seats could be used to carry further luggage if needed, but a family of two adults and two children would have had very little space to carry anything.

As a ploy to keep the basic price down, three items that were previously standard on the 100 were now expensive extras – overdrive, wire wheels and the heater. To make matters worse, although the C-series engines nominally produced 102bhp, 12bhp more than the previous engine, in practice there was a certain lack of torque. Combined with increased weight, this led to inferior acceleration. The

'an impressive increase in punch'

John Bolster and Roy Salvadori put the latest Austin Healey 100 Six through its paces.

BOLSTER How do you find her with the new cylinder head, Roy?

SALVADORI This new 6-port induction system gives her an impressive increase in punch, particularly in top from 50 to 80. You know the technical story — one port to each cylinder means vastly better gas flow. The upshot of it is, BHP is now 117 at 4,750 revs. The Austin Healey always had plenty of dig, but now it's really outstanding.

BOLSTER Does her handling match up to this performance?

SALVADORI Oh, more than that. Push her really hard (she's a first-rate sprint car) and she still handles beautifully. The gear-change is as slick as they come, and the ratios are just the job for fast work on the intermediates.

BOLSTER How about finish? Not exactly Spartan, is she?

SALVADORI No, thank goodness. I sell Austin Healeys and I know my customers. Sleek lines, modern colour schemes, leather upholstery, the lot — that's what they want and that's what they get. This car's a gem.

BOLSTER Speaking as a racing driver or a salesman, Roy?

SALVADORI Both, old boy.

AUSTIN HEALEY

THE AUSTIN MOTOR COMPANY LIMITED · LONGBRIDGE · BIRMINGHAM

In late 1957, the six-port head and its much-needed power boost arrived for the 100/6, so BMC felt compelled to shout about it. Who better to do the shouting than the splendidly eccentric and knowledgeable John Bolster of Autosport *magazine and top racing driver Roy Salvadori? At last the car went as well as its predecessor. (Author)*

We will see some part of this advertisement again in monotone in the 100/6 Overview section, but here it is in colour. Instead of the door interior and sidescreens, we are now treated to views of the engine and front suspension instead. This demonstrates that the BMC publicity department were not above a bit of recycling when it suited them. Note the position of the oil filter housing on the engine block; it was quite impossible to change the filter element without spilling prodigious quantities of old oil. (Author)

cylinder head design on this engine was poor, there being no separate inlet manifold, but the problem was rectified in September 1957, a year after 100/6 production commenced. A new type of six-port cylinder head released a further 15bhp, enough to restore performance to the old four-cylinder levels. At roughly the same time, construction of the 100/6 moved from Longbridge to the MG factory at Abingdon, which found itself designated as BMC's specialist sports car works.

Despite the wider appeal of the 2/4-seater Austin-Healey, there was a latent demand, particularly from competition-minded individuals, for a two-seater version to be re-introduced. BMC obliged during 1958 by making the BN6 model, which retained the longer wheelbase but had the small seats deleted and the spare wheel and battery (twin batteries in this case) back where they had been in the BN1 and BN2 cars. This variant sold very well for a time, but demand dropped off dramatically by the early 1960s, after which time all "big" Austin-Healeys had the 2/4-seater configuration.

A colour front cover on Motor magazine must have set the publicity budget back a bit in 1958. The gentleman is doing what one was told never to do – apply weight to a sports car windscreen. Still, I don't suppose it was his car... (Author)

The production life of the 100/6 was virtually the same as that of the four-cylinder car, lasting around three years from summer 1956 to summer 1959. Comparable numbers were sold too, and the Healey's greatest market by far was once again in the USA. A total of around 15,400 100/6s of both types were built, the majority of them at the Abingdon plant. 4150 of those cars were of the BN6 two-seater version.

3000 MARK I (BN7 AND BT7)

With the exception of a small batch of 50 cars built at Abingdon in late 1957 with four-wheel Dunlop disc brakes, all 100/6s had continued with the BN2-type Girling drum brakes on all wheels. By 1959, this was looking alarmingly outdated for a fast sports car, for the rival TR3 had been fitted with front-wheel disc brakes since September 1956 and even relatively ordinary saloon cars were now appearing with this superior type of fade-free braking system. As a result, the Healey was granted 11-inch Girling front discs and at the same time the opportunity was taken to increase engine capacity by 10% to 2912cc. This change unleashed around

12% more torque and an increase in compression ratio at the same time improved the brake horsepower figure to 124 from 117. Taken together, these changes were quite noticeable on the road, and the marketing department lost no time in renaming the car the Austin-Healey 3000. It was indeed a superior car to the superseded 100/6 and was launched with some fanfare in June 1959. Both body styles remained available, the 2/4-seater being type BT7 and the two-seater carrying type number BN7.

The Austin-Healey 3000 was current for 8½ years, although during that time there were a number of variations and improvements, as this book will later reveal. The first type was built at Abingdon, in common with all the 3000 variants, until May 1961 – a total of 13,650 cars made up of 2825 BN7 two-seaters and 10,825 BT7 2/4-seaters. This period, between 1959 and 1961-62, was very much the heyday of the 3000 as a successful international rally car, campaigned under the banner of BMC's Competition Department at Abingdon and also by a number of keen private owners. The 3000 became very much the "must have" rally car, succeeding Triumph's now outdated TR3/3A series and predating the 1963 emergence of the Mini Cooper in its tuned "S" form. The high point of the Austin-Healey's competition career was probably the outright win in 1960's gruelling Liège-Rome-Liège rally by the indomitable combination of Pat Moss and Ann Wisdom.

Nor was the 3000 just a formidable and virtually unbreakable rally car, for it was also found on the world's racing circuits at all levels. It provided enthusiastic amateurs with a relatively cheap way into racing, using the car in virtually standard form, and appeared in high-level international sports car racing in lightweight and highly tuned guise. Indeed, it was the desire of the Competition Department to wring more power from the ageing 3-litre engine that led indirectly, in May 1961, to the introduction of the 3000 Mark II model.

A most unusual photograph showing a police officer with what one presumes to be his patrol car, albeit unmarked. Finished unsurprisingly for the period in black and with disc wheels, this Mark I 3000 carries a Devon registration, so one assumes that the Devon Constabulary ran a sports car or two to try to keep up with the villains in their 3.8 Jaguars. (By courtesy of Bill Cummings)

AUSTIN HEALEY 3000
MARK II

faster off the mark for three good reasons

Three reasons: Get into an Austin Healey 3000 Mark II. Accelerate. You feel a new response. A joyous surge-forward you never experienced before—not even in an Austin Healey 3000. The previous one didn't waste any time, but this one has an unfair advantage. It's got three carburettors where the other had two. That means in simple terms you've got 130 b.h.p. to play with as compared with the previous 124. That means an even finer rally car. An even finer pleasure car. And the extra price of the extra carburettor is frankly nil: the car costs

£824 plus £378.18.1 Purchase Tax and Surcharge.
More points: The Mark II is not only an even faster car. it's also an even safer car. It's still got disc brakes on the front of course, but as an optional extra the braking can now be servo-assisted. And inside the car are all the necessary fittings for seat belts.
Still more points: New camshaft. New air cleaner. New heat shield for silencer. New grille and air-intake slats.

GET INTO AN AUSTIN AND OUT OF THE ORDINARY!

THE AUSTIN MOTOR COMPANY LIMITED · LONGBRIDGE · BIRMINGHAM · Personal Exports Division: 41/46 Piccadilly · London · W1

BMC's publicity people felt that maybe they should crow about the new triple-carburettor engine in November 1961, as well as a number of other changes detailed in the small print. Strangely, though, nothing is said about the new centre gear-change lever that arrived that same month. (Author)

A further example of a recycled advert, as this same basic drawing of the car was used in several guises. Here it is superimposed on a hunting scene and the car has turned into a Mark II with vertical-barred grille. As it is still a two-seater, it must represent the exceedingly rare RHD Mark II BN7. (Author)

3000 MARK II (BN7, BT7 AND BJ7)

This time, the main specification change was the incorporation of triple SU carburettors in place of the previous two. This allowed the Abingdon works to homologate their rally cars with three carburettors – even twin-choke Webers. It also meant that Healeys at Warwick, who still looked after the Austin-Healey racing team, could do the same with their circuit 3000s. Visually, the Mark II cars could be distinguished by a new front grille with a series of upright bars rather than the horizontal "wavy" type of the 100/6 and Mark I 3000s.

This pleased Donald Healey, who had a theory (which seemed at the time to be true in practice) that expensive cars had vertical grille bars and cheaper cars had horizontal ones!

The production period of the BN7 and BT7 Mark II cars was relatively short, from April 1961 to June 1962, and in that 15-month period 5450 cars were made. Of these, a mere 355 or 6% were of the two-seater BN7 configuration. Demand was dropping rapidly for the roadster, so it was not surprising that the two-seater variant was dropped altogether when the new BJ7 model appeared in 1962, sporting vastly improved weather equipment. There was a considerable overlap in production at this time, for the first BJ7 cars (often called the Mark IIA) were built as early as February 1962, whereas the final BN7 and BT7 Mark II cars were made in June 1962.

To add to the confusion, the new BJ7 series was still called the 3000 Mark II, whereas by rights it should have been called a Mark III. Thus we have two different types of Austin-Healey 3000 Mark II. The first is the 1961-62 cars with triple carburettors, 132bhp, old-style clip-in sidescreens and a DIY hood. The second is the 1962-63 BJ7 cars, which returned to twin carburettors (albeit with no significant loss of power) but sported winding glass side windows, a more comfortable interior and a soft-top of the full convertible type which could simply be pulled over the cockpit in one movement and provided much improved weather sealing. 6113 examples of the BJ7 cars were built between February 1962 and late 1963, all being of 2/4-seater configuration.

through a Borg Warner automatic transmission. The engine produced 175bhp and plenty of torque and performance. In fact, those who have driven an example agree that the 4000 was quite a car, especially in the manual gearbox form used for the second and third cars. BMC went so far as to commission a short pre-production run of the cars, but this was cancelled when it became clear that making the 4000 comply with impending US legislation would cost just as much as doing the same for the well-tried 3000.

The Healey name did remain alive for a time on Sprites, and on the 1970s Jensen-Healey. In the meantime British Leyland made one more (fortunately abortive) attempt to revitalise it. They misguidedly tried to rebadge the lacklustre MGC as an Austin-Healey. The Healey family, however, refused to sanction the use of their name in this fashion and so, on the afternoon of 21 December 1967, the final production Big Healey left the assembly lines at Abingdon. I say "production" for there was actually one more car built as late as 14 March 1968. This vehicle, with chassis number BJ8-43026, was an ivory white home market car delivered to long-time BMC dealers H A Saunders Ltd in Worcester. Quite why this happened is not now known; it was built form spares in the Abingdon "show" shop rather than on the production line, and maybe there was some special influence at work – who knows? This final Healey 3000 has survived, been restored and is currently domiciled in the USA. In addition to this sole 1968 car, there were a couple of USA-bound cars still awaiting rectification work at the end of 1967, but otherwise that was it and the former Austin-Healey 3000 lines henceforth produced MGCs.

THE BIG HEALEY TODAY
Since its demise some 47 years ago, the legend of Donald's "hairy chested" Big Healey in all its forms has only grown, as has the value of the cars themselves. Taking inflation into account, to buy a top-condition 3000 Mk III today would cost roughly three times more in real terms than it cost to buy a new one in late 1967. All models of Big Healey are highly desirable in today's classic car market, a market which can now be said to be truly global.

Collectors from places as diverse as Japan, Australia, Latin America, Canada and all parts of Western Europe admire and seek out the Healey, not to mention of course enthusiasts from the car's spiritual home of the USA, for it must not be forgotten that overall almost 90% of all 100/6 and 3000 production was sold new in that country. In no way is it exaggerating to state that, without the North American market, not only would there have been no Austin-Healey but none of the other large-scale production British sports cars of the 1950s, 1960s and 1970s would have existed either. It would have made no commercial sense just to build them for UK customers or even for the wider European market. The Austin-Healey was a tremendous export success

This is one of the two prototype Mark III 3000 fixed-head coupés built circa 1965 as possible contenders for production. Sadly for Healey enthusiasts, management preferred the somewhat insipid MGB GT; based on its subsequent popularity and 15-year production life, who is to say that they were wrong? A pity, though – the 3000 coupé was quite a car. It was yet another BMC/BL "might have been"... (By courtesy of John Wheatley)

The last gasp of the Big Healey was the magnificent 4000, fitted with the 4-litre Rolls-Royce engine. Six inches wider and somewhat longer than production cars, it looked like a 3000 on steroids. One of the three prototypes is seen on an Austin-Healey club rally in Scotland. (Author)

The 4-litre Rolls-Royce engine as installed in the Austin-Healey 4000. Even that illustrious name could not save the Big Healey from extinction at the end of 1967. (Author)

as well as a success in both rallies and races.

Although all the models covered by this book are perennially sought after, it is true that some variants are more desirable than others. The 100/6 models, particularly the 2/4-seater BN4 type, are less valuable than their later brothers, although there is a premium on the rarer BN6 two-seater version, as well as on the later BN7 3000 two-seaters. The most desired variant is still, as it has always been, the Phase II version of the 3000 Mark III, the final development of the car. Although the four-cylinder 100s are outside the remit of the present volume, it should be added that these cars, so long in the shadow of the six-cylinder models, have in recent years come to be recognised for the excellent and stylish vehicles that they are. As a result, values of good examples, particularly 100M and BN2 variants, have gone at least as high as the late Mark III 3000s.

In value and desirability terms, the Mark I and Mark II 3000s are placed roughly halfway between the 100/6 and

the 3000 Mark III. However, the later Mark IIs with the full convertible hood and winding windows are worth rather more than the earlier Mark IIs, which reflects both their rarity and increased practicality and comfort. Price variations aside, all models of Big Healey will provide their lucky owners with a vehicle that is both beautiful and purposeful at the same time, a car that always attracts admiring glances. Not only that, it is a car that can still deliver its original purpose – to be fast and fun to drive – and driven it has to be as there are no mod cons in a Big Healey!

Even in current traffic conditions, a Healey will not be left behind, although it must be accepted that fuel will be consumed at an alarming rate if the full performance is utilised. Even in their day, the six-cylinder Healeys were never the most economical of cars. But they are distinctive and wholly representative of a different, carefree, pre-social conscience, pre-green era – dinosaurs, in fact, but what wonderful dinosaurs!

AUSTIN-HEALEY 100/6 – AN OVERVIEW

This high-angle view of a well-restored 1957 BN4 car clearly shows the centre-line crease in the bonnet only found on 100/6s – and even then, not on all of them. Although the chromed wire wheels look smart, it is very doubtful whether they were available new on home market cars at this date, even as a dealer fitment.

The Austin-Healey 100/6 was announced at the end of September 1956 and became available to purchase with almost immediate effect, from October that year. Not an ideal time in the UK as it coincided with the Suez Crisis and the imposition of petrol rationing! At introduction, only the 2/4-seater model was available, type BN4. Availability of this continued until the introduction of the 3000 in June 1959, although the final cars were actually built in March 1959.

In fact, no BN4 cars were built between 28 April 1958 and 22 September 1958, allegedly because Abingdon production was concentrating on the 2-seater BN6 model. However, it is believed that a stockpile of unsold BN4 cars had built up, which may have been a secondary reason for this hiatus. The basic UK price of the BN4 was £762 on its 1956 introduction,

but this did not include wire wheels, overdrive or a heater. With these items added and including UK purchase tax, a BN4 would have cost £1223.

The two-seater 100/6, type BN6, was built between April 1958 and March 1959. Basic UK price at introduction was £817 without overdrive, heater or wire wheels. When UK tax and these fitments were added, the April 1958 price of the BN6 became £1306, although this had reduced to £1235 by the time that the car was discontinued.

The 100/6 was assembled in the BMC plants at Longbridge in south-west Birmingham and at Abingdon, then in Berkshire but now in Oxfordshire. Series production of the BN4 at Longbridge commenced in August 1956 immediately after that of the four-cylinder BN2 had stopped, and it continued

AUSTIN-HEALEY 100/6 – GENERAL SPECIFICATIONS

Engine capacity	2639cc (161 cubic inches) six-cylinder, with overhead valves
Bore and stroke	79.4mm x 89mm (3.125in x 3.50in)
Compression ratio	8.25 to 1 (later 8.7 to 1)
Maximum power	102bhp at 4600rpm (later 117bhp at 4750rpm)
Maximum torque	142 lb ft at 2400rpm (later 149 lb ft at 3000rpm)
Carburettors	Two SU type H4 with 1½-inch throat (later two H6, then HD6 with 1¾-inch throat)
Transmission	Four-speed gearbox with synchromesh on second, third and top gears. Optional overdrive by Laycock de Normanville operating on third and fourth gears.

Gear ratios	(Main gearbox)		(Overdrive)
	1st	3.076:1	
	2nd	1.913:1	
	3rd	1.333:1	1.037:1
	4th	1.000:1	0.778:1
	Reverse	4.176:1	

Clutch	Borg and Beck 9in single dry plate type with hydraulic operation
Propshaft	Hardy Spicer type with needle roller bearings
Rear Axle	Hypoid bevel type, ratios 3.909 to 1 (standard cars) or 4.1 to 1 (overdrive cars)
Brakes	Hydraulic operation, with mechanical handbrake operating on rear wheels by means of cable and rod linkage Front: Girling 11in drums, 2¼in wide with twin leading shoes Rear: Girling 11in drums, 2¼in wide with single leading shoe
Suspension	Front: Independent, with double wishbones, coil springs, double-acting lever-arm dampers and an anti-roll bar Rear: Live axle suspended on seven-leaf semi-elliptic springs; double-acting lever-arm dampers and Panhard rod location
Steering	Cam Gears cam and peg type, ratio 14:1 to July 1958 or 15:1 thereafter
Steering wheel	Wire spoked, 16½in or 17in diameter
Turning Circle	35 ft (10.7m) left and right
Wheels	4J x 15in five-stud disc wheels with chromed hubcaps Optional 48-spoke 4J centre-lock knock-on wire wheels in silver paint or chromed (certain export markets)
Tyres	Dunlop RS4 5.90 x 15 tubeless cross-ply on disc wheels; tubed type RS4 tyres with wire wheels

Dimensions		
	Length	13ft 1½in (4.0m)
	Width	5ft ½in (1.54m)
	Height	with top erect, 4ft 1in (1.24m)
	Wheelbase	7ft 8in (2.34m)
	Track	Front 4ft ¾in (1.24m)
		Rear 4ft 2in (1.27m)

Ground clearance	5½in (140mm)
Weight	(with fluids and 5 gallons fuel) standard cars 21½cwt (1092kg) with overdrive 21¾cwt (1105kg)

there until December 1957; 7053 cars, all BN4 2/4-seaters, were constructed. Of these Longbridge BN4 cars, the great majority had the 102bhp "galleried head" engine (see later) although an unknown number, maybe even several hundred, of the final examples had the 117bhp engine fitted with the "six-port" head which is more usually associated with the Abingdon-built cars. Of the 7053 Longbridge cars, 5541 were built in the 1956-57 model year, with 1512 in the 1957-58 year.

When production of the 100/6 started in November 1957 at Abingdon, there was an overlap of several weeks when cars were being built at both plants. As indicated above, the Abingdon BN4 2/4-seater model was constructed in two batches, from November 1957 to April 1958 and from September 1958 to March 1959. In total, these two batches accounted for 4241 cars. Incidentally, when the six-port head cars were first introduced into the USA, they were marketed for a brief period as the 100/6 MM model, MM standing for Mille Miglia.

The Abingdon-only 100/6 BN6 two-seaters, all of which had the six-port head and 117bhp engine, ran from April 1958 until March 1959 and amounted to 4150 cars. Thus the total number of Austin-Healey 100/6s of both types and from both plants is 15,444 cars. Note that much more about numbering and production breakdowns will be found later in this book.

PERFORMANCE
(For cars with "galleried head" 102bhp engine, as tested by *Motor* magazine, 2 November 1956)

Top speed	107mph (172km/h)	
	0-50mph (0-80km/h)	9.3 sec
	0-60mph (0-96km/h)	12.9 sec
	0-70mph (0-112km/h)	17.5 sec
	0-80mph (0-128km/h)	22.6 sec
	0-90mph (0-144km/h)	32.3 sec
Standing start quarter mile (402m)		18.8 sec
Average fuel consumption		23.2mpg
	(12.1 litres/100km)	

(For cars with "six-port" head and 117bhp, as tested by *Autocar* magazine, 30 May 1958)

Top speed	111 mph (179km/h)	
	0-50mph (80km/h)	8.2 sec
	0-60mph (96km/h)	11.2 sec
	0-70mph (112km/h)	14.8 sec
	0-80mph (128km/h)	20.1 sec
	0-90mph (144km/h)	25.8 sec
	0-100mph (160km/h)	37.7 sec
Standing start quarter mile (402 m)		18.1 sec
Average fuel consumption		23.2mpg
	(12.1 litres/100 km)	
Overall test fuel consumption		21.2mpg

The rare and attractive Primrose Yellow finish sets this very correct 100/6 BN4 off nicely; only the later fitment of 72-spoke wire wheels jars slightly.

Speed is emphasised in this early 100/6 advertisement. The artist seems to have forgotten the central bonnet crease, but the occupants nevertheless still look delighted with their purchase. (Author)

The front view of the very rare right-hand-drive BN6 two-seater demonstrates that the bonnet of this model did not have the central crease line. Period wing mirrors (almost useless in modern traffic) are in evidence. The wheels have received a non-original white painted finish. (By courtesy of Brightwells of Leominster)

From the USA comes this view of a LHD BN6 two-seater, again a Primrose Yellow car but this time a rare standard specification vehicle with disc wheels and no overdrive. It was restored some years ago by Healey expert Roger Moment, and clearly shows how the hood on the BN6 is significantly shorter than that of the BN4.
(By courtesy of Roger Moment)

The side view of the same car emphasises the much shallower cockpit of the BN6. The whole car looks shorter than the BN4 2/4-seater, but this is an illusion as they are exactly the same length.
(By courtesy of Roger Moment)

This delightful American advertisement from 1956/57 features Donald Healey himself at the wheel of a new 100/6 in the Bahamas. (Author)

Two 1950s chaps discuss the merits of the 100/6; smoking was still "de rigueur", as was the flat cap, and a sporting driver needs a sports jacket to emphasize his credentials. Note that the inset refers to the archaic practice of hand signalling.

On the 100/6, the body colour correctly extends up the side of the windscreen mounting stanchions. The ride height on this car looks to be just right, whereas tired rear springs cause the rear end to sag on many Healeys, so reducing an already marginal ground clearance.

Although period in style, the placing of these external mirrors much nearer to the cockpit makes them considerably more useful. The classic Austin-Healey colour scheme of Healey Blue over Ivory white is perennially popular and always looks smart, whatever the weather.

AUSTIN-HEALEY 3000 – AN OVERVIEW

Although a somewhat modified car and missing its front over-riders, this Abingdon-registered 3000 Mark I is an interesting "crossover" vehicle. It was built as a late 100/6 and used by Abingdon Works as a development car for the 3000 model, being converted into one of the earliest 3000s prior to sale. It also saw use as a "recce" car for the Alpine Rally. Later 72-spoked wire wheels are in evidence.

The Autin-Healey 3000 model commenced series production in March 1959, three months prior to its public launch in June. As with the later 100/6 there were both two-seater (BN7) and 2/4-seater (BT7) versions, the latter proving much more popular. The early 3000s looked very similar to the 100/6s, though the presence of disc brakes on the front wheels was a good recognition point, as of course was the badgework. The central pressed line running fore and aft on the 100/6 bonnet was deleted for the 3000, but other than that, there were no significant external visual differences.

Under the bonnet sat the larger engine, but again it looked much the same as the 10% smaller capacity 100/6 motor. Compression ratio had increased to 9.0:1 and power output rose from 117bhp to 124bhp, with the larger cubic capacity ensuring a notable increase in torque. Gear and axle ratios were raised to give the 3000 a more relaxed cruising gait, but fuel consumption increased by perhaps 10% compared to the earlier car.

As before, everything was done to keep the basic price

down, the BN7 two-seater costing £824 in the UK (£1168 with tax) while the 2/4-seater BT7 was a little more expensive at £829 (£1175 with tax). Those prices were for unadorned cars, of which relatively few were made. Overdrive added £66, wire wheels another £35 and a heater cost £15. The very smart hardtop added a further £85, and all these prices included tax. So a fully equipped BT7 could cost its owner almost £1400 in the UK, which was sending the car almost into XK Jaguar territory. Nevertheless, sales took off well, almost all of the cars going to North America, and by the end of 1959 just over 7000 Healey 3000s had been assembled at Abingdon in around nine months. This was the highest production rate so far achieved by the Big Healey.

Note that when I use the word "assembled", I mean just that, for it should not be forgotten that Jensens put the body/chassis units together, even painting and partly trimming the cars before they ever reached Abingdon. Not only that, but the body panels themselves came from Boulton and Paul, the chassis came from John Thompson Motor Pressings, the engines from Morris Engines at Coventry and the gearboxes and axles from BMC's transmissions plant in Birmingham. Not a lot was actually manufactured at Abingdon.

The retrospectively named Mark I 3000 continued to be built until May 1961, by which time 2825 BN7 two-seaters had emerged along with roughly four times as many BT7 2/4-seaters; there were 10,825 of these, making 13,650 cars in all. To demonstrate how much of a USA property the Healey 3000 was, a mere 829 of these cars found UK buyers, whereas just over 11,000 examples went Stateside, the rest of the world accounting for the balance.

As often occurred during Autin-Healey production, there was a blurring of the change-over point when the Mark I cars gave way to the Mark IIs, the first of the latter being constructed in April 1961. Specifically called the Mark II from inception, this model was immediately distinguishable from its predecessor by a much more sophisticated and smarter front grille of chrome vertical bars; gone were the Austin corporate "crinkles". The vertical bar theme was echoed in the subsidiary air-intake grille at the front of the raised bonnet pressing. A little "Mark II" badge was mounted below the winged Autin-Healey front badge to dispel any lingering doubts about the car's identity. As previously, both BN7 two-seater and BT7 2/4-seater versions were available.

Under the bonnet, the Mark II immediately proclaimed itself by being the proud possessor of three rather than two carburettors – "Wow, now that really is a sports car," the small boys would chorus! Although they proved somewhat trickier to keep in tune, these three HS4 1½in carburettors, together with an appropriately more sporting camshaft, helped lift the theoretical power output of the Mark II 3000

to 132bhp from 124bhp. However, contemporary road test results recorded that the car was no faster than before and used somewhat more fuel; it must also have cost BMC a little more to build, yet no price increase was made on the outgoing Mark I... So why did this evidently regressive change occur?

Two answers have been suggested; onc is that things *looked* more impressive under the bonnet and thus gave the USA dealerships a new selling point, and the other is that it allowed BMC's Competition Department to fit three carburettors to the works rally Healey 3000s, to the great benefit of their competitiveness and while still complying with homologation rules. So what was in effect a first series of Mark II 3000 ran with this specification for just over a year, giving way in May-June 1962 to the second series which sported the much improved full convertible soft top and winding glass windows. However, during that first year a significant change took place in November 1961, when the long-established Healey tradition of using an offset gear lever with a side-change mechanism came to an end. A new version of BMC's C-series gearbox with a top-mounted centrally positioned selector mechanism was

This 3000 Mark I is to an unusual specification, carrying the expensive hardtop yet fitted with the "basic" steel disc wheels.

PERFORMANCE

3000 Mark I
As tested by *Motor* magazine, 13 July 1960

Top speed	115mph (186km/h)	
	0-50mph (0-80km/h)	8.5 sec
	0-60mph (0-96 km/h)	11.7 sec
	0-70mph (0-112km/h)	15.5 sec
	0-80mph (0-128km/h)	19.9 sec
	0-90mph (0-144km/h)	27.2 sec
	0-100mph (0-160km/h)	39.3 sec
Standing start quarter mile (402 m)		17.7 sec
Average fuel consumption	21mpg (13.51 litres/100km)	
Overall test consumption	18.8 mpg (15.0 litres/100km)	

PERFORMANCE

3000 Mark II with three carburettors
As tested by *Motor* magazine, 26 July 1961

Top speed	113 mph (182km/h)	
	0-50mph (0-80km/h)	8.3 sec
	0-60mph (0-96 km/h)	10.9 sec
	0-70mph (0-112km/h)	14.3 sec
	0-80mph (0-128km/h)	19.2 sec
	0-90mph (0-144km/h)	25.9 sec
	0-100mph (0-160km/h)	36.4 sec
Standing start quarter mile (402 m)		18.3 sec
Average fuel consumption	21mpg (13.51 litres/100km)	
Overall test fuel consumption	20.8mpg (13.61 litres/100km)	

PERFORMANCE

3000 Mark II Convertible
As tested by *Motor* magazine, 10 April 1963

Top speed	116 mph (187km/h)	
	0-50mph (0-80km/h)	7.2 sec
	0-60mph (0-96km/h)	10.3 sec
	0-70mph (0-112km/h)	12.9 sec
	0-80mph (0-128km/h)	16.7 sec
	0-90mph (0-144 km/h)	21.3 sec
	0-100mph (0-160km/h)	29.4 sec
Standing start quarter mile (402 m)		17.3 sec
Average fuel consumption	19.5mpg (14.01 litres/100km)	
Overall test fuel consumption	17.7mpg (15.9 litres/100km)	

AUTIN-HEALEY 3000 – GENERAL SPECIFICATIONS

Engine capacity	2912cc (178 cubic inches) six-cylinder, with overhead valves, BMC C-series type	
Bore and stroke	83.36mm x 89mm (3.28in x 3.50in)	
Compression ratio	9.0:1	
Maximum power	3000 Mark I	124bhp at 4600rpm
	3000 Mark II (triple carburettors)	132bhp at 4750rpm
	3000 Mark II Convertible	131bhp at 4750rpm
	3000 Mark III	148bhp at 5250rpm
Maximum torque	3000 Mark I	162 lb ft at 2700rpm
	3000 Mark II (triple carburettors)	167 lb ft at 3000rpm
	3000 Mark II Convertible	158 lb ft at 3000rpm
	3000 Mark III	165 lb ft at 3500rpm
Carburettors	3000 Mark I	two SU type HD6 with 1¾in throat
	3000 Mark II	three SU type HD4 with 1½in throat
	3000 Mark II Convertible	two SU type HD6 with 1¾in throat
	3000 Mark III	two SU type HD8 with 2in throat
Transmission	four-speed gearbox with synchromesh on second, third and top gears. Optional overdrive by Laycock de Normanville operating on third and fourth gears.	

Gear ratios		(Main gearbox)	(Overdrive)
3000 Mark I	1st	2.93:1	
and side-change	2nd	2.05:1	
Mark II	3rd	1.31:1	1.07:1
	4th	1.00:1	0.82:1
	Reverse	3.78:1	
3000 Mark II	1st	2.83:1	
central change	2nd	2.06:1	
	3rd	1.31:1	1.07:1
	4th	1.00:1	0.82:1
	Reverse	3.72:1	
3000 Mark III	1st	2.637:1	
	2nd	2.071:1	
	3rd	1.306:1	1.07:1
	4th	1.000:1	0.82:1
	Reverse	3.391:1	

Clutch	3000 Mark I and II
	Borg and Beck 10in single dry plate type with hydraulic operation
	Later Mark II Convertible and early Mark III
	Borg and Beck 9½in diaphragm spring type with hydraulic operation
	Later Mark III (from October 1964)
	Borg and Beck 9in diaphragm spring type with hydraulic operation
Propshaft	Hardy Spicer type with needle roller bearings
Rear Axle	Hypoid Bevel type, ratios 3.545:1 (standard cars) or 3.909:1 (overdrive cars)

AUTIN-HEALEY 3000 – GENERAL SPECIFICATIONS (Continued)

Brakes	Hydraulic operation, with vacuum servo assistance optional on Mark II cars and standard on Mark III cars; mechanical hand-brake operating on rear wheels by means of cable and rod linkage Front: Girling 11¼in discs Rear: Girling 11 in drums, 2¼in wide
Suspension	Front: Independent, with double wishbones, coil springs, double-acting lever arm dampers and an anti-roll bar Rear: (Up to chassis number HBJ8 26704) Live axle suspended on seven-leaf semi-elliptic springs; double-acting lever-arm dampers and Panhard rod (From chassis number HBJ8 26705) Live axle, modified chassis frame and axle with six-leaf semi-elliptic springs, double-acting lever-arm dampers and radius arms
Steering	Cam Gears cam and peg type, ratio 15:1, giving three turns lock to lock
Steering wheel	Wire spoked, 16½in or 17in diameter
Turning Circle -	35½ft (10.8 m) left and right
Wheels	4J x 15in five-stud disc wheels with chromed hubcaps Optional 48-spoke 4J centre-lock knock-on wire wheels in silver paint or chromed (as a dealer fitment) (Late Mark II Convertibles and Mark III cars had optional 60-spoke 4½J wire wheels; these may have been available earlier as an option)
Tyres	Dunlop RS4 (later RS5) 5.90 x 15 tubed cross-ply tyres; 165 x 15 radial tyres optional from circa 1962
Dimensions	Length 13ft 1½in (4.0m) Width 5ft ½in (1.54m) Height with top erect, 4ft ¾in (1.24m) Wheelbase 7ft 8in (2.34m) Track Front 4ft 0¾in (1.24m) Rear 4ft 2in (1.27m)
Ground clearance	5in (140mm); 6½in 178 mm) from HBJ8-26705 onwards
Weight	(with fluids and 5 gallons fuel) Mark I and Mark II standard cars 22½cwt (1143kg) with overdrive 22¾cwt (1156kg) Mark II Convertible standard cars 23cwt (1166kg) with overdrive 23¼cwt (1181kg) Mark III standard cars 23¼cwt (1181kg) with overdrive 23½cwt (1197kg)

PERFORMANCE
3000 Mark III
As tested by *Motor* magazine, 26 March 1964

Top speed	122.5 mph (197km/h)
0-50mph (0-80km/h)	6.9 sec
0-60mph (0-96km/h)	9.8 sec
0-70mph (0-112km/h)	12.1 sec
0-80mph (0-128km/h)	14.8 sec
0-90mph (0-144km/h)	18.2 sec
0-100mph (0-160km/h)	23.7 sec
Standing start quarter mile (402 m)	17.0 sec
Average fuel consumption	21mpg (13.51 litres/100km)
Overall test fuel consumption	17.7mpg (15.9 litres/100km)

introduced for the company's big saloon cars and therefore found its way into the Autin-Healey 3000.

In total, 5451 first-series Mark II 3000s were made, but what is striking is how few there were of the BN7 two-seater configuration – just 355 cars in total, a mere 39 of which were right-hand-drive models. Indeed, these figures make such cars rarer than the 1955 100 S racers and therefore the rarest production Autin-Healey of all. Not surprisingly, this drop in popularity led to the two-seater being abandoned when the second series of Mark II cars was introduced, and

all these were built as 2/4-seaters, type BJ7. The first few of the new BJ7s were built as early as February 1962, but true series production of what was a much improved car did not commence until June, while the public launch was delayed until August that year.

Not only were the outdated and unlamented side screens lost in this re-vamp, but these was also a not unexpected reversion to twin carburettors of the type fitted to the Mark I cars. However, because of a clever camshaft redesign, no significant power was lost despite the missing carburettor –

From this angle, only the more substantial wrap-around windscreen differentiates the BJ7 from its immediate predecessors, the Mark II BN7 and BT7 cars.

indeed, road test results found the car to be faster than its predecessor even though weight was increased. Additional soundproofing, heat insulation and better trim were added to this new model, which should properly be called the Austin-Healey 3000 Mark II Convertible, though the shorthand "Mark IIA" is in common use amongst Healey enthusiasts.

These additional items, plus the weight of the new soft top, its mechanism and the accompanying windows, meant that the new car was some 5% heavier than the earlier Mark IIs. Basic price also increased by around 5%, the home market tax-free cost of a standard Mark II Convertible being £865 without overdrive or wire wheels. However, most enthusiasts agreed that this extra cost and weight were prices well worth paying for the increased civilisation and practicality of the new version of an old favourite. An additional bonus for UK

customers was a dramatic reduction in Purchase Tax made in November 1962 in a government effort to stimulate a flagging economy. This hated tax fell from 45% of the basic price to 25%, the net result being that home market Mark II Convertibles became around £150 (or 12½%) cheaper despite their multiple improvements. Allowing for inflation, this latest Healey actually cost less than any of its predecessors. Surprisingly, for what was now a civilised coupé, the heater was still an optional extra at £19, though few (if any) UK cars were built without it. During a manufacturing run from early 1962 to October 1963, 6113 Mark II Convertibles were built, over 90% of which had left-hand drive.

Sales of the Healey had held up reasonably well through all its various guises, but by 1963 a long-term declining trend was becoming apparent. The basic deign was more than 10 years old and this was now the era of the E-type Jaguar and the MGB, both of them much more modern in concept and execution than Donald Healey's ageing but much-loved masterpiece. Continuing success in international competition still came the Healey's way, but if the car was to continue a further major upgrade was necessary. That upgrade came in February 1964 with the launch of the Mark III version of the 3000, which had in fact taken over on the production lines from the Mark II in November 1963. Initially not all the changes were ready for incorporation; the chassis and suspension modifications described later did not arrive until after the first 1390 cars had been built. However, these first cars did feature the much-revised interior which included for the first time a full walnut-veneered dashboard, and they also had a further uprated engine.

The full Mark III specification was finally incorporated into the car around May 1964. Externally the vehicle looked very similar to the first Mark III models, but a keen eye would detect a higher ride height. This was particularly so at the rear for at last an attempt, reasonably successful, had

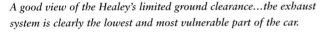

A good view of the Healey's limited ground clearance...the exhaust system is clearly the lowest and most vulnerable part of the car.

been made to address the perennial shortcoming of poor ground clearance and dented exhaust systems. Doing this entailed a redesign of the rear chassis frame, dropping it slightly under the axle to allow greater axle movement. Radius arms were added to provide positive axle location and the old transverse Panhard rod was deleted. A completely new exhaust system helped ground clearance a little, and incorporated no fewer than four silencer boxes, which did much to tame the old Healey rasp. Despite appearances to the contrary, this new and quieter system sapped no more power than the old type. Such is progress!

Under the bonnet a number of engine revisions resulted in

This colourful page from the 1965 3000 brochure still relied on artist's impressions rather than photographs, but then that adds to its period charm. The 125mph claim was a little optimistic, as was the amount of luggage forced behind the seats... maybe the cases were just very small? (Author)

A side view of the 1962-63 BJ 7 Mark II Convertible shows the new civilised folding hood erected, plus front quarter-lights and the deep chromed trim at the tops of the doors.

This contemporary Austin publicity shot shows a late 3000, a Phase III as it sports the separate front side and indicator lamps. One assumes that the car is finished in Healey Blue, but time has caused the original transparency to discolour somewhat. (By courtesy of John Wheatley)

almost 15% more power, which was now a gross 150bhp. Twin 2in SUs and yet another camshaft revision made this possible and, although there was a slight loss of torque at low revolutions, overall the engine was much livelier, resulting in the fastest series production Healey yet. The fully equipped Mark III 3000 was capable of a genuine 120mph, though at the cost of considerable wind noise, and could accelerate from 0-60mph in slightly under 10 seconds. To make sure it stopped, for the first time a vacuum servo was fitted to the brakes as a standard item.

To cap all this, the car was actually more economical than the earlier 3000s had been, despite the greater weight penalty, and up to 25mpg could be had with reasonable driving. The type number of this final development was BJ8 and, surprisingly, more of this last type of Big Healey were sold than of any other previous model, including the BN1 100s of 1953-55. In total 17,712 examples found homes, all but 2,300 of

these in the USA. This total includes the first 1390 cars built without the rear chassis modifications. In the UK the basic price had risen by £50 over the Mark II Convertible, starting at £915, which tax inflated to £1107. As usual, this was for the basic vehicle, for even the heater was still an extra at £19. However, even fewer standard cars were actually sold than previously and a Mark III without wire wheels and overdrive is a rare beast indeed.

From mid-1964, the specification of the 3000 remained constant, although the price rose by £20 in 1966. The only revision worthy of note was the fitment in April 1965 of separate orange flashing indicators for the first time, at least on UK market cars.

And so it was that the Austin-Healey 3000, by then a motoring anachronism, continued to be made and to sell surprisingly well right into 1967. In that last year, Abingdon was still turning them out at an average rate of around 10 per day, for 3057 were constructed between January and December 1967, when the last series-production 3000 rolled off the line with little fanfare just prior to Christmas. One later car was built up from spare parts in March 1968, presumably to special order, but that was that. As the Introduction explains, the Austin-Healey was the victim of new US pollution and safety legislation effective from January 1968, which brought requirements that the car could not be made to meet in any economic or aesthetic way. With its major market gone, cessation was the only option, sadly.

Nevertheless, the Big Healey can be counted as a great success for what was in essence a specialist car. More than 72,000 examples of all types were built over a period of 15 years and a good proportion of these both survive and are cherished today. The car was simply tremendous value for money!

Another Austin publicity shot from 1965 shows a car in classic British Racing Green – the later, and darker, of the two BRG shades used on 3000s. What could be better? A sunny day, a timeless English location and a brand new Austin-Healey to play with, and at someone else's expense! (By courtesy of John Wheatley)

This is the view that most other motorists would have had of a well-driven 3000 in 1966, the year of this car's build.

The power plant of the 3000 is a sturdy six-cylinder overhead-valve unit of 2,912 c.c. capacity. It is fitted with two HD 8 semi-downdraught S.U. carburettors and its oil circulation is protected by a full-flow oil filter which traps all damaging foreign bodies in a replaceable element. Developing 150 b.h.p. at 5,250 r.p.m. this long-lasting engine has already proved itself capable of sustained high-speed motoring in excess of 100 m.p.h. Its smooth, effortless power over long periods of very fast driving is delightfully exhilarating to experience and its lively response through the gears gives to the Austin Healey 3000 Sports Convertible the magnificent sports car performance it deserves!

The BMC 2·9 litre power unit

The robust, four-bearing, fully-balanced crankshaft is fitted with an external vibration damper on its forward end to eliminate any whip at high revs.

With some justification, BMC made much in their advertising of the new 150bhp output of the 3000 Mark III engine when it arrived in 1963-64. Note the paragraph concerning "export availability" and extra cost options, including the display of a 220kph speedometer face. (Author)

Export Availability

The specification covers the general availability of the Austin Healey 3000 Sports Convertible. Certain Production variations are available, however, to equip this car for the markets of the world. The following items of equipment are therefore alternatively available at no extra charge:

Right- or left-hand steering — M.P.H. or Km.P.H. speedometer
Lighting equipment to suit any specific requirement — Six-blade fan
Centigrade or Fahrenheit water temperature gauge.

The following items of equipment can also be supplied at extra cost, provided they are requested at the time of the original order:

Adjustable steering column	Luggage rack
Cigar Lighter	Overdrive
Exterior wing mirrors	Radio
Fog lamp and/or Spot Lamp	Wire-spoke knock-on wheels
Heater and Demister	Tonneau cover
Locking petrol filler cap	Whitewall tyres
Wheel trims (disc wheels only)	Leather trim

A bright red 3000 Mark III squats purposefully on the cobbles in Georgian Bath.

ENGINE

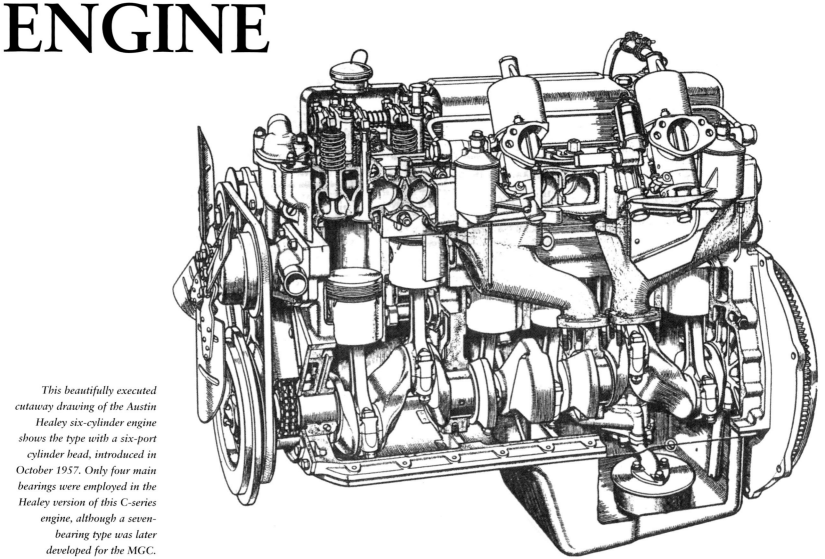

This beautifully executed cutaway drawing of the Austin Healey six-cylinder engine shows the type with a six-port cylinder head, introduced in October 1957. Only four main bearings were employed in the Healey version of this C-series engine, although a seven-bearing type was later developed for the MGC.

The main mechanical difference between the four-cylinder Austin-Healey 100 and the 100/6 was of course the fitment of the BMC "corporate" six cylinder engine known as the C-series. This was designed using the existing Austin B- series engine as a basis in 1953-54 at the Morris Engines branch of BMC in Coventry, principally to power the large saloon cars in the company's range.

This engine was part of Sir Leonard Lord's master plan to have all the company's passenger cars powered by just three types of engine by the mid-1950s. There would be the A-series for the A30 and Morris Minor small cars, the B-series for the medium-sized Morris Oxford and Austin Cambridge, and the C-series to propel the Austin Westminster, Morris Isis and Wolseley 6/90. In fact, Lord's plan failed to some extent, for not only did the old Austin Atlantic four cylinder engine used in the Healey 100 carry on, but so did the large 2½-litre Riley four-cylinder motor that had powered the original

Healey cars. Although little remembered now, there also remained in production the D-series 4-litre six-cylinder, built in limited quantities to power the Austin Sheerline and Princess Limousines and an engine which eventually found itself in the unlikely position of powering Jensen's 541 coupé.

When the C-series was conceived in 1953, it seems unlikely that there were thoughts of eventually using it in the Austin-Healey. The Healey had only just commenced production and nobody knew how well it would sell in the long term, or that it was destined to remain a current model for 14 years. Nevertheless, when the time came, it proved surprisingly easy to swap the much longer and heavier six-cylinder for the old four-cylinder in the Austin-Healey's engine bay. Only the radiator had to be moved forward and a bonnet top pressing incorporated to allow clearance. The extra wheelbase of the 100/6 did not really assist with accommodating the larger engine, for the space it created was used to increase cockpit room.

THE 2639CC ENGINES

When the C-series motor first appeared publicly in October 1954, it was fitted with just a single downdraught Zenith carburettor for use in the Austin Westminster and in this form it produced only around 90bhp, which was hardly a brilliant output for a supposedly modern design of more than 2½ litres. The Riley 2½-litre engine had been providing more power 10 years earlier! When given twin SU carburettors for its Wolseley 6/90 incarnation, the C-series' output crept up to around 95bhp, which was still not what might have been expected. Something around 110bhp would have been nearer the mark.

The problem really lay in the cylinder head and "inlet manifold" design. I use inverted commas here as there was in effect no inlet manifold, simply a mixture distribution gallery cast into the cylinder head itself and to which the H4 carburettors were directly bolted. These were the earlier type of carburettors with vertical dashpots, not the later semi-downdraught variety. This design of what has become known as the "galleried" cylinder head proved somewhat inefficient and, as would soon become clear, materially restricted power output. That did not meet with the Healey family's pleasure. This early engine, producing 102bhp in Austin-Healey form, carried the serial prefix 1C-H, the H standing for high compression. Compression ratio was in fact 8.25:1, the cylinder capacity of 2639cc being achieved by a bore of 79.4mm and a stroke of 88.9mm, the latter considerably shorter than the old 111mm stroke of the engine used in BN1 and BN2 cars. This led to a noticeable loss of low speed torque. Piston speed at maximum power was calculated at 2680 feet per minute and the total piston area was 46.2 square inches.

The basis of the engine, including the head, was cast iron, and the sump, rocker cover and timing chain cover were all of sheet steel. The forged-steel crankshaft featured four main bearings; like the big-end bearings, these were of the white-metal-lined shell type up to 1959, and were replaced by the more durable lead-indium type thereafter. Vertical overhead valves activated by pushrods were used, and were driven from a side camshaft journalled low down on the right hand side of the block. A duplex timing chain drove the camshaft from the crankshaft, with a chain tensioner fitted inside the timing cover. From 1962 a vibration damper was added as well. The camshaft itself was jounalled in four bearings.

THE GALLERIED-HEAD ENGINES

On the galleried-head 1C-H engine, the valves had diameters of 1.69in (inlet) and 1.42in (exhaust). Valve timing was a relatively conservative 5°/45°/40°/10°. Oil was circulated by a

Hobourn-Eaton rotary vane oil pump, oil pressure at 2000rpm when the engine was hot being approximately 55-60psi. Water circulation was provided by a fan-belt driven pump bolted to the front of the block and temperature was regulated both by a fan and by a thermostat housed at the forward end of the cylinder head. Depending on seasons and markets, this could open at any given point between 72° C and 88° C.

On the 2639cc engine there were internal water passages between each cylinder, but to enable capacity to be stretched to 2912cc for the Austin-Healey 3000, the engine was bored out to 83.36mm, which meant the loss of some cooling passages, the cylinders being siamesed in three pairs. Fortunately cooling did not seem to be adversely affected.

Oil filtration was dealt with by a canister-type filter housing with a replaceable felt inner forming the filtering system. On the 1C-H engines the filters were of Tecalemit or Vokes manufacture, and on the various 29-series engines by Tecalemit or Purolator. Filter housings were painted to match the engine itself, and the oil filtration system was of the "full-flow" type.

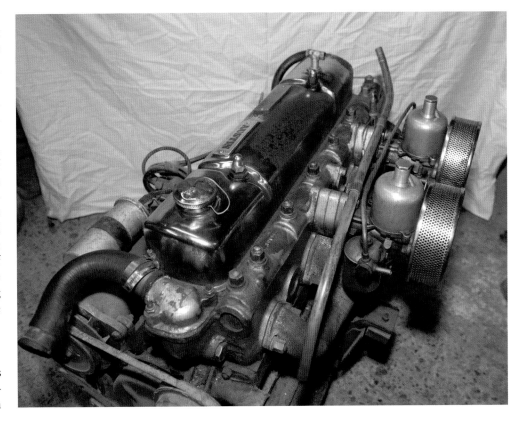

A close-up view of the original type of 100/6 "gallery head" engine: the gallery for mixture distribution which forms part of the cylinder head casting can clearly be seen, with the SU carburettors bolted directly to it. The H4 1½in SUs are of the sidedraught type, with vertical dashpot housings. It did not prove possible to find such an engine still installed in a 100/6 for photography, almost all surviving UK 100/6s having been given the later type of cylinder head over the years. However, this "out of car " view allows more detail to be seen (by courtesy of Bob Kemp).

THE SIX-PORT HEAD ENGINES

Even before the public introduction of the 100/6, both Austin and Healey engineers had been aware of the power deficiencies of the 1C-H engine and accepted that a radical solution was needed. So during the first year of 100/6 production, an entirely new cylinder head was developed. This had six separate circular inlet ports and a conventional detachable inlet manifold. Combined with larger 1¾in HD6 semi-downdraught SU carburettors, this provided better breathing. Valve sizes were increased to 1.75in (inlet) and 1.56in (exhaust), and new flat-topped pistons raised the compression ratio to 8.7:1. Exhaust manifolding was also improved and a very necessary heat-shield between exhaust system and carburettors was introduced. These changes allowed the release of an extra 15bhp and, more importantly, an increase in torque throughout the engine's speed range. Nor was economy significantly affected. This revised engine was given the code prefix 26D and cars fitted with it were introduced, at least in the USA, as 100/6 "MMs", those letters standing for Mille Miglia.

The introduction of the "six-port" engine, as it became known, was slightly slurred in that for a few weeks, cars were being built fitted with both old and new engine types. This kind of thing was not uncommon with BMC. The fact that the engine's public launch coincided with the move of 100/6 production from Longbridge to Abingdon does not help our understanding of what happened. However, several facts are clear. All Abingdon-built 100/6s, whether BN4s or the new BN6s, were fitted with the revised six-port engine, which in effect means that all 100/6s built after November 1957 had it. All pre-October 1957 Longbridge-built 100/6s had the galleried-head 1C-H engine, but BN4 cars built at Longbridge in October and November 1957 could have been fitted with either type, seemingly at random. This was presumably a way of using up the existing stocks of the 1C-H motor as rapidly as possible.

As for the numbers of Longbridge BN4s built in those few weeks with the six-port engine, the records are insufficiently detailed to help, but one source quotes the number as 305 cars. Records nevertheless indicate that the first car so fitted was BN4-48863 and that from BN4-52602 all cars were so fitted. One can only sympathise with a buyer at that period who discovered shortly after taking delivery of his new Austin-Healey that a much superior engine was about to be available!

Those who drove the new car rapidly confirmed that it was a much livelier vehicle throughout the speed ranges at almost no cost in fuel consumption terms. Once the new cylinder head and induction arrangement was settled, it continued throughout the rest of Big Healey production with only relatively minor changes to facilitate power upgrades, as explained below. Incidentally, despite the obvious benefit of the engine upgrades and despite the fact that it could hardly have cost any more to manufacture than the 1C-H gallery head engine, it seems that no other vehicle in the BMC range that used the C-series engine was ever given the benefit of this six-port head and its associated improvements. It was an Austin-Healey exclusive!

These two views show both sides of a 3000 engine with most ancillaries removed. The 12 ports, six exhaust and six inlet, can be clearly seen, as can the fact that the deep part of the oil sump extends only about half-way along the length of the engine. The paint colour is the correct "steel dust grey" – actually a light green. The heater outlet tap is visible towards the rear of the cylinder head in the illustration below.

THE 2912cc ENGINES

Early spring 1959 saw the start of Austin-Healey 3000 assembly at Abingdon, this being the next stage in engine upgrading. In common with all other C-series engined cars, cubic capacity of the 26D engine was increased by 10% to 2912cc by the simple expedient of an overbore to 83.36mm from 79.4mm.

29D ENGINES

This engine became type 29D, the increased cylinder size combined with an unchanged cylinder head automatically raising the compression ratio to 9.0:1. The simple increase in capacity raised power to 124bhp at 4600rpm with a corresponding addition to torque, which now peaked at 167 lb ft at 2700rpm. Oil pressure was somewhat reduced from the 100/6 to be 50psi at 2000rpm in a hot engine. In order to allow the cylinder bore increase the water coolant passages between each pair of cylinders had to be "siamesed", and to cope with the increased torque, extra external stiffening ribs were cast into the crankcase. Otherwise, however, there were no significant differences between the 29D and 26D engines.

29E ENGINES

The 29D engine continued unchanged for almost two years, at which point the 29E series was introduced for the revised 3000 Mark II cars. This was the somewhat infamous version with three 1½in SU carburettors. I say infamous because it introduced both extra cost and complication for, by all accounts, no increase in performance on the road – even though the power output on paper went up to 132bhp. Fuel consumption was also increased to compound the felony, and the reasons for this strange change are discussed elsewhere in this book. In addition, the 29E engine fitted to BN7 and BT7 cars had a higher-lift camshaft which sported a more aggressive valve timing of 5°/45°/51°/15°.

29F ENGINES

When barely a year later the BJ7 Mark II Convertible replaced the BN7 and BT7 duo, yet another engine specifica-

The engine of a Mark I 3000 shows the red-painted shroud over the cooling fan that is an original feature of most cars. The copper heater return pipe is visible, and just behind it can be seen the capillary tube for the earlier type of water temperature gauge.

This is the earlier type of engraved valve clearance setting information plate. It was held to the cover by copper rivets.

tion materialised. This was the 29F series, although it is believed that some early BJ7s still had the 29E valve timing quoted above. For the 29F, valve timing was changed to 10°/50°/45°/15°, but the main change was a sensible reversion to just two carburettors which were of the 1¾in SU HS6 type. Power output was every bit as good as with the three carburettor set-up, but the engine was noticeably easier to keep in tune. Torque was somewhat reduced, but on the road this was not noticeable.

29K ENGINES

Again, however, this 29F engine did not run for long, for when build of the yet to be announced Mark III cars started in October 1963, the final version of the C-series engine was installed, type 29K. This time there was a major increase in output to between 148bhp and 150bhp, depending upon which source one credits. Torque rose to 173 lb ft at 3000rpm, which helped to propel the significantly heavier Mark III from 0–60mph in just under 10 seconds and on to a top speed exceeding 120mph. These figures were virtually the same as the much lighter, out-and-out racing 100 S model of eight years earlier.

This magic was conjured by yet another camshaft profile with valve timings of 16°/56°/51°/21°, fitted together with stronger valve springs. Carburation was revised yet again to utilise two 2in HD8 SUs, and a quieter yet less restrictive exhaust system was fitted. Not only was power increased by nearly 15%, but the 29K engine actually proved more economical than its immediate predecessors. Having finally achieved this state of tune with reliability, BMC's engineers left the engine well alone, and the 29K series ran unchanged until the 3000 model's demise at the end of 1967.

The correct oil filler cap, finished in engine colour and attached by wire to the valve cover. Embossed on the cap are the names of the approved manufacturers of oil for the car.

The same 3000 Mark I engine viewed from the other side. The vacuum ignition advance diaphragm housing is attached to the distributor, which is partially visible. A brass nut held the small-diameter brass pipe to the housing. The other end of the pipe can be seen just in front of the rear carburettor.

FRENCH-MARKET 29FF AND 29KF ENGINES

One small point to note is that an underbored engine of just 2860 cc was used in most (but not all) cars for the French market between 1962 and 1967. This engine was not used anywhere else, and came about entirely due to the vagaries of French horsepower taxation; the smaller capacity made the car qualify for a lower tax rate. For the Mark II Convertibles, these engines were designated 29FF and for the Mark III models the type prefix was 29KF.

ENGINE SPECIFICATIONS

This tabular summary of 100/6 and 3000 engine specifications is used by courtesy of Anders Clausager.

Model	100/6 BN4 (early series)	100/6 BN6 & later BN4	3000 Mark I BN7 and BT7	3000 Mark II BN7 and BT7	3000 Mark II BJ7	3000 Mark III BJ8
Engine type	1C-H	26D	29D	29E	29F	29K
Capacity	2639cc	2639cc	2912cc	2912cc	2912cc	2912cc
Carburation	2 x SU H4	2 x SU HD6	2 x SU HD6	3 x SU HS4	2 x SU HS6	2 x SU HD8
Compression ratio	8.25:1	8.7:1	9:1	9:1	9:1	9:1
Maximum power	102bhp at 4600rpm	117bhp at 4750rpm	124bhp at 4600rpm	132bhp at 4750rpm	131bhp at 4750rpm	150bhp at 5050rpm
Maximum torque	142 lb ft at 2400rpm	149 lb ft at 3000rpm	167 lb ft at 2700rpm	167 lb ft at 3000rpm	158 lb ft at 3000rpm	173 lb ft at 3000rpm

The oil capacity of all these engines was approximately 13 pints (Imperial), including the oil filter assembly.

This shot of a 3000 engine gives a good view of the bonnet release mechanism and return spring. A non-standard fuel filter is in evidence by the forward carburettor – a sensible idea even though not original. The air filter housings should not have a polished finish, and the overflow pipe from the radiator filler should be black rather than red. Shown clearly is the slight angle at which the carburettors are mounted, these being known as the "semi-downdraught" type of SU.

EXTERNAL APPEARANCE

Colours: All engines were painted at their plant of origin, not at Abingdon or Longbridge. The great majority of 100/6 and 3000 engines were painted a grey/green metallic colour known officially as Steel-dust Grey. An unknown number of early Abingdon built 100/6s did however have their engines painted in the standard Morris olive green engine paint.

Engine colour paint was used also on the dynamo, starter motor, engine mounts, including the rubbers, heater valve, oil filter housing, heater return pipe and oil breather tube. It was sometimes (but not always) used on other small standard engine fittings.

Top end: All engines had a pressed steel rocker (valve) cover that fitted over two threaded studs. On the 1C-H engines, the rocker cover was secured by domed nuts. The later engines initially had flat washers under T-headed fasteners, and then from around 1960 shallow cup washers with a rubber interface were fitted below the T-headed fastener. All rocker cover fastenings were painted engine colour.

The rocker cover also had an oil filler cap with a twist-lock action, the cap being wired to the cover to avoid loss. All 100/6 and 3000 engines were labelled on the rocker cover simply "Austin" – never Austin-Healey – and most also carried a plate on the cover that detailed correct valve (tappet) clearances. These two plates were riveted to the cover by tubular alloy or copper rivets. The Austin label was in blue letters on a silver background, and the tappet clearance label was initially of unpainted brass with engraved lettering, but later a printed transfer label on aluminium was employed. The rear of the rocker cover carried a T-shaped breather tube, which on one side vented into the rear engine tappet cover and on the other side into the rear air cleaner.

Tubes and hoses: The breather tubes were originally made with a woven finish, these later being replaced by smooth rubber. The rubber hose between tappet cover and rocker cover was painted engine colour. Hoses were originally secured with flat clamp-type clips, but these were later replaced by wire clips in most cases.

Engine numbers: The engine number, which included the engine type prefix, was stamped or pressed into an aluminium plate secured to a plinth on the left-hand side of the cylinder block below the manifold. On some engines this number plate was left unpainted, but on others it was painted the same colour as the engine.

Views from each side of a late 3000 Mark III engine. The larger 2in HD8 SU carburettors are in evidence. The Tudor screenwash bottle has migrated to under the bonnet because its former home on the under-dash parcels shelf no longer existed on the Mark III cars. They had full-width polished wooden dashboards instead.

The later information plate was a printed transfer type fastened by aluminium rivets. The engine always simply carried the Austin name rather than Austin-Healey. The bolts, washers and black rubber sealing rings that held the cover down are visible.

CARBURETTORS AND FUEL SYSTEM

The twin H4 SU carburettors on the "gallery head" early 100/6 engine were sidedraught types with vertical rather than inclined dashpots. These have the correct brass hexagon tops to the piston dampers. The air-cleaners shown are the original drum type with oil-wetted gauze filters. (Courtesy of Bob Kemp)

When introduced in 1956, the 100/6 was equipped with twin SU H4 1½in throat carburettors. These were somewhat unusual and differed from the H4 units used on the four-cylinder cars in that they were of the older sidedraught type, rather than the later semi-downdraught type. The airflow was horizontal through the instruments and the piston dashpots were vertical.

The standard needle fitted was AJ, the weak needle being M1 with the rich needle being a number 4. The piston springs fitted were red type. Early examples of the 100/6 with the 1C-H engine used the same Burgess air filters as had the BN2 models, a drum type with oil-wetted metal gauze as the filtering medium. They were painted Hammertone green with black and silver Burgess nameplates. From car number BN4-48862, Coopers air filters that were similar in design were substituted, the Coopers name being pressed into the cover in raised letters.

There were no float bowl overflow tubes on these H4 carburettors. A copper fuel feed pipe connected the two float bowls with banjo fittings; the forward carburettor float chamber was connected to the chassis fuel line by a reinforced flexible pipe to allow for engine movement. A metal heat shield was attached to the exhaust manifold studs in a not wholly successful attempt to protect the carburettors from exhaust heat. The choke mechanism was manual, and a black central bracket fixed between the air cleaners provided an anchor point for the Bowden cable that ran through the bulkhead to a choke control knob mounted under the dashboard.

SIX-PORT ENGINES

When the six-port or 26D engine was introduced in October 1957, carburation was considerably changed. Twin semi-downdraught SU carburettors with 1¾in diameter throats were fitted, type HD6. These carburettors are immediately differentiated from the sidedraught H4 type by their angled mounting. For the first time, a separate inlet manifold was used and although this was painted green, the paint failed to adhere properly to the cast aluminium and rapidly disappeared. The inlet manifold was equipped with two small-diameter steel drain tubes, one at each end. At their lower ends they were fastened to a bracket held by a long oil sump bolt on the left-hand side of the engine. Quite why this venting of the inlet manifold to atmosphere did not cause upset to the mixture is a mystery to the author!

Standard needles for these HD6 instruments were type CV, with rich and weak needles types RD and SQ respectively. Yellow piston springs were fitted. The heat shield was improved with a layer of asbestos attached to its underside, and its position was changed so that it was now interposed between the carburettors and the inlet manifold. Revised Coopers air cleaners were used, being of the thinner "pancake" type, one bolted to each carburettor. They were painted either engine colour or, more commonly, silver and had Coopers decals visible at their tops.

Oil-soaked, reusable gauze mesh was once again the filter medium. Metal overflow tubes were fitted on the HD6 instruments, attached through a banjo fitting under the float bowl lid bolt. These overflow tubes extended below the exhaust manifold for safety's sake on the 100/6, but when the same HD6 carburettors were used on the 3000 Mark I,

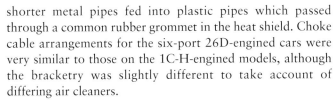

shorter metal pipes fed into plastic pipes which passed through a common rubber grommet in the heat shield. Choke cable arrangements for the six-port 26D-engined cars were very similar to those on the 1C-H-engined models, although the bracketry was slightly different to take account of differing air cleaners.

AUTOMATIC CHOKE

The HD6 carburettors with the same needles continued (despite the larger engine capacity) for the 3000 Mark I. However, after roughly 2000 cars had been built, there was a brief and somewhat unsuccessful flirtation with the SU automatic choke system, known as a "thermo" or "starting" carburettor. The system was used reasonably successfully on several Jaguar models. No manual choke was fitted, but a small auxiliary carburettor was interposed between the two main instruments. This drew fuel from the rear float chamber and dumped it directly into the inlet manifold when the engine was cold, control being by a thermal switch fitted at the front of the cylinder head. As soon as the engine achieved a measure of heat, this switch cut the starting carburettor out by means of an electrical connection. The whole arrangement proved unreliable and was prone to sticking "on" for far too long, causing flooding problems. It introduced unnecessary complication and, in any event, most enthusiastic Austin-Healey buyers much preferred to have manual control over the choke.

The thermo carburettor was introduced at engine number 29D-2864 in mid-1959 and was deleted that November at engine number 29D-6395. After its deletion, a manual choke was re-instated and at the dashboard end was re-sited to the main dash panel above the heater controls. Incidentally, at this same change point, the SU carburettors received indented black plastic tops to their piston dampers, replacing the nicer

The later 100/6s and earlier 3000s had HD6 1¾in carburettors, which were of the later semi-downdraught type. The linkages and choke cable are clear here. Note also the small-diameter pipe connecting to the left-hand carburettor; this conveyed the inlet manifold vacuum to the distributor. Again, the brass hexagon tops to the dampers are in evidence.

Above left: This detail shot of the HD6 carburettor shows the correct type of Cooper "pancake" air filter, with correct decals and colour. The level of shine on the dashpot is just about correct; SUs did not come from the factory highly polished. The Lucas flasher unit can be seen just to the right of the air filter.

Carburettors on the 3000 Mark I were much as on the later 100/6, and brass hexagons were still in evidence. The clamp for the choke cable can clearly be seen by the left-hand air filter, and again, Cooper air filters finished in engine colour are in evidence. The brass banjo-type connections on the float chambers can be seen, connected to each other by a rigid steel pipe.

Mark II 3000s of both types, BN7 and BT7, featured these triple SU carburettors, which were HS4 types with a 1½ in throat diameter. By this time in 1961, the brass hexagon tops to the dashpots had been replaced by cheapskate plastic versions. The air filters on this engine are not correct, and should be of the Coopers type. A transverse balance pipe is connected to each individual inlet manifold by short black rubber hoses. The complex throttle linkage can be seen, as can the bell crank on the bulkhead. The choke mechanism pivot is also on view with its "2 to 1" lever. This car features the optional brake servo, and so there is a rubber pipe leading from the front manifold across the top of the engine to the servo unit. The polished alloy valve rocker cover is a nice touch, though non-original.

The triple-carburettor engine is seen here in a different car, viewed from the other side. The air filters are correct here, but an in-line fuel filter has been added. This car sports after-market polished dashpot covers, and the brake servo pipe appears to take off from the balance pipe, which is unusual.

traditional brass hexagon tops. These plastic tops continued for the rest of the Healey 3000 production run.

The automatic choke arrangement is very rarely seen now, as a large number of the cars built with it have been converted to manual choke operation. Others have had the thermal switch replaced by a manual electrical switch so that the driver can control when the auxiliary carburettor cuts in and out. Post-November 1959 3000 Mark I cars reverted to the same twin HD6 carburettor arrangements as their pre-automatic choke brethren.

TRIPLE CARBURETTORS

March 1961 saw the introduction of further complication, for the Mark II 3000 was announced sporting triple SU carburettors, each mounted on a separate cast alloy inlet manifold. This change took effect from car number 13751. Further concurrent changes were necessary both to throttle and choke linkages. The carburettors on these 29E-series engines were of the new HS type, which differed quite considerably from the previous HD and H types of SU. Three 1½in semi-downdraught HS4 instruments were used, standard needles being type DJ, with DK and DH as the rich and weak needles respectively. Piston spring colour was red. The three individual inlet manifolds were connected by a transverse balance pipe with right-angled stubs that were attached to the manifolds by short rubber hoses with wire clips. Mounted on top of this pipe was a bracket, and on it pivoted a choke linkage lever, mounted so that it gave a 2:1 mechanical advantage. One end of this lever was pushed or pulled by the Bowden cable from the choke knob on the dashboard, while the other end was attached to three individual cables, one to each of the three carburettor choke mechanisms. It was an arrangement that did not look as though it would work satisfactorily for very long.

Throttle linkage also proved complex on these "tri-carb" cars, access not being at all easy for tuning purposes. Their three slim Coopers air cleaners, finished in hammered silver

After the excess of the triple-carburettor era, the Mark II Convertible reverted to twin instruments. They were 1¾in HS6 types, as shown here, a modernised version of the earlier IID6 carburettors. Older brass hexagon tops on the carburettors seem to have replaced the plastic type.

paint with decals, further hampered access. Carburettor float chambers were interconnected by flexible braided fuel hoses, the front carburettor feeding the other two and receiving fuel through a further flexible hose with a support bracket, fed from the fixed chassis fuel line. To allow for fuel overflow, each float chamber lid had a clear plastic reinforced tube elbow which was connected to a black plastic tube reaching downwards. The rear two of these tubes descended through holes in the bulkhead chassis brace, the front one through the opening between the inner wheel arch and the shock absorber mounting tower.

During the brief run of the 29E engined "tri-carb" Mark II, several fuel system changes were made. From engine 29E-2995 in November 1961, the carburettors were fitted with nylon, rather than metal floats, this being so for all subsequent SUs used on Healey 3000s. It was also found necessary to increase the diameter of the inter-manifold balance pipe and to improve the operation of the float chamber overflow pipes. Major difficulties occurred with fuel vaporisation, always something of a problem with Big Healeys principally because the relatively large engine inhabited a relatively small space. Therefore the heat shield was now covered in asbestos on both sides, as a partially successful solution. Do not tell the Health and Safety folk, or you may find your Healey condemned and taken away in a polythene bag!

29F TWIN-CARBURETTOR ENGINES

Problems with the cost, complexity and tuning of the 29E engine "tri-carb" arrangement saw a reversion to twin 1¾in SUs when the Mark II Convertible BJ7 models were introduced in spring 1962 with 29F series engines. Updated HS6 carburettors were used, which had as their standard needles type BC, the weak and rich needles being respectively TZ and RD. A green piston spring was employed.

As already mentioned, these HS-series carburettors had significant differences from earlier types in the area of the jet and float design and also the fuel mixture adjustment mechanism. As on the Mark I 3000s, the carburettors had overflow tubes fixed to the float bowls to avoid fuel getting near to the exhaust system, which would have been a fire risk. On each of the HS6 carburettors, the overflow outlet was part of the float bowl lid; reinforced plastic tubes connected to this and passed downwards through a common grommeted hole in the heat shield, venting to atmosphere approximately level with the lower edge of the engine block.

Throttle and choke linkage and the associated bracketry on the 29F engine were very similar to their equivalents on the later 29D engines previously described. The inlet manifold still had the two steel drain tubes running from each lower corner of the manifold down the side of the engine and fixed by extended sump bolts at the bottom. The carburettors were attached to the inlet manifold by four studs each. Interposed

All Mark III cars had the distinctly fatter HD8 carburettors. The new choke mechanism included a bracket on the bulkhead, with the twin choke cables coming from it. The front cable was given a support stay, which is visible here. This otherwise very original, low-mileage car has a non-original chromed valve rocker cover.

A close-up shot of the HD8 instruments clearly shows the fatter air filters that Mark III 3000s carried. The braided fuel hose is a good idea from a safety point of view, but is a replacement for the original type.

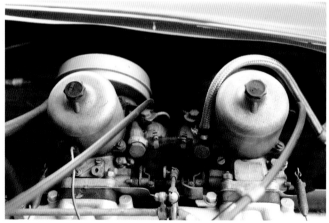

between the manifold and the carburettors was the usual heat shield, painted engine colour, now with asbestos lining only on the manifold side. Further heat insulation was provided by two insulator blocks made of grey or buff-coloured composite material for each carburettor, one mounted on each side of the heat shield. Blocks and heat shield were all carried by the same four elongated studs that located the carburettors.

CARBURATION FOR THE 29K SERIES ENGINES

Not surprisingly, yet another carburation set-up was required for the more highly tuned 29K series engine employed in the Mark III 3000 of 1963-67. For the first time, the largest production type of SU was required, the 2in throat HD8 instrument. Two were fitted and, as before, they were of semi-downdraught design canted at a 30° angle from horizontal. The HD8s had piston chambers (commonly called "dash-pots") that were both shorter and fatter than those on the carburettors previously described. They were also attached to the main carburettor body by four rather than the normal three setscrews. The standard needles used were type UH, the rich and weak needles being UN and UL respectively. Red and green piston springs were used – unique to this application.

Once again Coopers hammered silver painted air-cleaners were used, broadly similar to the previous types but somewhat thicker and flatter in cross-section. They also had larger exit holes to suit the 2in carburettor throats. Instead of a single Bowden cable being used throughout from dash control to carburettors, the single choke cable extended only as far as the engine side of the bulkhead. A bracket on the bulkhead was used at this point, and the single cable pushed or pulled on twin cables that ran from it, one to each carbu-

This view of the HD8 carburettors shows the linkage and also the position of the return springs. Again, the fuel feed pipe appears to be of a later style.

Behind the rear bulkhead near the rear axle was maybe not the most sensible place to locate an electric fuel pump, where it was susceptible to attack by road dirt and salt. This is the pump in its later location on the right-hand side of the car. It was in the equivalent position on the other side on earlier cars, and fairly near the hot exhaust pipe, which is why it was repositioned.

rettor. These cables were covered in black plastic sleeves, the shorter cable running direct to the nearer (rear) carburettor whereas the longer cable to the front carburettor needed the support of a black metal bracket fixed to the inlet manifold.

Carburettor linkages and associated pipework were broadly as on the 29F engines, but instead of each carburettor having an insulating block on each side of the heat shield, the 29K engine had a thick black plastic block on the manifold side and just a thin fibre gasket on the carburettor side. Another minor difference was that on the HD instruments the float chamber overflow outlet was a banjo type fitting, rather than the integral type of the HS6 carburettors.

FUEL PUMP
Fuel reached the carburettors from the tank by courtesy of an SU fuel pump on all the Big Healeys from 1956 to 1967. The early 100/6 cars used a round-bodied type HP pump, located on a bracket in a somewhat inaccessible position behind the heelboard at the rear of the cockpit on the left-hand side of the car. The bracket was bolted through the heelboard panel with the bolt heads under the cockpit carpeting. The easiest way to get at the pump was to remove the left-hand rear wheel!

Although still in that position, from car 60413 in March 1958, a high-capacity type LCS pump with a rectangular shape was fitted. This continued through a minor capacity upgrade in March 1961 until August 1964. However, from car 17352 in January 1962, the fuel pump was moved to the same relative position, but on the other side of the car. This was a sensible precaution which took it further away from the heat of the exhaust system. The run of the fuel line, from the tank and forward to the engine, was altered as a consequence.

The last change was a further upgrade to a new design of an SU pump, type AUF 301. This provided a boost in output and was fitted from 3000 Mark III car number 28225 in August 1964.

Each of these pump types had a filter that was removable for cleaning, and a wide black band of rubber covered the join between the pump body and the removable cap to prevent ingress of water – particularly important in view of the pump's exposed location.

FUEL TANK

The fuel tank on all 100/6 and 3000 cars was in the same position as on the four-cylinder cars at the rear. It was a flattish tank, the top of which in effect formed the boot floor and was covered by a mat, as described in the Interior section. The bottom of the tank rested within the rear of the bodyshell with the central part of the underside of the tank visible from below, as was the hexagonal drain plug. The tank was secured by two black metal straps running front to back. The capacity was always 12 imperial gallons (54 litres).

A major change was that the tank filler was no longer situated in the boot. The filler pipe now extended via a short rubber connecting pipe with wire clips, from the front right corner of the tank up through the rear tonneau panel to allow for external filling. The filler pipe had a twist-fit, bayonet-style cap that was chrome plated or stainless steel, and a lockable cap was available on all types of 3000s at small extra cost.

Fuel lines were of zinc-plated $\frac{5}{16}$in steel tube with brass fittings. One line ran from the tank to the pump through a hole and grommet in the boot bulkhead. The other ran from the pump along the inside of the chassis rail, to which it was attached by either hairpin-type metal clips or by clips similar to those used for the wiring loom. It then ascended the front shroud support member where it connected to the flexible fuel pipe that fed the carburettors, the flexible pipe allowing for engine movement.

Not at all "original" but nevertheless interesting is this engine fitted with triple twin-choke Weber carburettors for maximum power output, as used on the later works 3000 rally cars.

COOLING SYSTEM

The cooling system was more important on the Big Healeys than on most cars, for with a largish engine confined within a smallish space, it would be called upon to work hard, especially in the western USA where many of the cars were sold. Provided the water passages in the block and the radiator are clear, the cooling system will cope, even on hot days. If the cylinder head or block passages are silted up, however, there is likely to be trouble and even a car fitted with a modern auxiliary electric fan will struggle.

The radiator itself was carried over from the BN1 and BN2 models with only minor modifications to the fixings. It ran pressurised at 7psi rather than the 4psi of the earlier cars, and an eared type of pressure cap was fitted. Late BJ8 Mark III cars are thought to have had a 10psi radiator cap fitted from new. Due to the extra engine length, the radiator had to be positioned further forward than in the four-cylinder cars, so that it actually sat ahead of the front chassis cross-members. Water capacity was 18 imperial pints, with a further 2 pints within the heater system if this was fitted, making a total capacity of 2½ Imperial gallons or more than 11 litres.

FAN BELT AND FAN

A fan belt driven from a bottom pulley on the front of the crankshaft operated both the dynamo and a water pump which was bolted to the front of the engine block and painted engine colour. The fan itself was bolted to the water pump pulley with four bolts and was covered for safety at the top by a pressed steel shroud projecting backwards from the radiator header tank. Early water pumps had the pulley bolted on, but from engine 29E-2247 the pulley was press-fitted. The fan belt was ⅜in wide and was plain with no teeth cut into it up to engine number 29K-10271; thereafter it was ½in wide and the pulley grooves were widened to take account of this.

The fan itself was a metal two-piece affair of four blades disposed in a cross shape. Up to 1960 the fan was painted bright red, but thereafter yellow became the colour of choice. The four holding bolts were not painted, however. In January 1961 at car number 13601, a six-bladed fan became optional This improved airflow somewhat and was frequently fitted to cars destined for hot climates. By 1964, at car 26705, an

This type of AC radiator cap with a 7lbs pressure rating is correct for all but the later Mark III cars, which ran at 10lbs pressure. Also visible is the correct black rubber small diameter overflow hose.

eight-blade fan became available in a further attempt to improve cooling; this was again painted yellow. Finally a 16-blade fan, painted orange, became available as a dealer fitment. These multi-bladed fans obviously shifted more air through the radiator and improved cooling, but at a cost of consuming somewhat more power than the four-bladed type.

THERMOSTAT

Temperature was controlled by a thermostat fitted in a housing at the forward end of the cylinder head, and this housing also formed the top water outlet elbow. The radiator top hose connected this outlet with the radiator header tank. There were a number of different thermostat specifications depending on local climatic conditions and whether it was summer or winter.

Although the fan on earlier cars was usually painted red, it could be yellow on later models like this one. The safety shroud was almost always coloured red as a warning. Also visible in this picture are the radiator top hose, the thermostat housing, the fan belt and water pump pulley onto which the fan is bolted, and also the polished copper heater return pipe which discharges into the cooling system's bottom hose.

The wide radiator header tank, correctly painted dull black. Seen on the left is the cold-air intake trunking; similar trunking caries fresh air to the heater just out of sight on the opposite side.

Abingdon build in late 1957 or from summer 1958 (sources differ), this was moved to a tapping below the thermostat housing. Original radiator hoses, always black, had the textured fabric "stockingette" finish, but modern replacements are of the smooth finish variety. Both the radiator top and bottom hoses were moulded, the bottom hose having a subsidiary moulding which formed the inlet for the heater return pipe. Longbridge-built cars featured hose clips with a thin steel band tightened by a cotter pin, but it is thought that all Abingdon-built cars used wire hose clips with a screw tightening arrangement.

HEATING AND VENTILATION SYSTEMS

The majority, possibly the great majority, of six-cylinder Healeys were fitted with a heater, even though this always remained an extra-cost option. Cars destined for hot and dry countries usually had no heater, but most cars sent to the USA, which was of course nearly 90% of all production, had the heater fitted – even some cars ordered for the hotter parts of that country.

Even if not used as such, the heater performed a useful secondary function in that it increased the cooling water capacity by at least 10%. In emergencies, it could be brought into action as a "heat sink" on a car that was reaching boiling point in heavy traffic, albeit at the cost of roast passengers! The heater was manufactured by Smiths Industries and was nominally of 3½kw, though many would doubt that rating in cold weather! For cars built without a heater where owners regretted this fact, the factory made available a complete retro-fitting kit.

Unlike the standard fitment recirculating drum-type heater on the BN1 and BN2 cars, the unit fitted to the six-cylinder cars was of the more efficient fresh- air type. Air was taken in at the front of the car, unpolluted by engine fumes, ducted to the heater unit and then directed to the cockpit. This system had the additional benefit of a ram-effect that was denied to the four-cylinder cars, because forward motion of the car forced air through the system without the necessity for the heater fan motor to run constantly.

The heater unit consisted of two main parts. There was a fan or blower unit mounted on the right-hand inner wheel arch, to which it was fixed by a bracket and four hexagon-headed sheet metal screws. The second part was a heater matrix box sited on the cockpit side of the front bulkhead under the dashboard. Large-diameter black trunking picked up air from just behind the front grille on the right side and carried it to the blower unit. From there, the air was conveyed through similar but slightly smaller trunking through the bulkhead to the matrix box. This box was fitted with two footwell outlets, which could be closed off by shutters, and two demisting outlets for the windscreen.

The blower unit was partly black plastic, which was left in its natural state, and the metallic parts were painted black.

The opening temperatures could be as low as 68°C (154° F) or as high as 83°C (182°F), depending upon what was required. Cars supplied for the UK home market were usually supplied with thermostats opening at around 72°C (162°F), as this was a reasonable compromise figure. The earlier cars had the older bellows type of thermostat but the later wax type was fitted from engine number 29F-2592 onwards in 1962.

RADIATOR

Cooling difficulties led to upgrades to the radiator itself; the 100/6 radiator had nine gills per inch, and this was increased to 10 for the earliest 3000s. At the start of 1960, the definitive radiator with 12 gills per inch arrived and was fitted to all subsequent cars. All radiators and their associated bracketry were painted black. However, the fan shroud was frequently, but not always, painted red, presumably as a warning of the rapidly rotating fan.

Radiator caps were zinc-plated and otherwise unpainted. They had a central brass rivet visible from above which formed part of the cap spring mechanism. The correct depth for a radiator cap is exactly one inch. They were stamped with their correct pressure, and removal instructions were embossed into the top surface. An overflow pipe, made of ribbed black rubber, emanated from the side of the radiator filler neck via a small outlet stub and passed down the right side of the radiator frame, clipped to it in four places by clips integral with the radiator.

This is the later, more efficient, six-blade cooling fan, invariably painted yellow.

HOSES AND TEMPERATURE SENDER

Earlier 100/6s had the water temperature gauge sender fitted in the radiator header tank, but from either the start of

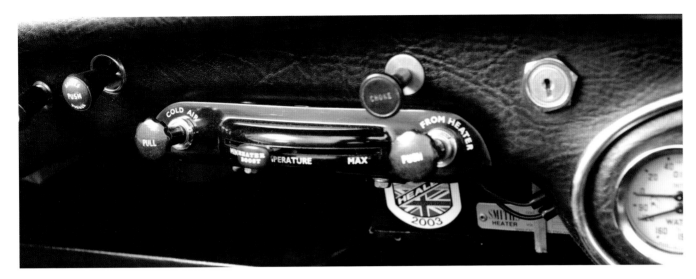

Fixings were generally zinc-plated. The trunking was fastened where necessary by large wire screw-type clips and was itself made of a paper and foil laminate reinforced by wire and coloured matt black. The blower unit received its electricity supply from the wiring loom via a bullet connector, and was earthed through a large metal eyelet fixed to the inner body brace by a self-tapping cross-head screw.

All cars, whether fitted with a heater or not, had a separate fresh-air intake system intended to counteract continued complaints about cockpit heat from the exhaust system and the engine. Trunking with the same diameter as that between the blower and the heater matrix box ran from a metal intake tube fixed just behind the front grille on the opposite side of the car to the heater trunking. It ran to the bulkhead where it was secured by a wire clip to a circular bulkhead mounted flange fitted with a wire mesh anti-insect screen. This allowed fresh air directly into the left-hand side footwell, which was of course the driver's side on the great majority of cars built. Air could be shut off by a flap situated within the metal tube at the front, and that flap was operated by a Bowden cable with a control knob on the left-hand side of the heater control panel.

Heating was controlled by a laterally sliding knob and short Bowden cable which regulated the water inlet valve on the top of the heater matrix box. This sliding control knob had a dual function, as pulling it out switched on the heater blower motor to boost throughput when the car was either motionless or moving slowly. The final control adjusted the volume of air that the heater was giving out. This knob was on the right-hand side of the heater control panel and it was pulled fully out to shut off hot air flow altogether. When the cables were correctly adjusted and kept lubricated, this control system worked well, but it was prone to stiffen up if not used regularly.

The same basic heater control panel was used throughout the six-cylinder cars' run. On the pre-1964 cars it was sited at the centre of the dashboard under the point where the dash panel indented upwards, but on the Mark III cars with the full-depth dash and centre console, it was set into the dash panel itself centrally at the top.

Water reached the heater matrix box from a lever-operated tap on the right-hand side of the cylinder block. On cars with no heater, a suitable blanking plate was substituted. The hose from this valve passed through a hole with a protective grommet towards the top of the bulkhead. Water returned from the matrix to the engine through another hose which passed through the bulkhead; again, the hole had a protective grommet. This return hose was connected to the copper heater return pipe secured to the cylinder head manifold studs, and the return pipe joined the moulded outlet towards the top of the radiator bottom hose mentioned above.

Heater hoses were secured by wire clips tightened by screw and captive nut. The original hoses had the "stockingette" fabric type finish, but these are no longer available and smooth-finish black rubber hosing is an accepted substitute.

EXHAUST SYSTEM

This view of the exhaust box on a 3000 Mark I shows that ground clearance was pretty minimal even on a well maintained car. Forward of the silencer box can be seen the short section of flexible pipe fitted to allow for slight engine movement. Small wonder that the occupant of the seat above the silencer got warm legs....

Two views of how the exhaust gases escaped to atmosphere. The angled ends of the exhaust pipes are correct, though the angle can vary slightly from car to car.

The exhaust manifolds were made of cast iron in two separate pieces, each delivering the exhaust gases from three cylinders to a downpipe. They were secured to the cylinder head studs with flat steel washers and long nuts made of brass which prevented them corroding, although this made them vulnerable to damage during removal and fitting because they were relatively soft. These exhaust manifolds were painted green on new cars, but as high-temperature paint was not used, the finish did not last long.

EARLY TWIN-PIPE SYSTEM

The two manifolds exhausted into twin downpipes, which had flexible sections to allow for some measure of engine movement. A single silencer box with twin inlets was mounted hard up under the floor on the left-hand side of the car, thus heating the floor and seat nicely! The silencer boxes were originally of Burgess manufacture and were painted in semi-matt black. On the BN4 cars with the 1C-H gallery head engine, the silencer box had only a single exit point and a single tailpipe was used. However, cars with the six-port engine had twin tailpipes connected to a silencer with twin outlets. These two pipes were braced to each other at two points by welded spacer bars.

The tailpipe(s) exited at the left-hand rear of the car, roughly in line with the left-hand rear over-rider, the pipe end(s) being cut at an angle. Exhaust sections were originally connected by black-painted band clamps rather than the more commonly seen U-clamps. Exhaust hangers with rubber block cushioning suspended the exhaust system from the chassis frame in three places, at the front and rear of the silencer and aft of the rear axle. Excess heat was transmitted to the floor, and so later cars had an asbestos heat shield between the floor and the silencer box, with asbestos spacers on the shield's four mounting points to allow some cooling airflow through. It is not clear when this was added; it may have been from the 3000 Mark II onwards, although the change could have occurred earlier.

THE "CONTINENTAL" EXHAUST SYSTEM

The twin-pipe system with the straight-through Burgess silencer was notoriously (and gloriously) noisy, leading to not a few complaints. Therefore at the start of 1961 a so-called "Continental" exhaust system was developed, and was fitted to some cars for Continental European export. Not all cars

On the 3000 Mark III model, the twin pipes emerge on the other side of the car. Again, angled ends are usual, though not very apparent here.

sent to the Continent after 1960 had the system, and it is not clear whether it was fitted only for certain countries or only by request.

After passing through a slightly modified version of the usual main silencer, the twin tailpipes turned 90° across the car behind the rear axle and a secondary silencer box was fitted transversely at the rear on additional flexible mountings. Twin pipes emerged from this second silencer and turned a further 90° to exit under the rear bumper but on the right of the car rather than the left. This new system tamed the raucous noise somewhat, but presumably at the expense of some power loss through extra back pressure.

THE FOUR-SILENCER SYSTEM

For the Mark III BJ8 cars there was a major exhaust system revision, following on the lines of the "Continental" type. This featured no fewer than four silencer boxes, all having crimped ends and rolled bodies. The exhaust system was in effect dualled throughout, with no communication between the exhaust gases from the front three and rear three cylinders until they escaped to the atmosphere.

Again the rear silencers were fitted transversely across the back of the car with the tailpipes each performing two right-angled bends to exit on the right-hand side just outboard of the right rear over-rider. Additional rubber-bushed exhaust hangers carried the extra weight and the tailpipes were again cut off at their ends at about a 60° angle. This exhaust system was fitted to all BJ8 Mark III cars, irrespective of their destination, and surprisingly did not need revising when the new rear suspension arrangement arrived on the Phase II cars.

It certainly quietened the Healey's exhaust, and BMC claimed that no power loss resulted despite the use of four silencers – something that seems somewhat doubtful to the author. Quieter it may have been, but the new system was certainly more expensive to replace! Tailpipe fixings and silencers were usually painted black from the factory, although there is some evidence that a number of late BJ8s had silver-painted exhaust systems.

The complex four-silencer exhaust system fitted to the Mark III cars was a successful attempt to quieten them down without losing power to back pressure and while providing more ground clearance. This system required numerous fittings and fixings and clearly had more potential for blowing joints than the earlier, simpler systems. It also cost a lot more to replace. The original silencer boxes would have had crimped ends, but the type shown here is the usual modern replacment.

TRANSMISSION AND REAR AXLE

The later BN2 version of the four-cylinder Austin-Healey 100 model had used the standard BMC four-speed gearbox designed to go with the C-series engine, but with a mechanically operated clutch. This gearbox was carried over to the 100/6 and later cars, but the clutch operation was changed to hydraulic. The gear ratios were also left unchanged for the 100/6, but for the first time a different rear axle ratio was fitted depending upon whether a car was supplied new with overdrive or not – 3.909:1 for non-overdrive cars and 4.1:1 for the much more common overdrive cars. As an aside, it seems that cars were built with overdrive as the default specification, non-overdrive cars having to be specifically ordered as such. Those who have driven any Big Healey without overdrive would not disagree with the policy!

Paint finishes on gearboxes, bell housings and overdrive units appear to have been the usual "steel dust" grey/green metallic throughout, with no variation reported.

GEARBOX

Four major varieties of the BMC C-series gearbox were used during production of the Big Healeys, and the details of these are set out in separate panels for clarity.

OVERDRIVE

Despite four different sets of gear ratios, there was only one change to the overdrive ratio, which went from 0.778:1 to 0.822:1 at the introduction of the 3000 models. There appear to have been no other significant changes to the overdrive unit.

An underside view of the transmission. Just visible forward of the X-bracing is the small gearbox mounting cross-member with the overdrive unit forward of that; note the large brass plug which unscrews to allow the overdrive unit to be drained of oil. The gearbox itself sits between the overdrive unit and the bellhousing bolted to the back of the engine. The underneath of the starter motor can just be seen beside the rear end of the sump. The gearbox is painted the correct engine "Steel Dust Grey". The flexible sections of the exhaust system are also in evidence.

GEAR CHANGE LEVER

A major and immediately noticeable change occurred in November 1961, half-way through Mark II 3000 BN7 and BT7 production. The mildly eccentric offset cranked gear change lever which had existed since the 1955 BN2 model was replaced by a more conventional central gear lever, short and vertical, as befitted a proper sports car. Both types of gear lever had a chrome shaft surmounted by a ball-shaped black plastic knob with the gear positions engraved into it

GEAR RATIOS – 100/6

	Internal ratios	Overall ratios (non-overdrive)	Overall ratios (overdrive)
First	3.076	12.02	12.61
Second	1.913	7.48	7.84
Third	1.333	5.21	5.47
Third o/d	1.037	–	4.25
Fourth	1.00	3.909	4.1
Fourth o/d	0.778	–	3.19
Reverse	4.17	16.30	17.1

Mph per 1000 revolutions in top gear:

Overdrive cars	18.0mph in fourth
	23.3 mph in fourth overdrive
Non-overdrive cars	18.9mph in fourth

With 18.9mph per 1000 revs in top gear, the non-overdrive 100/6 was hopelessly under-geared, even by the standards of the day. Overdrive really was an essential fitting.

GEAR RATIOS – 3000, 1959-1960

Gearbox ratios changed in spring 1959 when the 3000 models entered production.

	Internal ratios	Overall ratios (non-overdrive)	Overall ratios (overdrive)
First	2.93	10.386	11.453
Second	2.053	7.277	8.025
Third	1.309	4.640	5.120
Third o/d	1.073	–	4.198
Fourth	1.00	3.545	3.909
Fourth o/d	0.822	–	3.205
Reverse	3.78	13.40	14.541

The non-overdrive cars benefitted from a higher axle ratio of 3.545:1, which produced 20.9mph per 1000 revolutions in top gear. This was a considerable improvement over the 100/6 figure, but the cars were still marginally under-geared.

The overdrive-equipped cars produced 23.2mph per 1000 revolutions in overdrive top. There was no increase over the 100/6 figure because the overdrive ratio itself had been lowered to 0.822:1 from the earlier 0.778:1. It was possible to request the higher non-overdrive 3.545:1 axle ratio for a car with over-drive. Although this was not listed as an official option, a few cars were so built. This specification produced a relaxed 25.2mph per 1000 revolutions in overdrive, gearing which the torquey 3000 engine could easily handle.

Just to the right of the right-hand hose passing through the front bulkhead is the overdrive throttle switch box. This prevents overdrive from being disengaged on a trailing throttle. The rod which connects this box to the accelerator linkage from the crank on the side of the box can just be seen. Although always fitted to overdrive-equipped Healeys, for some reason this complex mechanism was not found necessary on Triumph's TR range.

and picked out in white.

When the central gear lever arrived, so did a fibreglass transmission tunnel cover, somewhat narrower than the previous tunnel with its flattish top made necessary by the old offset gear lever. The new tunnel therefore created a little more room in the cockpit. The gear lever and tunnel changes were introduced from chassis numbers BT7-15881 and BN7-16039.

CLUTCH

The clutch was a single dry plate unit throughout the 100/6 and 3000 production run, manufactured by Borg and Beck. Unlike on the four-cylinder cars, it was hydraulically operated, and the pendant clutch pedal operated directly on a master cylinder bolted to the pedal box. The master cylinder shared a fluid reservoir with the braking system.

The clutch slave cylinder was situated on the right-hand side below the bell-housing. Clutch plate diameter was 9in on all 100/6 cars, but the increased torque of the 3000 engine required an increase in plate diameter to 10in. Half-way through the run of the Mark II BJ7 Convertible in 1963, at engine number 29F-4898, a diaphragm spring clutch was introduced. More efficient and lighter to operate than before, this allowed a reduction in plate diameter to 9½in. Things then came full circle nearly a year after the 3000 Mark III's arrival, for the clutch plate reverted to the original 9in diameter of the 100/6. This change occurred from engine number 29K-4108 in approximately October 1964.

This 1957 100/6 displays the wide transmission tunnel and the gearlever offset to the left, which operated what became known as the "side-change" gearbox. This arrangement was in production until late 1961.

A close-up of the straight gear lever used on the side-change box. The round gear knob is correct. Later in production, a slightly cranked gear lever was introduced to make changing gear marginally easier.

GEAR RATIOS – 3000, 1960-1963

Gear ratios were changed yet again in March 1960 when stronger gear clusters were introduced to combat a known weakness. This unannounced change occurred from engine number 29D-10897 (gearbox number 6656) on overdrive cars and from engine number 29D-11342 (gearbox number 1177) on non-overdrive cars. The ratios then became:

	Internal ratios	Overall ratios (non-overdrive)	Overall ratios (overdrive)
First	2.88	10.209	11.257
Second	2.06	7.302	8.052
Third	1.31	4.643	5.120
Third o/d	1.074	–	4.198
Fourth	1.00	3.545	3.909
Fourth o/d	0.822	–	3.205
Reverse	3.72	13.1	14.541

The miles per hour per 1000 revolutions figures remained unaffected.

In November 1961, not long before the end of BN7 and BT7 production, the BMC standard C-series gearbox received a long overdue revision. This included provision of a central gearchange, which enabled the Healey 3000 at last to have a proper sports car type short-throw central gear lever. This is it on a BJ7. A new transmission tunnel had to be provided, and the lever was sealed at its base by a rubber boot.

On the Mark III 3000 with its fashionable centre console, the new central gear lever looked even more at home and appropriate. Such a console would not have been possible with the old offset lever and side-change arrangement.

PROPSHAFT

The propeller shaft was always of Hardy Spicer manufacture and was a carry-over from the four-cylinder models but with slight length variations. Universal joints with grease nipples were provided at both ends, a further nipple being provided on the forward end sliding spline. The propeller shaft was always finished in black paint.

GEAR RATIOS – 3000, 1963-1967

The introduction of the 3000 Mark III model in October 1963 saw yet further gearbox ratio revisions.

	Internal ratios	Overall ratios (non-overdrive)	Overall ratios (overdrive)
First	2.637	9.348	10.308
Second	2.071	7.341	8.095
Third	1.306	4.629	5.105
Third o/d	1.071	–	4.188
Fourth	1.00	3.545	3.909
Fourth o/d	0.82	–	3.207
Reverse	3.391	12.021	13.255

Once again, the mph per 1000 revolutions figures were unaffected.

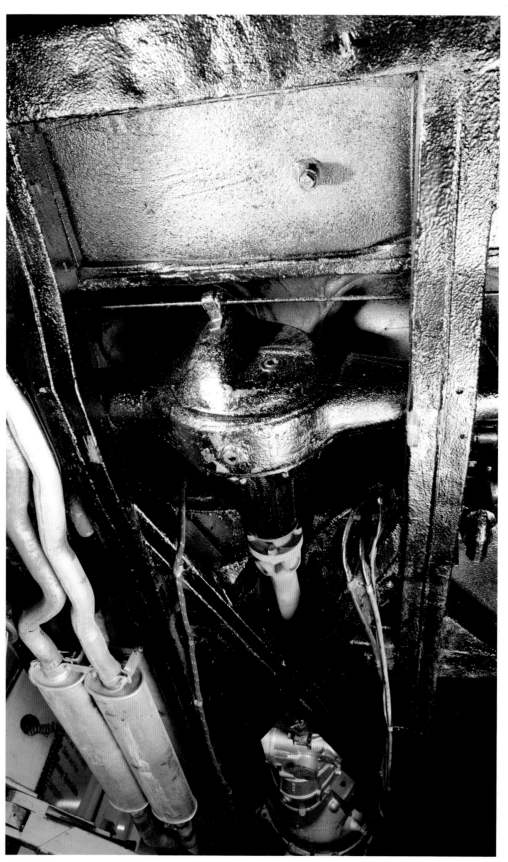

REAR AXLE

The final element in the transmission system was the rear axle. Again, this was a carry-over from the late BN1 and all BN2 models. It was equipped with hypoid bevel gears mounted in a "banjo" casing. The axle was of the ¾ floating type and had a bolted-on differential carrier. The same basic axle was used in various of the larger BMC cars and was of Morris Motors design, both stronger and heavier than the spiral bevel design used on the earlier BN1 cars.

As it was such a well-tried and over-engineered component, the hypoid bevel axle required almost no internal modifications during the Big Healey production run. Indeed, those who race Healey 3000s have found it possible to transmit more than 200bhp through this axle without modification and with reliability. The only production modification of any significance occurred when the Phase II version of the Mark III 3000 was introduced, at chassis number BJ8-26705. The axle casing had to be changed to allow for the deletion of the Panhard rod and substitution of the radius arm rear suspension. These changes of course required different mounting points on the axle casing.

Somewhat unusually, the rear axle passed over the chassis side rails, and attached to it on each side were black bump rubbers which restrained its upward movement by impacting on the bump boxes attached to the body. Thin rubber pads fitted to the top of the chassis rails under the axle casing cushioned the axle as it dropped due to suspension movement. The axle and differential casings were always painted black, as were the brake lines and other attached fasteners.

The final drive came with three different ratios – 3.545:1, 3.909:1 and 4.1:1 – and all these are discussed in the Gearbox section. All rear axle units and gearboxes were manufactured by BMC Ltd themselves at their Tractors and Transmissions plant in Ward End, Birmingham.

The rear axle is very difficult to photograph satisfactorily, as it is tucked above the main chassis rails. This view shows the centre section housing the crown wheel and pinion plus differential unit. The drain plug is at the base, with the level/filler plug showing on the back of the casing. The rod journalled in the loop attached to the back of the axle casing is part of the handbrake mechanism. The rear portion of the propshaft, including the universal joint, can also be seen. Note how part of the bottom of the fuel tank, with its drain plug, is visible between the chassis rails.

CHASSIS

One basic single design of chassis frame sufficed for the entire Big Healey run from 1953 to 1967 with little modification, a testament to how "right" the initial Healey family design had been. The only changes of real significance were firstly the increase in wheelbase of almost two inches to allow fitment of the "+2" rear seats and, secondly, the 3000 Mark III Phase II rear suspension changes to produce more ground clearance.

Unlike Triumph's TR range, which had a basic ladder-frame chassis with cross-tubes and X-style cross-bracing, the frame of the Healey was more closely integrated with the bodywork itself. Welded to the bare frame were bulkhead and bodywork support bracing. This assisted in providing a very strong and rigid front end, which was necessary to allow the independent front suspension to operate properly.

This semi-monocoque design made it necessary to spray-paint the whole construction as one, so Jensen's painted the body/chassis units together in the same basic colour, which of course was the colour of the finished car.

MAIN CHASSIS MEMBERS AND CROSS-MEMBERS

The basis of the chassis was formed by two main box section members, 3in wide and 3½in deep, set 15in apart and running parallel to each other from front to rear. These box sections were constructed from two channel halves welded together, the weld seam remaining clearly visible. The members were braced centrally by a cruciform structure, and at their front ends they were connected by dual transverse cross-members. These cross-members were dipped at the centre and at each outer end they incorporated suspension towers. These in turn formed the mountings for the front shock-absorbers and seating points for the tops of the front springs. The upper part of the cross-member had had to be reshaped into a shallow V to give clearance for the six-cylinder motor.

The rear cross-member, which ran adjacent to the petrol tank, was braced for strength and carried an extension piece on either side which acted as the rear bumper support. Main body support was provided by two outriggers each side, one located under the forward door pillar and one under the rear one. These were welded to the two main members.

Just forward of the central X-bracing, situated under the

The front end of a restored car with the engine removed affords good views of the structure. The main members can be seen, with the box-section bases upon which the engine mounts are bolted. Also visible are the top front cross-member and the drilled bracing members, the bonnet release mechanism, the rubber pads around the bonnet aperture lip, and the front suspension towers, one of which has the shock absorber on view.

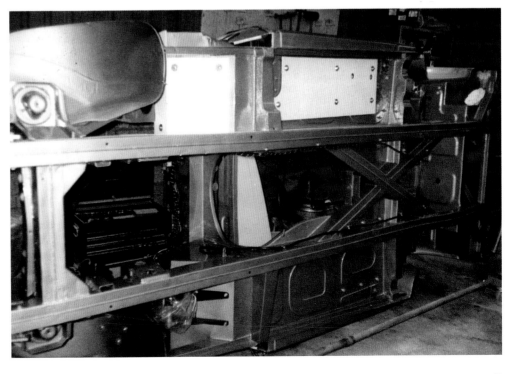

This excellent underside view of a restored chassis shows the substantial main longitudinal members, cross-members, X-bracing at the centre, the floor pans and the box section outriggers supporting the sills and central sections of the body. Note the white heat shields fitted to deflect exhaust heat.

The twin front chassis cross-members show well here, along with a lower inner wishbone pivot point, the steering track rod, a shock absorber, the steering idler and the X-bracing for the front shroud assembly.

This frontal view shows the cross bracing, the front inner wings, the front suspension pivot points and the front body mounting points at the extreme forward end of the main chassis rails. The two circular holes allow the trunking for the cold air ventilation on one side and the heater air inlet on the other side to pass through.

overdrive unit, was a short cross-member which carried the mountings for the rear of the engine-gearbox unit. The forward location points for the rear springs were located on the rear of the two outriggers, and the other end of each spring was attached by a shackle to the top face of the rear cross-member. All the various chassis frame members were of square or rectangular section; there were no round tubes used at all. Unusually, the main chassis members passed under the rear axle, which made for a low centre of gravity but was also the principal reason for the Healey's lack of useful ground clearance.

FRONT BULKHEAD

Also welded to the two main members was the front bulkhead and scuttle framing, which consisted of two cross-braced, channel-section hoops, strengthened towards their bases by an inverted triangular structure that formed the toeboard. The bulkhead was substantially strengthened by a forward-facing box-section member on each side. These ran from the top of the bulkhead area to the chassis frame itself, just aft of the suspension towers. Holes were punched into these members, presumably for lightness, and the box-section members provided not only rigidity but also strength in the event of frontal impact.

The bulkhead area was formed by several pressings welded together, and the whole was angled backwards at the rear. Hinge mounting points for the forward-hinged doors were formed by pressings that filled the spaces on either side of the bulkhead framework.

FLOORS AND SILLS

The floors rested on and were welded to the top of the chassis frame. They were made in two sections, one fitted each side of the propshaft tunnel. Floors had raised pressings to give additional stiffness and to provide anchoring points for the seat runners.

Inner body sills, again welded to the floors and body outriggers, attached to the outer sides of the floor pans. Surprisingly, despite the extra two inches added to the chassis, these inner sills were the same length as those on the earlier cars with the original wheelbase; they simply did not extend as far back into the rear wing area.

CHASSIS DETAILS (FRONT)

Two built-up pressed steel engine mounts, one on each side, supported the front of the engine. These were bolted to box sections welded to the top of the chassis frame. Rubber vibration absorbing blocks were employed, which also allowed a degree of engine movement.

Still at the front of the chassis, it was found necessary shortly after 100/6 production began to add air deflector panels behind the grille to direct air more effectively through the radiator.

CHASSIS DETAILS (REAR)

At the rear of the car there were chassis frame differences between the two-seater BN6 and BN7 cars and the 2/4-seaters. The two-seaters had twin 6-volt batteries in the same position as on the BN1 and BN2 cars; they were clamped to small frames located behind the rear tonneau bulkhead and accessed through a trapdoor in the shelf behind the seats. These battery frames were welded to the top of the main chassis frame.

Interestingly, despite the extra two inches of wheelbase length that were added for the benefit of the extra seats in the 2/4-seaters, the reintroduced two-seater did not revert to the original wheelbase length of the BN1 and BN2 models. This was presumably in the interests of standardis-ation. The further differences between the two-seaters and the 2/4-seaters are more fully described later, in the Body section of this book.

There were significant modifications to the rear of the chassis in mid-1964 when the Phase II version of the Mark III 3000 arrived. These were an attempt finally to address the Healey's perennial ground clearance difficulties, and were introduced from car number 26705. Where the two main longitudinal members passed under the axle, they were now made to dip somewhat to allow the axle to drop down further, this allowing the car to ride higher. The Panhard rod mounting point on the right of the chassis was deleted, and a new mounting was added on each side to secure the forward ends of the radius arms that had taken over the job of axle location.

Floor pans are on view in this shot, along with the propeller shaft tunnel. The short cross-member which carries the rear engine/gearbox mount is visible forward of the tunnel. This car is a two-seater, as the hinged battery access panel makes clear.

The inner rear wheel arch and rear part of the main chassis rails are depicted here, together with a rear shock absorber mounting plate. Also on view are the body B-post and its supporting bracket, plus (at lower left) one outer end of the rear chassis cross-member.

This photograph clearly demonstrates how the rear chassis rails were dropped under the rear axle on the Phase II and III versions of the Mark III 3000. This arrangement allowed the axle more vertical movement and gave more ground clearance.

STEERING

The same basic wire-spoked steering wheel was carried over from the 100 models to the 100/6, and indeed carried on right through Big Healey production with only detail changes. On the 100/6, the Healey "lightning flash" motif appeared on the horn push, and superimposed on top were the "100" figures with a tiny figure "6" in a diminutive medallion on the right-hand end of the flash.

Big Healeys were built with both left-hand and right-hand drive, but a precise breakdown of quantities cannot be deduced. Although the Abingdon works kept accurate records, cars built at Longbridge were less well recorded, and for the first 15 months of production show no details of steering position. Anders Clausager states that surviving records reveal just 7% of Abingdon-built Big Healeys of all types to have had RHD, the actual number of

cars being 3673 from a total of 51,317. If the same 7% factor is applied to the 7053 Longbridge built 100/6s, we arrive at 494 cars. This is an approximate figure, but it seems doubtful if many more than 500 right-hand-drive Longbridge 100/6s were made. Therefore total RHD six-cylinder Healey production is unlikely to have been more than 4200 cars out of more than 58,000 cars in total.

The cars had a cam and peg steering gear of a design that

dated from the introduction of the Austin A70 and A90 in the 1940s. For some reason, rack and pinion Morris Minor type steering was not considered and hence the Austin-Healey was saddled with an exceedingly long steering column, for the steering box was mounted right towards the front of the chassis. As a result, in the event of a heavy frontal impact, the Healey driver was vulnerable to injury from the column into his chest. One cannot imagine such a layout being sanctioned today.

Steering boxes, associated bracketry and columns were invariably painted black, as were track and tie rods and the various steering levers and arms. The body of the steering idler could be either painted black or left in its natural metal finish. Bolts and fastenings used in the steering system were generally zinc-plated.

STEERING BOX AND STEERING ARMS

The steering system on all the six-cylinder Healeys was of Cam Gears manufacture, like that on the later four-cylinder models. However, the gear ratio was lowered from 12.6:1 to 14:1, in order to take account of the extra weight of the six-cylinder engine over the front wheels. From car BN6-1995 in July 1958 and for all subsequent cars, the ratio was lowered yet again to 15:1. This produced three turns lock-to-lock as compared to two and a half turns for the BN1 and BN2. The turning circle nevertheless remained approximately 35 feet left or right, increasing very slightly on the later 3000s. Correct toe-in was between 1/16in and 1/8in.

The steering box was bolted to the chassis at its front end by a bracket that incorporated an unpainted cast aluminium spacer. On the opposite side sat the steering idler unit, mounted similarly. The box and the idler were connected through short levers by a transverse and adjustable track rod, ball-jointed at its outer ends. Tie rods, likewise ball-jointed at either end, were linked to the track rod and conveyed the steering motion to the front wheels through steering levers bolted to the front hubs. Grease nipples were deleted from steering joints at car 19191 in April 1962, thereafter the joints were of the "sealed for life" type. Adjustment was achieved by a screw-type adjuster acting on the rocker shaft. Both the steering box and the idler had external oil-filler plugs.

STEERING COLUMN AND WHEEL

The steering column was supported along its length by two black-painted brackets, and on the early BN4s was adjustable. From car number BN4-68960 and on all BN6s, a non-adjustable column became standard, but this soon had to be lengthened by half an inch to give a little more clearance between the dashboard and the steering wheel. The longer column arrived at cars BN4-70165 and BN6-3375 in September 1958. The adjustable column did however remain as an extra-cost option right through six-cylinder car production.

The steering wheels were different for adjustable and non-adjustable systems.

All steering wheels came with three four-wire spokes, disposed in the fashion of the Mercedes-Benz logo. On cars with adjustable steering, the wheel had a smaller horn-push surrounded by a chrome-plated bezel. Both the wheel rim and the centre boss horn-push were made of hard black plastic, and within the rim was a wire reinforcement. Diameter of the wheel could be either 16½in or 17in, depending upon manufacturer. Bluemels made the former and Clifford Casing Co of Birmingham made the latter, which was the rarer type.

All wheels carried the Austin-Healey lightning-flash motif, with the figure 6 in a tiny circular medallion off-set to the right-hand side when the wheel was in the straight-ahead position. 100/6 cars additionally had the figure 100 added to the 6. The horn was operated by pressing the spring-loaded push, and the direction indicators were controlled by a black or chromed plastic lever at the top of the centre boss which clicked either left or right depending on the turn to be made. A self-cancelling mechanism was fitted. This lever differed slightly between cars with adjustable steering and those without it.

One peculiarity worthy of mention is that from September 1961 cars built specifically for Germany, Sweden and also possibly Switzerland had steering column locks fitted, presumably to comply with local legislation. As became the norm on most cars later, the lock inhibited the ignition and starter switches.

The horn push and steering wheel boss differed depending upon whether adjustable or non-adjustable steering was specified. This is the horn push usually employed for non-adjustable steering, whereas the type shown on page 68 is that used throughout production for adjustable steering. The "lightning flash" was still present, but the "100" figures had disappeared to leave just the figure "6" in the tiny medallion. For some reason, the figures "3000" did not appear at all.

SUSPENSION

The front suspension changed hardly at all during the Big Healey's run. Here on a late 3000 is the end of the anti-roll bar with its rubber-bushed link to the lower wishbone and spring pan. Also seen are the spring itself, the outer steering tie rod with its ball-jointed end, the shock absorber arms at the top forming the top wishbone, the flexible brake pipe and its union with the rigid pipe. Just visible above the inner part of the tie rod is the bottom of the steering box with the steering lever splined onto its shaft. The brake disc, splined wire wheel hub and knock-off nut are also on view.

As with the chassis, the original design of the Healey's front and rear suspension needed very little modification over the years, the last Mark III 3000s using much the same suspension as had the early BN1s.

FRONT SUSPENSION

This had been purloined from Austin's late-1940s A70 and A90 range of saloon cars. It had been found to work well, was proven to be robust and cost-effective, so why change it?

Of conventional double-wishbone design, incorporating coil springs, this suspension had top wishbones formed from the A-shaped arms of the lever-arm shock absorbers bolted to the top of the suspension towers. A ⅝in diameter anti-roll bar was incorporated, this being attached to each main chassis rail below the front bumper supports by rubber-bushed brackets. A thicker bar was available as a competition option. The bar connected to the front suspension lower wishbones by way of drop links, again rubber-bushed, and triangular pressed steel plates. Note that the nuts used should

be castellated with split pins and not the Nyloc type. A black rubber bump stop was incorporated within the coil spring. Lower wishbones were bolted to the spring pan and pivoted at their inner end from brackets welded to the chassis frame.

Swivelling kingpins connected the outer ends of the A-shaped shock absorber arms and lower wishbones, and these carried the housings which incorporated the stub axle. The castor angle on all 100/6s and 3000s was 2°, the camber angle 1° and the swivel (king) pin inclination was 6½°. Hub bearings were adjustable Timken taper roller types. The shock absorbers were Armstrong double-acting types, and the Armstrong reference number was 1S9/10RXP.

There were two different types of front wheel hub, depending upon whether wire wheels or disc wheels were specified. The wire wheel hubs were changed from car number 26705 in May 1964 from having twelve threads per inch to eight. This of course means that the knock-on nuts are not interchangeable before and after this point.

Front springs and spring rates, which were upgraded to take account of the heavier engine, were changed during six-cylinder production more than once. From 100/6s number 35707 (LHD) and 35827 (RHD) in February 1957, longer coil springs were fitted. Although these were painted black, they carried a ½in-wide green paint stripe to mark them out from the earlier spring types. Uprated stiffer springs arrived in June 1960, fitted from BN7-10329 and BT7-10303. These springs were distinguished by a red paint stripe and continued in use until the Mark II Convertible arrived.

For both the BJ7 and BJ8 models, an even stiffer set of front springs was provided, denoted by vertical stripes of red and white, parallel to each other. A final front suspension change occurred in May 1964 with the arrival of the Phase II BJ8 cars. These used a new type of front swivel and axle assembly which for the first time was handed; quite why this was done is unclear.

Coil springs were black, as already noted, and so were shock absorbers sometimes. However the bodies were more often left in their natural alloy metal finish, with black painted arms. Anti-roll bars and most other suspension parts were also painted black, but inner lower wishbone brackets attached to the chassis and the suspension towers themselves

This is as good a view as one is likely to get of the rear axle installed in a car. The handbrake linkage and pivot point are visible, as are the rear of the propeller shaft, the rear brake drums and the base plates of the spring clamps. The spring leaves and U-bolts can also be seen, along with the bottom of the fuel tank with its drain plug, and the main rear chassis cross-member. The bottom of one of the rear shock absorbers and its connecting link are forward of the axle case on the right-hand side of the picture, and the drain plug at the bottom of the differential housing in the centre of the axle casing can also be made out.

were painted body colour. The links from wishbones to the anti-roll bar were left unpainted in their natural metal finish.

REAR SUSPENSION

This was of very conventional, robust and simple design and remained in principle largely unchanged throughout the Big Healey production run. The first cars had seven-leaf semi-elliptic springs, but Phase II BJ8 cars differed, as detailed later. The leaves were held together by U-shaped clamps, closed at their open end by a countersunk, flat-headed screw which passed through a spacer tube on its way to being threaded into the other side of the U-clamp. Zinc sheet was placed between the longer leaves to allow them to slide better against one another. The rear axle casing passed above both the springs and the chassis members and was attached to the springs by U-bolts that clamped onto a spring bottom plate. Also fixed to this was a bracket for the rubber-bushed link which connected the springs to the rear shock absorbers.

Clamped to the top of the axle casing by the U-bolts was a bullet-shaped black rubber bump stop. This acted on a bump box bolted to the underside of the body directly above the axle and restricted its upward movement. These bump boxes were added after the body-chassis unit was painted and so

were painted black rather than in body colour.

Rear shock absorbers, like the front ones, were double-acting lever-arm units by Armstrong. Their type number was DAS 9 RXP. Although these remained the standard units throughout six-cylinder Healey production, the arms were modified slightly when the Phase II Mark III rear modifications arrived in May 1964. These modifications were described earlier, in the Chassis section.

Other differences introduced at that point included the use of six rather than seven spring leaves, which provided a softer ride than the previous type. These springs featured polypropylene interlinings instead of zinc sheet and were held together with metal clips rather than the previous U-shaped brackets and screws. By way of comparison, the seven-leaf springs had a free length of 34.9in with ½in of laden negative camber, while the six-leaf springs had a free length of 32.625in and 1in of positive camber measured from the top leaf. The laden length of both springs was 36in.

On the Phase II cars, the previous Panhard rod was of course deleted, with twin radius arms being provided in its place to locate the axle. All springs were finished in black paint, as were the brackets and rear shackle bars. However, the fastenings attaching the springs to the axle and at their forward and rear ends were zinc-plated rather than black-painted.

BRAKES

It is quite unusual now in the UK to find a 100/6 still with its original front drum brakes; many have been converted to discs. This very correct car has drum brakes with the drums finished in the right silver paint, similar to that on the wire wheels. It is also fitted with the original style of 48-spoke wheels, again a rare find today. (Author)

When the 100/6 was introduced, the brakes themselves remained the same as on the BN2 100s, being hydraulically operated and made by Girling. However the operating method varied in that the brake and clutch pedals were now pendant types, acting directly on unpainted master cylinders mounted on a bracket above the pedal box from which the pedals pivoted.

Brake light operation on all cars was provided by a pressure switch, which had screw terminals on early cars and push-on terminals on later cars. The switch was threaded into the fluid distribution manifold that fed the individual brake pipes and which bolted to the lower portion of the dual front chassis cross-member, at a point roughly below the dynamo.

MASTER CYLINDER

The Longbridge-built early 100/6s had brake and clutch master cylinders each with their own integral fluid reservoir. However, once Abingdon build commenced, clutch and brakes were supplied with hydraulic fluid from a common reservoir. This was shaped like a tin can, painted black, and had a vented screw-type lid that was embossed with the

manufacturer's name. It combined both an inner and an outer reservoir and had separate outlets. On RHD cars, this reservoir was mounted on the chassis brace, but on LHD cars it was fixed to the left-hand vertical front shroud support. A black band-type clamp was used to attach the reservoir.

On the Phase II Mark III 3000s, the diameters of the master cylinder and brake calliper pistons were slightly increased. However, local legislation forced a final modification in June 1967 on cars from BJ8-41930 onwards, built for France and the Benelux countries. A transparent plastic brake fluid reservoir was provided with a clear plastic lid, this being separate from the clutch reservoir. As a result, the clutch was given its own reservoir, a black painted metal can as previously but only about half the size of the previous combined item and having only one bottom outlet. As only approximately 1100 BJ8s were built after this point, and as nearly 90% of these would have gone to North America, plus others for the home market and the rest of the world, this modification with its attendant costs could only have affected a tiny number of cars – no more than 50 I would guess. However, it is indicative of how complying with safety legislation was beginning to affect even the Big Healey. It was a trend that, as we have seen, ultimately led to the model's demise.

DRUMS, PIPES AND HOSES

The 100/6 used the same 11in brake drums as had the BN2 models, both front and rear, and these were painted the same silver colour as the wheels. The front brakes had two leading shoes, each operated by a separate slave cylinder, whereas the rear brakes had leading and trailing shoes activated by a single cylinder. Screw-type adjustment was provided through the brake backplates. Brake linings were 2¼in wide, providing a total friction area of 188 square inches. 3000 rear brake drums usually had circumferential finning, though plain drums were occasionally found.

Zinc-plated ³⁄₁₆in diameter steel brake pipes (unpainted) connected the brake slave cylinders to the master cylinder, and three flexible black reinforced rubber hoses with longitudinal ribbing were used to allow for wheel and axle movement. There was one for each front wheel, and a single hose reinforced by a steel coil ran to the rear axle, along which were clipped the cupro-nickel hydraulic pipes leading to each rear wheel cylinder. Standard UNF threads were used on the brake hose unions.

COCKPIT CONTROLS

Brake and clutch pedal ends were of square section, bowed in side view, and covered with rubber pads that were studded for extra grip. The handbrake was operated from a central cockpit lever and activated the rear brakes by a combination of rods, cranks and cables. Due partly to the relatively long lever provided, the handbrake was very efficient if maintained in good order. Even though the Healey was a sporting car, no fly-off action was ever fitted to the handbrake, the chromed lever of which locked on with a push-button at the top. The handbrake lever was always fitted on the right hand side of the transmission tunnel, irrespective of whether the car had left-hand or right-hand drive. No modifications were made to the handbrake during the whole of the six-cylinder Healey run, although it was found necessary to give a little more clearance to the lever from May 1957 by alterations to the right-hand seat and surrounding carpet.

FRONT DISCS AND SERVO

BMC finally caught up with its rivals in March 1959 when the 3000 entered production with front disc brakes. Like the drums, these were of Girling manufacture. Discs had an 11in diameter and each was acted upon by a twin-piston calliper mounted on the appropriate front wheel's swivelling hub housing. At first no dust shields were provided, but these were found necessary and introduced in March 1960. Like the callipers, these shields were painted black although some callipers, finished in either silver paint or else left in natural metal finish, have been claimed as original.

No factory brake servo was initially available for this disc-drum brake system, although a number of owners fitted proprietary items to counteract heavy pedal pressure. However, from car number 15104 during the run of the Mark II 3000, a Girling vacuum servo unit became available as an extra cost option. When build of the Mark III cars commenced towards the end of 1963, the servo unit became a standard fitting.

The servo was mounted on two black-painted pressed steel brackets fixed to engine compartment side of the sloping part of the right-hand footwell. The servo unit vacuum tank was painted gloss black but the hydraulic cylinder body remained as an unpainted aluminium casting. The servo was operated by inlet manifold vacuum through a rubber hose connected to the manifold. This hose had a similar black fabric style finish to the hoses used in the heater and engine breather systems. It was secured at each end by clips with a thin steel band tightened by a cotter pin.

THE ALL-DISC-BRAKED CARS

One final obscure aspect of the 100/6 braking system needs to be clarified. In the latter part of 1957 a small series of

Rear drum brakes remained remarkably similar right through from late BN1 100s to the end of 3000 production. The bolt-on splined hub extension for a wire wheel is seen here, and the drum is finished in the correct colour. Circumferential fins, as seen here, were found on most, but not all, rear drums. The nuts holding the drum and splined hub extension were specially shaped "Nylok" type

The dust shield is visible behind this front brake disc and calliper. Original callipers were usually painted black, although most replacements are silver, like this one. The top of the shock absorber arm can just be seen above the disc.

The fluid reservoir which fed both clutch and brake systems is seen here on a Mark III 3000. The two master cylinders are shown mounted on the bulkhead, connected to the pedals on the cockpit side. Fresh air trunking can be seen at the top, and at left is one of the horns. The bonnet release operating rod is also on view.

This 100/6 handbrake lever has the correct black hand grip, with the chromed locking button at the top. Fly-off operation was never fitted to the Big Healey.

probably 50 100/6s were built with a Dunlop four-wheel disc brake system and vacuum servo fitted. Some were certainly built at Longbridge, but there may have been Abingdon-built cars as well, for this was taking place at the precise time that the change of assembly plant was occurring.

I owned one of them, registered XNX 56, in the early 1980s and by sheer coincidence this very car, still with its four-wheel wheel disc brakes, is one of those featured in this book. When I owned the car I was puzzled by this seemingly non-standard set-up and I asked Geoffrey Healey himself about this feature. I was told the following story, later corroborated when I met former Donald Healey Motor Co experimental engineer Roger Menadue years later.

When the 100 S production-racing Healeys were being built in 1955, it had originally been proposed that 100 examples should be made, although for reasons unknown only 50 were actually constructed. However, Dunlop had been asked to supply 100 sets of their then revolutionary four-wheel disc braking system, an order which could not be amended. As a result, there remained at the Warwick Healey works 50 unused sets of these brakes.

Never ones to waste anything, the Healey family arranged for these sets to be used on 50 100/6 cars which were then marketed as "extra special" vehicles at a premium price. It is thought that all these cars had the then new six-port head engines as well. Whether the cars were built with these brakes or converted when new by Healeys at Warwick remains unclear, but they certainly did (and do) exist, and must have provided headaches for parts department managers over the years by their differences from standard and their absence from official documentation. Some contemporary Jaguars used a similar Dunlop system and brake parts for these rare 100/6s can, I believe, still be obtained via Jaguar specialists. I was also told that an ancillary benefit of this disc brake fitment on "production" cars was the possibility that the Works might be able to gain homologation papers for competition 100/6s so fitted, and I believe a handful of such cars were built.

WHEELS AND TYRES

The BN1 and BN2 100s were granted wire wheels as a standard fitting, but the 100/6 and 3000s were not so fortunate, and had disc wheels as standard with wire wheels as an extra cost option. There were, and are, owners who consider wire wheels to be a liability, with their propensity to break spokes and the perennial difficulty of cleaning them. However, the general opinion is that the Healey looks right on wire wheels and a little odd on steel disc wheels, even though these might be more practical. Wire wheels also allow for better brake cooling.

What is in no doubt is that a Big Healey on disc wheels is a pretty rare beast and that the later the model, the rarer it is; only a tiny percentage of Mark III cars were fitted with disc wheels, although they were undoubtedly available until the end of production. However, they may not have been available on very late cars in North America, where the wire wheel seems to have become the standard fitment.

WIRE WHEELS

Wire wheels were manufactured by Dunlop and were of 4Jx15 size, having 48 spokes. In truth, a 48-spoked wheel was barely adequate for a car of the Healey's power and weight, and from roughly the start of 3000 production a considerably stronger Dunlop 60-spoked wire wheel of 4½J section could be had as an option. Apparently, there were difficulties in fitting this early version of the slightly wider wheel over the front drum brakes of the 100/6, which explains why it was not offered for that model. In mid-1963, at car number 29367 towards the end of the Mark II Convertible's run, the 60-spoke wire wheels replaced the 48-spoke type as the normal optional fitment. It should be noted that the now commonly seen 72-spoke wire wheel was never available for the Austin-Healey during its build period.

One of the plus points of the knock-on wire wheel as originally developed by Rudge-Whitworth was its quick-change facility, clearly of great use when racing. The ears on the hub

The original wire wheel for all cars with this option had 48 spokes, right up to 1962-63. This was barely adequate for the job in view of the car's power and weight, and most owners these days opt for the stronger 60-spoke variety. This original example of the 100/6 nevertheless still sports the correct, if somewhat fragile, 48-spoke wheels. (Author)

This is the 60-spoke wire wheel, which was standard on cars with this option from 1963. It was, however, available at extra cost before then. This one has the correct silver-grey paint finish. Today, the 165x15 radial tyre shown here represents the size and type most commonly used.

Those buyers not prepared to pay for the wire wheel option made do with this steel disc wheel, fitted with eight elongated cooling holes. The wheel was finished in the same silver-grey paint as the wire wheels, and always came with this chromed hub cap plate with its Austin "winged A" motif.

negated the quick-change facility. This took place from as early as 1958 for cars sent to Germany and Switzerland and, somewhat later, cars for Holland and even sometimes France suffered the same indignity. By 1966 the safety disease had even spread to some parts of North America and a good number of the late Mark III cars sent there had these octagonal wheel nuts.

From the introduction of the Phase II version of the Mark III, the threads on the wheel nuts and hub splines were made coarser at eight threads per inch as compared to slightly more than 12 per inch on earlier cars. The wheels themselves remained interchangeable, even though the nuts no longer were. As was usual with knock-on wire wheels, the hubs and nuts on the right-hand side had a left-hand thread, whereas those on the left-hand side had a conventional thread. This was done so that the wheel nut had a natural tendency to tighten itself during the forward motion of the car, but of course it also meant that the wheel nuts were not interchangeable from side to side.

All nuts were engraved on their centres with the word "undo" and an appropriate arrow and the words "left side" or "right side" as appropriate. For cars fitted with eared wheel nuts, a copper-faced hammer was provided in the tool kit. Cars with "safety" nuts were provided with both the hammer and a large black-painted spanner that fitted over the octagonal nut and which was belaboured with the hammer to tighten or loosen the wheel.

nuts were simply struck several times with a copper- or leather-faced hammer and the wheel was loosened or tightened in a few seconds. In common with many other British sports cars of the 1950s, the Healey had chromed knock-on securing nuts with ears – at least until meddling politicians got busy and in several countries declared these a safety hazard. Octagonal style hub nuts had to be substituted, which did nothing for the look of the assemblage and rather

Wire wheels were painted with a semi-matt aluminium-silver paint of a standard BMC type, code AL1. The vexed question of the originality of chromed wire wheels arises at this point. Without doubt there were Healeys which reached their first

A close-up of the knock-on hub nut which retained the wire wheel. These were "handed" left and right, and were engraved to ensure correct fitting.

owners with chromed wire wheels, particularly in the USA, this being so as far back as the early BN1 cars. However, the factory did not list these as an option and it seems that they were usually fitted by the dealer before the customer took delivery. It had long been held that the simple act of chroming wire wheel spokes weakened them, and for this reason BMC refused to list these as an original option.

DISC WHEELS

The disc wheels were made by Rubery Owen Ltd and, like the 48-spoke wire wheels, were of 4J section and 15in diameter. They fitted over five studs mounted on the hubs and were fastened by five nuts, domed on one side. Eight ventilation holes were provided in each wheel, arranged in four pairs of two with a space between the pairs. The holes were oval rather than circular.

The wheel was finished by a chromed hub cap or naveplate which, like the wheel itself, was the same as that used on the big Austin saloons of the day. Pressed into its centre was the Austin winged-A motif.

TYRES

Tyres on basic 100/6 cars with disc wheels were of the tubeless type, size 5.90 x 15 and of cross-ply construction. They were normally of Dunlop manufacture and of the Gold Seal variety. Cars supplied with wire wheels (and, it seems, disc-wheeled cars supplied new with overdrive) were given the higher specification Dunlop Roadspeed RS4 5.90 x 15 cross-ply tyres, and these came with inner tubes fitted. RS4 tyres could be ordered specially on an otherwise basic specification car.

The 3000 models came as standard with Dunlop Roadspeed tyres, tubed type, irrespective of the type of wheel fitted. The RS4 specification tyre was superseded in mid-1960 by the new RS5 upgraded variety. By the time of the 3000 Mark II Convertible, radial-ply tyres were gaining general acceptance and as a result, Dunlop's SP41 tyre, size 165 x 15 in an HR rating became available as an option. Dunlop RS5 cross-plies continued to be the basic fitment, however, and North American export cars almost always had them, the radial-ply type being much slower to gain a foothold in the USA market. A large proportion of the later cars supplied new to Continental Europe had radial-ply tyres, particularly cars to France, the home of the radial-ply design.

SPARE WHEEL

All cars were provided with a spare wheel identical to the other four. On 2/4-seater cars, this was fitted in the left-hand side of the boot, so taking up considerable valuable luggage space. On the BN6 and BN7 two-seaters, the spare was placed as it had been on the BN1 and BN2 100s, on a ledge at the forward end of the boot where it protruded into the rear of the cockpit under a cover. Further details about spare wheel fittings will be found in the Body section.

This chromed 60-spoke wire wheel features the emasculated octagonal "safety" hub nut demanded by legislation in some export markets. A number of the last 3000s supplied to the USA also suffered this indignity. Chromed wire wheels were always frowned upon by BMC, as chroming the spokes tended to weaken them. Red painted brake callipers are highly unoriginal and not at all nice in the author's personal view.

Not available in period, but quite commonly fitted today, is this type of 72-spoke wire wheel. It gives an even greater margin of safety than the 60-spoke type.

ELECTRICAL EQUIPMENT

This is the earlier type of regulator or control box, a Lucas RB106/2. The wire clip holding the cover is clear.

As with the BN1 and BN2 cars, and in common with almost all of the British motor industry at the time, all electrical fittings were by Joseph Lucas and Co from Birmingham.

This general view of a 100/6 engine shows the dynamo in position, with the coil mounted to it. The saddle and clamp arrangement for holding the coil is visible. The dynamo shown is a Lucas type C45/PV5. When the car was built, the coil supplied would probably have been coloured silver, although some were finished in dull black.

DYNAMO
Electricity was generated by a Lucas dynamo driven by the fan belt and bolted to the engine on the right-hand side using a three-point mounting. This had an adjustable slide at the forward end. The slide was usually locked with a Nyloc nut, although on earlier 100/6s, a split washer and plain nut was used. Alternators were not a standard fitting for Healey 3000s in period, although they were used on the various works rally cars.

The model of dynamo was updated twice. The 100/6 and early 3000 Mark I cars had a C45 PV5 type, which had screw-type electrical connectors. This changed to C45 PV6 on the later Mark I and all Mark II 3000s, with spade-type, push-on connectors. The Mark III cars had a type C42 PVC dynamo.

Dynamos were always finished in engine-colour paint.

STARTER MOTOR
Like the dynamo, the starter motor was always finished in engine-colour paint. It was not changed during the production run, remaining a Lucas type L3M418G.

The starter motor solenoid was Lucas type ST950 and again remained unchanged. It was located under the bonnet near the base of the oil filter housing.

VOLTAGE CONTROL BOX
Voltage regulation was dealt with by a Lucas RB106/2 control box, which on the 3000 Mark III was replaced by the updated RB340 type. The RB106/2 box was mounted on the right-hand side of the bulkhead and had screw-type wire fixing points. The cover was made of black or, more commonly, dark brown Bakelite plastic and carried the word "Lucas" moulded in. A simple wire clip held the cover in place. The later RB340 control box was square in shape without the rounded off corners of the RB106/2 type. There was no wire clip and the case, which was of black plastic, had a rough textured finish to it. Its wire terminals were of the push-on spade type.

IGNITION COIL
The ignition coil was always attached by a band clamp to the top of the dynamo. A saddle was incorporated into the clamp and a further clamp secured the coil to the band clamp. This was tightened by a screw. The coil was left unpainted but the

The distributor on the six-cylinder Healeys was easily accessible and was, on earlier cars, a Lucas type DM6A, as seen here. Note the clamp at the base which was loosened to provide timing adjustment, and also the cable-drive for the rev counter on earlier cars. emerging from the side of the distributor pedestal. Just visible towards the centre right of the picture is the heater outlet cock from the cylinder head.

Here we see the later type of Lucas control box as used on the Mark III 3000s, a type RB340. This has a cover with squared-off ends, which is held down by screws rather than a wire clip.

clamp was finished in engine colour. The saddle was absent on the BJ8 cars which used the C42 PVC dynamo, which was smaller in diameter.

The nose of the coil was in black Bakelite with a threaded knurled knob that held the high-tension lead from the distributor. Some late cars had the later type coil with a push-on connector. All Lucas coils had their date of manufacture stamped into their bases, and all coils supplied for six-cylinder Healeys were of the heavy-duty type, model HA12. An uprated Lucas "sports coil" could be specially ordered for those with competition in mind. This was recognisable by having a red instead of a black plastic nose.

DISTRIBUTOR AND IGNITION LEADS

The distributor was a Lucas type DM6A for the 100/6, 3000 Mark I and Mark II BN7 and BT7. This was changed during Mark II Convertible production to type 25D6. The change point was at engine number 29F-3563 and this later distributor was used on Mark III 3000s as well. Contact breaker gap remained at .016 of an inch throughout. The distributor cap had the word "Lucas" moulded into the black or dark brown plastic of which it was made.

The plug leads entered the cap at the side rather than from the top, as they had on the BN1 and BN2 cars. They were gripped by small brass screws accessed from inside the cap, as was the coil lead at the centre of the cap. Plug leads were plain black and had braided metal cores.

Spark plug connectors were of hard black plastic, and a straight type was used on the Longbridge-built BN4s. Most Abingdon-built cars reverted to the moulded black rubber

connectors used in the four-cylinder Healeys, but right-angled rubber connectors were used for the BJ8. Plug leads to the first and second cylinders, and those to the fifth and sixth cylinders, were clipped together by black rubber rings, but for some reason this was not done on cylinders three and four! Plug leads on many cars bore numbers (1 to 6) to identify their cylinder. These numbers were in black on yellow sleeves fitted around the leads just above the point where the lead entered the connector. The firing order on all the six-cylinder Healeys was 1,5,3,6,2,4.

These plug leads carry the yellow sleeves that show which cylinder they serve. The vacuum advance diaphragm can be seen on the side of the distributor. Note that this car is fitted with an alternator rather than the original dynamo, just visible to the right of the picture.

SPARK PLUGS

Spark plugs were invariably of Champion manufacture, with a 14mm diameter and a ¾in reach. Plug gap was always set to .025in.

Longbridge-built 100/6s had Champion NA8 plugs, with N5 plugs being substituted in Abingdon-built 100/6s and 3000s, although some late BJ7s and all BJ8s had type UN12Y plugs. In addition the harder type N3 plug was sometimes supplied for Mark I 3000s and could be specifically requested as it was much more suitable for high-speed or competition work. The nearest modern equivalent Champion plug is type N12YC, which is suitable for all road-going six-cylinder Healeys.

IGNITION TIMING

Static ignition timing varied by model, too. The 1C-H galleried-head 100/6 originally had ignition timing set at 5° *after* Top Dead Centre, amazingly; no wonder it didn't go well! This was rapidly revised to 6° before TDC, which held good for the six-port head cars as well. The Mark I 3000 required a setting of 5° BTDC, but on the Mark II, timing was advanced considerably to 12° BTDC. Mark III 150bhp 29K engines were quoted as requiring 10° BTDC static timing, or 15° BTDC if measured stroboscopically.

Ignition timing was advanced automatically both by centrifugal weights within the distributor and also by vacuum advance. The vacuum advance pipe which connected the distributor vacuum unit to the rear carburettor was made of ⅛in copper tubing painted engine colour, as were its clamps. It was fastened to the engine by means of two securing clamps, one fixed to the heater valve rear bolt and the other attached to the left rear cylinder head stud.

These are the twin Lucas horns in their correct position on a Mark III BJ8 car. Note the tension spring on the bonnet release rod above the horns and the bracket for receiving the end of the bonnet prop.

HORNS

Twin horns were always fitted to the Big Healeys, one with a high note and the other with a low note. The actual note emitted was adjustable. The 100/6 and Mark I 3000s had Lucas type HF1748 horns, which were mounted behind the front grille on brackets welded to the upper front crossmember. Such horns were normally painted a metallic silver colour, although black examples are not unknown.

The horn type changed to Lucas 9H on the introduction of the Mark II cars, and these were always coloured black. Mounting points changed too, and there were now one on the left and the other on the right-hand front shroud support in the engine compartment just under the bonnet. On Mark III BJ8 cars, the same horns were used, but both were now mounted on the right-hand front shroud support, quite near the coil mounting.

WINDSCREEN WIPERS AND WASHERS

As it had been on BN1 and BN2 cars, the windscreen wiper motor was seated on a bracket under the front scuttle on the cockpit side of the bulkhead and on the left-hand side of the car. It remained in this position throughout and was always the self-parking type. On cars up to the late Mark II Convertibles in August 1963 it was Lucas type DR2, and thereafter type DR3A. The motor acted directly on a rack within a tube that passed across the car and below the scuttle, engaging the gear wheels fixed at the base of the wiper spindles. Lucas wiper motors always carried a date of manufacture stamp.

Somewhat unusually for the late 1950s, the 100/6 always had as standard equipment a windscreen washer system, albeit an early primitive one. This was carried over to the 3000s and things did not improve much. No Healey was made with an electric washer system, although many owners fitted them later and some were dealer-fitted on new cars. On all cars bar the Mark III 3000s, the manual screenwash bottle was fitted under the left-hand side of the dashboard, where it was not exactly easy to fill. It was located in a circular hole cut into the parcel shelf situated in that area, towards the bulkhead and on the right side of this shelf. A black-painted metal ring actually held the bottle steady.

The bottle itself was glass on the Longbridge-built cars and translucent white plastic on Abingdon-built cars. A brand name of Trafalgar appeared on the glass bottle, but the plastic type was not ascribed to any maker. The width of the bottle's neck was widened, presumably to make filling easier, after cars BT7-6344 and BN7-6486. Small-bore clear plastic piping connected the reservoir to the dashboard-mounted plunger and then to the screen washer jets on the scuttle just in front of the windscreen. The great majority of cars were fitted with two separate jets, but some 100/6s had a single central jet with a pair of angled nozzles.

On the BJ8 Mark III cars, revisions to the dashboard meant that the reservoir bottle had to be relocated under the bonnet.

On LHD cars it was located just in front of the right bonnet hinge, whereas on RHD cars it was on the left-hand side near the fuse box. Phase I BJ8s continued with the anonymous plastic bottle held by a black metal frame, but Phase II cars had bottles which carried the manufacturer's name of Tudor. The metal frame in this case had a slightly different shape and was painted blue.

WIRING LOOM AND FUSE BOX

All Big Healeys were wired with a positive earth system, even the last Mark IIIs. The wiring loom was made in several sections, which were joined by bullet connectors. As normal, colour-coded PVC plastic coated wires were used, wrapped together by a braided cotton casing. This had a colour trace pattern woven into it so that wiring looms for different models of Healey could be identified.

Earlier 100/6 cars used wires with colour-coded lacquered braid coverings. The main section of the wiring loom passed through the bulkhead in a single grommetted hole, splitting into various sub-sections behind the dashboard. Other smaller loom sections joined the main loom, such as those for the headlights, horns, dipswitch and overdrive. In addition, a subsidiary loom which fed the fuel pump, lights and indicators at the rear of the car joined the main loom near the fuse block and travelled along the left-hand chassis rail to the rear and into the boot. Here, it split into further sections for the left and right rear lights, and a central feed for the number plate light.

On this BJ8 3000 Mark III, the fuse box has a black plastic cover. To the right of it is the zinc-plated overdrive relay, and to the left is the overdrive throttle switch with its actuating rod in view. Note that the screenwash bottle on these cars is fitted under the bonnet.

Not surprisingly, the wiring looms were of Lucas manufacture and carried the maker's name on a label fastened around the main loom in the engine compartment. Wiring looms were installed into the chassis-body units at Jensen's, but the actual connections were made at Longbridge or Abingdon as the individual components requiring electricity were added. Bullet connectors were used for the great majority of wiring connections, the male bullet pushing into the female sleeve, which was covered by a heavy-duty black plastic insulation cover. Some female connectors were of the double sleeve type to accept two male bullets where a common feed was required.

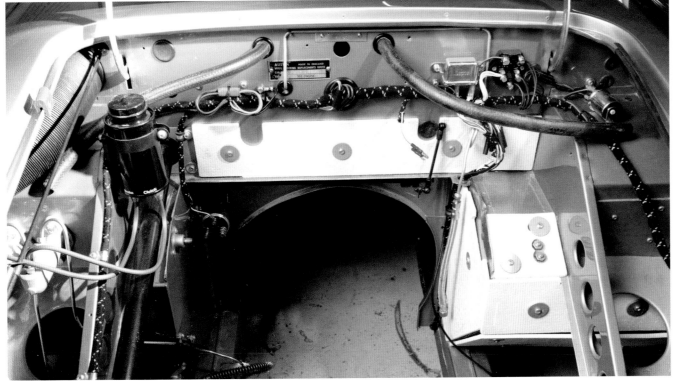

In this engine-less car one of the main parts of the wiring loom is visible, as is the large black rubber central grommet through which it passes on its way to behind the dashboard. The main loom carries a colour-coded thread, as explained in the text.

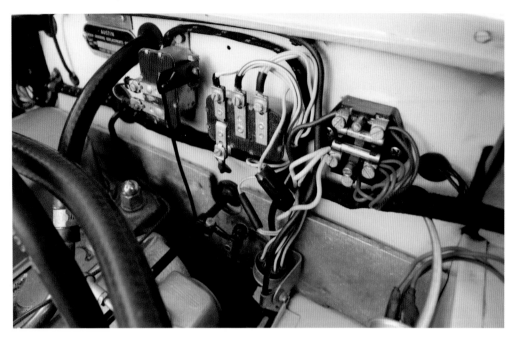

These are the electrical fittings on the front bulkhead of a 100/6. As was often the case, this fuse box did not have a cover. Two spare fuses are lodged in the box. The actuating rod and crank for the overdrive throttle switch are plainly visible.

Both the main wiring loom and its subsidiaries were held by metal wrap-round clips, zinc-plated and of several sizes appropriate to the wiring to be secured. These clips were fixed to the car's body-chassis by cross-head self-tapping screws.

As the car evolved through its various models from 1956 to 1967, there were a number of detail changes to the looms to reflect the relocation of various items and the introduction of other equipment. The dashboard redesign for the Mark III BJ8 cars, for instance, occasioned quite a few modifications. As a result there are a number of similar yet not identical wiring looms for the various Big Healeys and one needs to be aware of this if replacing the wiring.

The wiring incorporated a fuse box having one 50-amp fuse and one 35-amp one, together with screw fittings for the securing of the wiring. Not all electrical items were fused, the lighting system being a prime example. The 50-amp fuse protected the horns, and the 35-amp fuse covered all other fused circuits. The fuse box on all cars up to late 1963 was a Lucas type SF6 and was located on the left-hand side of the front bulkhead under the bonnet. In addition to the two fuses in use, the box was moulded to carry two spare fuses at 90° to the main fuses, one of each rating. Lucas fuse boxes of this type frequently, but not always, had a push-on black plastic cover.

The BJ8 cars used a different Lucas fuse box, type 13H252; this held two 35 amp fuses with two spares and had a soft plastic dust cover. Spade connections rather than screw terminals were used.

No other fuses were used elsewhere in the wiring, although a 10 amp in-line fuse was added into the rear number plate lamp wiring towards the end of Mark III production in 1967.

This new fuse was to prevent a short in the vulnerable wiring to this lamp from burning out the entire wiring system, a fault that had actually occurred on a number of cars.

OVERDRIVE CIRCUIT

The overdrive unit was activated by a Lucas solenoid attached to its side, and this was controlled through a relay operated by the overdrive switch. The zinc-plated relay box was mounted on the engine side of the front bulkhead adjacent to the fuse box. Screw terminals were used, clamping the Y-shaped booted connector ends of the overdrive wiring itself.

A further electrical control was also fitted in the overdrive circuit, and this was an electrical throttle switch that prevented overdrive from being disengaged when the car was running on a trailing throttle. The throttle had to be about one-third open to achieve disengagement, an arrangement that prevented unwelcome shocks to the transmission system. The switch was mechanically connected to the accelerator linkage by a black-painted wire rod that operated a lever on the side of the switch. Once again, this switch was sited in the front left bulkhead area under the bonnet, very near to the overdrive relay unit, and its body was similarly zinc-plated. On the Mark III cars, the overdrive relay was mounted higher up the bulkhead than on the earlier cars, but still near the fuse box and throttle switch.

BATTERY

The heart of the car's electrical system was the battery – or batteries in the case of the BN6 and BN7 cars. Once again, Lucas provided the original equipment batteries, a single 12-volt 58 amp/hour type for the BN4, BJ7 and BJ8 cars, and twin 6-volt batteries on the BN6 and BN7 cars. These were connected in series to give the same 58 amp/hour capacity.

All batteries were originally in hard black rubber cases with tar tops and moulded-in securing flanges. The type number for the original 12-volt battery was GTW9A, and this was fitted up to 1962, with type BTWGA fitted to the Mark II and III convertibles. The 6-volt batteries were type SLG11E. The lead terminals were always Lucas helmet types, marked plus or minus as appropriate and clamped to the battery by self-tapping screws.

THE TWIN 6-VOLT SYSTEM

On the two-seater BN6 and BN7 cars, the two 6-volt batteries were carried in metal frames fixed to the top of the chassis behind the rear tonneau panel in the flat deck and forward of the rear axle. They were accessible through a hinged trapdoor located above them and behind the seats. The batteries were held to their metal frames by bars and J-shaped rods that hooked into notches in the chassis brackets. These rods had screwed tops, and zinc-plated wing nuts held them in place.

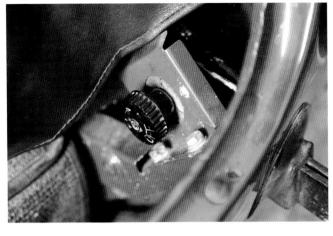

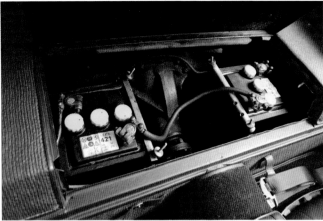

Here we see the twin 6-volt batteries connected in series that were found on the BN6 and BN7 two-seaters. They fitted in metal trays mounted on the chassis on either side of the rear of the propeller shaft. These restraining clamps are not quite as original, but the Hardura matting and vinyl surround to the battery trap door look to be original and correct.

This shows the battery master switch on a 2/4 seater car. Also to be seen are one of the tiny rubber buffers fitted around the boot rim lip, the rubber boot through which the bumper irons pass, the correct Hardura matting for the boot floor and a part of the thin cover that went over the battery.

A thoughtful touch was a cut-off master switch which also formed the earth connection. It was mounted on the front bulkhead of the boot, and was a useful anti-theft device, as it could only be accessed when the boot was opened. When the boot was locked shut, the car's electrical supply could not be energised. Battery cables were covered in black plastic, which was then encased in a black cotton sleeve.

On these twin-battery cars, one cable ran from the negative side of the right-hand battery to the engine compartment via the chassis rail, to which it was clipped. A further short cable connected the positive and negative terminals of the two batteries. The final (earth) cable ran from the positive side of the left-hand battery to the cut-off switch. The other terminal on the cut-off switch was connected by a braided, uninsulated cable to an earth point on one of the fixing bolts for the left-hand suspension bump box.

THE 12-VOLT SYSTEM

The 2/4-seater cars, BN4, BT7, BJ7 and BJ8, all had a totally different arrangement. Their single 12-volt battery was mounted in the boot on the right side, sitting in a heavy-duty acid-resistant black plastic tray. It was tethered by a right-angled steel strip fixed along its outer edge, and this was held down by a screwed holding rod at each end. The other ends of these rods were hooked under points at the bottom rear of the battery. A wooden spacer block braced the battery against the inside of the rear wing. There was a flexible plastic cover over the top of the battery to protect luggage from spilt acid.

The positive battery terminal was towards the rear of the car and was connected to a master or cut-off switch mounted on the right-hand rear shroud support bracket. A short earth cable earthed the other terminal on the cut-off switch to a

On the 2/4-seater cars, the battery had to be moved to the right-hand side of the boot, and was a large single 12-volt type. This battery has the correct external strapping and individual filler plugs. Note the heavy-duty acid-resistant black plastic tray under the battery. Also on view is the standard-fit battery master switch. Normally a thin black plastic cover was loosely fitted over the battery to protect the luggage, but it has been removed here for the photograph.

The fuel pump has been dealt with in the Carburettor section, but is shown again here as it is an item of electrical equipment. This car is a late Mark III 3000 with radius rods to control the rear suspension, and these are visible in the photograph. Showing also on top of the axle casing is the small ventilator, an item that is prone to blockage.

bolt on the same support bracket. The negative post on the battery was connected by a long cable to the starter solenoid in the engine compartment. This cable passed through a grommet in the inner wing, then under the car and along the right-hand chassis rail to the engine compartment. It was clipped to the chassis using metal wrap-round clips.

LAMPS AND LIGHTING

The standard Lucas headlamp unit used in the earlier Big Healeys was the type F700 seen here. This had a separate bulb, sealed beam units being reserved for the USA market once separate headlight bulbs became outlawed in that country. The small rivet at the top of the chromed headlight rim is clearly shown.

As with other electrical items, it was Lucas who supplied the lamps for all the cars under review. Note that number-plate lamps, which were Lucas type 467/2, are dealt with in the Bodywork section of this book.

HEADLAMPS

The usual headlamp fitted to home market cars, and to most of those not destined for North America, was the type F700. This did not have the well-known "tripod" arrangement used on other cars of the period, and in fact it seems that "tripod" headlamps were never fitted to 100/6s or 3000s. The F700 lamps had convex block-type lenses.

The earliest North American cars were built and shipped with no headlamps, and the lamps were fitted by dealerships on arrival. This was because sealed-beam units were required in the USA where separate headlamp bulbs were no longer legal, and sealed-beam lamps were not available from Lucas

A similar F700 headlight from a different car shows the later type of headlight rim, which had a slightly wider profile than that used on the 100/6s and earlier 3000s.

before about July 1959. The US dealers usually fitted sealed-beam units by Westinghouse or General Electric.

Once Lucas had sealed-beam headlamps available, these were fitted to North American cars at the factory, as well as to some cars for other export destinations. Eventually, they were used on home market cars as well, although it is not certain exactly when this began. In March 1962, the lens of the standard sealed-beam headlights changed to incorporate a ring around the Lucas name in the centre. From September 1965, the Lucas Mark X headlamp was used on Mark III cars, although possibly not for North America, at least at first.

There were a number of different variations in the headlamps supplied to European markets, and the type used depended on local regulations applying where the car was sold. For instance, cars for France were required to have yellow bulbs, whereas from 1960 cars sent to Sweden needed lamps with asymmetrical dipping, something which was later introduced for other Continental markets.

The headlamp units were fitted in black-painted metal bowls by means of three spring-loaded adjustment screws over which the clamping rings that held the actual lamp were fitted. The bowls themselves were attached to the car body by cross-headed, self-tapping screws, and there was a black rubber gasket between the headlamp bowl flange and the car body. Moulded into this were two hollow tubes with closed ends that covered the ends of the two adjustment screws and protected their threads from road dirt and corrosion.

A chromed rim around the headlamp concealed the adjustment screw heads and fixing screws. This rim had a brass rivet at its top. It was slipped over projections on the top of the headlight bowl and then secured by a self-tapping screw and further clip at the base of the rim. Some earlier cars had an internal clip at the top held by the rivet, and this located into a notch in the headlight bowl rim.

SIDELIGHTS, INDICATORS, TAIL LAMPS AND REFLECTORS

The smaller lights went through a number of changes over the production life of these cars. The major changes occurred in May 1964 and March 1965. There were also some changes specific to individual markets, and these are discussed separately.

Front sidelights and indicators

On cars built before May 1964, the front sidelights and indicators were combined in Lucas type 594 units. These had a clear glass beehive-shaped lens marked with the words "Lucas" and "Made in England". The lenses were held in place by being pressed into the rubber boot around the bulb holder, and further retained by a chromed ring that pressed into an outer ring on the same rubber boot.

From May 1964 at car number 26704, Lucas type 691 units were introduced for the front sidelights. These had lenses that were somewhat larger than before and were made of frosted plastic still with the central portion in "beehive" style. The lenses were fixed to the light body with two long screws, and a drain hole was provided. This should be fitted at the bottom.

The second and major change came in March 1965 at car number 31336. Separate front indicator lamps were provided, the shroud pressings being slightly modified

The Lucas 594 front sidelight had a "beehive" style of lens in either clear or slightly frosted glass. This unit doubled as the front turn indicator and had a twin-filament bulb. The lens is retained by the chromed ring, which itself is a push-fit into the rubber backing disc.

accordingly. These were of the same pattern as the sidelights, but of course orange/amber coloured. Although all cars for all markets from 31336 onwards had these new lamps, it seems that they may have been phased in gradually a little earlier and some cars with earlier chassis numbers are known to have had the updated lamps from new. Peter Healey's red 3000 Mark III, known to be original, proves that at the end of 1964/start of 1965, an additional number of "cross-over" cars were built. These had a Lucas L632 combined clear front sidelight and amber indicator light unit, as illustrated on page 87. This was a sort of "halfway house" towards the post-March 1965 arrangement. These cars also had separate rear indicators, although not of the post March 1965 type. Again see photographs on page 87.

Rear lights

The rear lights on pre-May 1964 cars were again Lucas 594 units, this time using a red lens. They achieved the clever trick of performing three separate functions with only two filaments in each unit: they acted as tail lamps, brake lamps and indicator lamps.

This miracle was achieved by clever wiring and a small zinc-plated steel box containing relays. The box ensured the correct priority of function when the car was braking and turning simultaneously at night: the brighter brake light filament flashed while the dimmer sidelight filament remained constantly illuminated. It was a system that caused confusion even then and yet which, amazingly, is still legal today in the UK on cars built at that time. It does, however, cause some younger MoT test men to have apoplexy! The box was mounted on the left front inner wing just in front of the shroud support, where it was partially hidden by the fresh air trunking.

This is a Mark II Convertible, BJ7. Again the later headlight rim is in use but the standard Lucas type 594 front sidelight lens was still fitted, as it had been from the start of 100/6 production.

Show below is an 1965 Mark III car with the Lucas L691 front sidelight lens used on most cars between May 1964 and March 1965, although note what is said in the text about "cross-over" cars with the combined Lucas L632 unit. (Author)

At the rear, a similar beehive 594 lens and lamp unit was employed, but the glass lens was coloured red. This style of lamp was used from the earliest 100/6s until May 1964. It was not only the tail lamp and turn indicator, but acted as brake light too. On this 100/6, the reflector can be seen with its broad chromed ring and conical lens cover. This type of reflector was used on the 100/6 and 3000 Mark Is.

This is the 100/6 and 3000 Mark I reflector, from which the conical lens cover was eventually deleted for the US market. The colours of this item varied all the way from red through amber and orange almost to yellow.

From car number 26704 in May 1964, Lucas type 692 units with red plastic lenses replaced the earlier type. The combined stop-tail-indicator system remained in use – at least for North American, UK and most non-European export market cars, which of course accounted for around 95% of production.

At car number 31336 in March 1965, the arrangement changed again, as proper separate indicator lamps were provided for all markets. Some earlier cars are known to have had the updated lamps from new, so the new arrangement may have been phased in over a period of time. With these separate lamps, the relay box controlling the three-way rear lamp function was no longer needed. The stop-tail lamps remained in their earlier positions, but the new indicator lamps took the place of the reflectors, fitting into pods that were slightly enlarged to suit the lamps' larger diameter. A similar arrangement had been used on cars for Germany and Sweden since 1961.

Rear reflectors

The 100/6 and the early 3000s had a stylish, bullet-shaped plastic cover over the reflector, which could be clear, red or orange, depending on the intended market. Likewise, the plastic reflector disc itself under the cover could be red, yellow or even white, again according to local regulations. This reflector was always mounted on a black rubber backing piece. A deep chromed bezel surrounded the "bullet" cover and secured it to the reflector body.

In May 1960, a change in US regulations outlawed covers over reflectors. As a result, a new and simpler design of reflector was introduced for all markets. This had a shal-

A close-up of the rear Lucas 594 multi-function light unit.

Mark II 3000s of all types, and the earlier Mark IIIs, had this style of rear reflector with no conical cover.

For a brief period around the turn of 1964-65, this type of Lucas L632 front lamp was used on what I have described as "Cross-over" cars. This lamp unit was the same as that fitted to the 1964-onwards Morris Minor. The sidelight showed at the bottom while the larger section of the lens was devoted to the orange indicator function.

lower, plain chromed ring surround and a rubber backing piece; it was fitted in the same pod as previously. Roger Moment reports from the USA that un-restored cars built at this period often have the earlier type of reflector with no "bullet" covers. He surmises that when the legislation changed, US dealers were simply instructed to remove the "bullet" covers on cars already built and shipped before the new type was used on production.

There was no change to the reflectors when other elements of the lighting system changed in May 64. However, when separate rear indicator lamps were introduced in March 65, the reflectors were displaced. They found a home on brackets that held them above the outer ends of the rear bumper. A silver painted bracket was used, attached to the outer bumper bolts, and the reflector itself was a Lucas RFR14, larger than the previous type. For some markets, it appears that this new reflector was fitted below, rather than above, the bumper bar.

FLASHER UNIT

The indicator flasher unit was always a Lucas type FL5, having the appearance of a small aluminium can. It was

During this same "crossover" period, some cars had this rear arrangement. They included this Mark III 3000, which is known to be original. A larger lens for the tail-and-stop light was used, together with the same reflector in the same position as before, but an amber indicator lamp was placed between them. It looks like very much like an afterthought. It is not clear how many cars had this little-known arrangement, or to which markets they were supplied. The same Lucas L692 red rear light unit and lens was used on cars built from May 1964 to March 1965, even where they were not given the separate indicator unit, as shown on this "cross-over" car. In this case, the brake light filament was arranged to flash as on the earlier cars.

By March 1965 the final indicator and side and tail lamp arrangement was in place. At the front, a small pressing was incorporated into the front shroud on each side, and the new separate front sidelight was mounted to it. The old sidelight position was occupied by a separator indicator lamp, as seen here.

mounted to the inboard side of the chassis brace, in front of and below the fuse block.

OVERSEAS VARIATIONS

From September 1961, regulations in Germany and Sweden required separate amber indicator lenses at both front and rear. So from car number 15163, cars for these markets had special arrangements.

At the front, a second type 594 lamp with an amber lens was mounted next to each sidelight; a slight modification to the front shroud was required. At the rear, the pods normally used for reflectors were sequestered to accept indicator lamps with amber lenses, and the original red lamps retained only their stop and tail functions. On cars with this arrangement, the displaced reflectors were fitted on bumper brackets, and showed above the bumper and just outboard of the rear lamps. The mystery is why BMC did not at that time adopt this separate indicator arrangment for all Big Healeys – it was much safer.

There was also a change in January 1963 that affected cars for Canada and possibly some other markets. These cars were given orange bulbs or orange lenses within the single front 594 unit. The front sidelight of course then showed the same orange as the indicator.

It is not at all easy to photograph the number plate light, which is sandwiched between the rear bumper and the rear shroud. The lamp was Lucas 467/2 and it was fitted in this position on the great majority of cars. There were, however, some later variations in position which are dealt with in the Bodywork section of this book. (Author)

From March 1965, the rear arrangement seen here was used. The old reflector pressing on the rear shroud was enlarged to take an indicator lamp similar to that now used at the front. The reflector was moved to the outer edge of the rear bumper, and was attached to it by a bracket.

The reflector lens was enlarged at the same time. The rear tail and stop lamp unit remained in its original position, and was a red-lens version of the white-lens type now used at the front. At last the turning intentions of Healey drivers were clear to following traffic!

DASHBOARD, INSTRUMENTS AND CONTROLS

Dashboards and instruments were items that were built into the body-chassis units whilst these were still at the Jensen factory. There were two distinct types of dashboard and instruments fitted to the six-cylinder Austin-Healeys, the first of which was very similar but not identical to that used on the four-cylinder cars. The second type was introduced with the Mark III models.

THE EARLY DASHBOARD
The first style of dashboard and instruments was found in all models from 100/6 to 3000 Mark II convertible.

The dashboard was an asymmetric pressing made usually of steel (but occasionally of aluminium) that crossed the car in a graceful curving swoop above the passenger's knees. A chromed grab handle was fitted at the passenger's end, mounted on the slant and dished to provide finger grip space. It was bolted through the dash to a wooden retainer. The instrument panel was a raised oval panel, set within the main dashboard in front of the driver. It contained the instruments and some switchgear. When the optional heater was fitted, its controls were situated below the central (shallowest) portion of the main dashboard.

This style of dashboard, upswept over the passenger's knees and with a parcel shelf underneath, was current from the 1956 100/6 to the 1963 Mark II Convertible. Here we see a Mark II BN7, which has the central gear change lever. The correct type of rear view mirror can be seen at the top, as can original-specification BMC seat belts. A non-original time clock and dash lamp have been added to this car.

This close-up of the passenger's grab handle shows the finger recess let into the dashboard.

The demister air outlets on the top of the dashboard were usually painted to match the trim colour, as here; again, a detail of the rear view mirror can be seen.

The heater control panel was located at the centre of the dashboard. The painted demister outlet can also be seen, as can a turn button for tonneau cover attachment. The large black central switch is not original.

The main dash also contained the ignition switch, with the ignition key number somewhat unwisely stamped on its face – although that was standard practice at the time. There was a manual screenwash plunger push, which was a plain back knob with a chromed bezel on early BN4s with Trafalgar screenwashers. On cars with the Tudor screenwasher, introduced at BN6-1183 in May 1958, there was a knob fitted into a chromed recess on the dashboard; the knob was labelled "screenwash push", or "windshield wash push" on cars for the USA.

The raised oval section was bounded by a chromed beading, secured to the dashboard by clips that passed right through the panel and were spread on the reverse side. In the centre of this oval, a further beading encircled the hole through which the steering column passed.

The chromed bezel surrounding the oval dash panel is visible here, and so is the windscreen wiper switch. Above this is the starter push button. This would once have had the letter "S" on it, but this has usually worn off over the years. The cable-driven rev counter, which contains the ignition warning light, has its red line at 4800rpm, for this car is a six-port engined 100/6.

Below the dashboard on the passenger's side was suspended a deep parcels tray with a lipped edge and the screenwash bottle set into it. The visible edges of this tray were trimmed to match the interior and its floor was lined with a loose piece of carpet. The parcels tray was fixed through its side edge to the side wall of the passenger's side footwell, and at its rear by a turned-down flange screwed to the front bulkhead. A support strut set vertically and painted black attached the tray to the bodywork at its inside edge.

On 100/6s and the earliest 3000s, the choke control knob was not on the dash, but located underneath on the left-hand side of the heater matrix box. During the brief period when the SU "starting carburettor" (see Carburettors section) was in use there was no need for a choke control, but when in November 1959 the manual choke returned, the choke control migrated to the main dashboard, located almost centrally just above the heater controls. Choke knobs can have either the word "choke" picked out in white on them, or just the simple letter C – both are found as original. The dash was braced centrally from behind, the chromed screw fixing the brace being visible on the front of the dash adjacent to the ignition switch.

Although the BN1 and BN2 dashboards had been painted, the six-cylinder cars had a fully trimmed dashboard with unpadded vinyl generally matching the main trim colour. The oval instrument panel was similarly trimmed. Unlike earlier cars, the area above the dashboard on the driver's side of the windscreen – the nearest part of the front shroud – was fully

On this early 3000, the rev counter red line has been repositioned at 5200rpm. At the top right of the picture can be seen the green indicator warning light.

This is the correct Smiths 120mph speedometer, complete with built-in high-beam warning light. The trip odometer was reset by a knurled knob behind the dashboard. This car is fitted with a non-original wood-rim steering wheel.

The fuel gauge occupied this position and was well known for its erratic swings when the car was cornering. The overdrive switch and its engraved escutcheon are visible.

trimmed, and had a certain amount of padding under the trim as a form of early crash protection. The two demisting vents, one each side and both painted to match the trim, protruded through this padded trimmed area to direct their hot air onto the inside of the screen.

The correct interior mirror was a non-dipping type that was oblong with rounded corners and made by Eversure. It was attached to the centre of the dash-top trimmed area by two cross-headed set screws bolted through the shroud with fixing nuts accessed from underneath. A ball fitting at the top of the mirror stem allowed for adjustment. The maker's name appeared on the two brackets that clamped to the mirror glass and its frame. The mirror surround had a chromed finish, as did the fixing stem.

The lower edge of the dashboard was finished with a Furflex clip-on trim that was in two parts, each running from the end of the dashboard and finishing either side of the heater control panel. These strips matched the basic trim colour of the car.

Not many cars were fitted with radio sets in period, and radios were a dealer rather than a factory fitment. When supplied, the radio and its separate power pack were usually mounted on brackets under the dashboard somewhere on the passenger's side. There was no official position, so a variety of mounting arrangements were found. Some radios were even fixed to the parcel shelf, both below and actually on it. Aerials were usually found positioned on the front wings just forward of the windscreen. Sometimes the radio power pack was fitted in the passenger's footwell area.

The heater controls have been dealt with in the Cooling System section, but a number of cars were supplied without heaters. On these, the place where the heater control sub-panel was usually found was fitted instead with a polished aluminium blanking plate that carried the Austin name. Cars

with no heater nevertheless retained the knob that operated the fresh-air inlet at the front of the car. This was mounted through an opening in the blanking plate.

SPEEDOMETER AND REV COUNTER

The instruments were made by Smiths Industries and consisted of four dials, one of which contained two gauges. The two larger dials were placed towards the centre of the oval instrument panel, and were the speedometer and rev counter. Between them, towards the top of the instrument panel, was found a green flashing indicator warning light with a chromed bezel surround. The 120mph speedometer (reading in 20mph increments) was on the left on LHD cars, and the cable-driven revolution counter set on the right. On RHD vehicles, these positions were reversed. Both instruments had matt black circular centres surrounded by dished outers with a silver-beige finish; the figures were outlined in black. They had deep chromed bezels, and flat rather than domed glasses. Needles on both speedometer and rev-counter were black with polished central bosses.

On the face of the speedometer was the legend "mph" (although a kilometre version was always available for those markets which needed it), and a tiny red ignition warning

The combined oil pressure and water temperature gauge was always positioned on the left-hand side of the oval raised panel. The ignition key switch with its hexagonal bezel is also on view.

This 100/6 dashboard is almost entirely correct; only the extension to the overdrive flick switch looks to be wrong. The knurled ring that allowed for steering wheel adjustment can just be seen behind the centre boss. The wiper and light switches both carry initial letters rather than the words in full; either appears to have been correct at various times, although the "initial letter" type is less common.

light was let into the silver-beige area of the face towards the bottom. Inset into the centre matt black circle were a trip counter and, below it, a total mileage recorder that read to 99999. The trip could be re-set by a black knurled knob that protruded downwards to the bottom of the panel.

The rev-counter read to 6000rpm, expressed as "60" but with an explanatory "X100" under the letters "rpm" set in the matt black centre circle. The maximum revolutions warning line was put at 5200 rpm on 3000 models, but Longbridge-built cars with the galleried-head engines had this marked at a lowly 4600 rpm; it was raised to 4800 for the six-port head 100/6. Matching the ignition light on the speedometer, the rev counter had a red warning light for the headlight main beam. This was changed to blue for some later export cars.

MINOR DIALS

The positions of the minor instruments remained the same, irrespective of which side the steering was installed. The fuel gauge was on the outer right and the combined water temperature and oil pressure gauge on the outer left. Strangely, for a sports car built at this time, there never was an ammeter fitted, although many owners later added one.

Both minor instruments had chromed bezels and faces painted the same colour as on the larger ones. Both also had plain black needles. The fuel gauge had its needle pivoted from the top and was marked in ¼ increments from "0" (zero) to "F" (full). This gauge was notorious for its prodigious swings, particularly when the car was cornering hard or on a gradient. To give an accurate reading, the car needed to be stationary and standing level.

The combined gauge on the left had the oil pressure section positioned at the top, reading from zero to 100psi. The capillary operated water temperature gauge at the bottom was marked on the Fahrenheit scale, reading from 90°F to 230°F. This type of gauge continued to read even after the ignition was switched off.

To suit continental markets, a water temperature gauge marked in Centigrade was offered from June 1961. There seems never to have been a metric oil pressure gauge available at all.

SWITCHES AND CONTROLS

Further controls were set within the instrument panel. The black starter push button carried a white letter S and was set in a small chromed bezel, located between the speedometer and the combined gauge towards the top. Below it was the wiper switch, which was a pull-out type set in a hexagonal bezel. Some of these switches were simply marked with a W, but others had the full word "wipers" inscribed on the black knob.

Between the rev counter and the fuel gauge on the right were the switches for the lights and the overdrive, if fitted.

The gear positions, both forward and reverse, were shown on the gear lever knob.

An offset gear lever was used on all cars up to November 1961

The black lighting switch was at the top, and was a two-stage pull-out type; again, it was sometimes labelled simply with an L or, more commonly, the full words "side" and "head" were embossed in white. The first stage put on the side and number plate lights, the second stage illuminated the headlights. The overdrive switch was a metal flick-type switch retained by a hexagonal chromed nut. There was also a chromed circular bezel, engraved "overdrive" in red at the top and "normal" in black at the bottom.

Direction indicators were controlled by a three-position chromed lever-type switch fitted above the boss which contained the horn push in the centre of the steering wheel. The central position was "off", and flicking the switch left or right controlled the appropriate indicators. There was a self-cancelling mechanism. The steering wheel itself and its horn-push boss were covered in the Steering section of this

The parcel shelf would have been commodious but for the fitment of the screen wash bottle in its centre. This must have been exceedingly difficult to fill in situ. The black-painted circular grille is a fresh air outlet, and the grille acted as an insect trap. In the top left on the small shelf is the windscreen wiper motor, again painted black. Towards the right-hand side are the heater matrix box and the heater control cables. Also visible is the choke knob and its associated Bowden cable.

Screen washer plungers could take various forms, this being one of the more common types.

The pedal arrangement, showing the rubber pads fitted to the brake and clutch pedals. Also on view is the foot-operated dip switch, and towards the top of the picture is a heater outlet trap door.

book, and the gear lever is detailed in the Transmission section.

The headlights were dipped by a Lucas push-type switch fixed to the driver's side footwell floor by a U-shaped bracket. The switch was always fitted so that it could be operated by the left foot. It was left unpainted and the wiring from it did not pass through the floor, as might have been expected, but was left exposed and ran upwards from the switch to join the loom behind the bulkhead. The bracket was painted black and was screwed to the floor through the carpet with two cross-head screws.

The three pedals were all pendant types. Unlike the other two, the accelerator had no rubber covering. It was a curved oblong metal pad, no more than an inch wide and roughly twice as long. The top of the pedal shaft had a crank in it and an integral return spring which was finished in black.

The brake and clutch pedals were finished in black, and as a safety measure both had black rubber grip pads pressed in place. There was no motif incorporated in the pedal pads, simply a raised fine grid pattern with an edging around the sides.

The Mark III 3000 had a completely revised dashboard, with a touch of walnut veneered luxury. The slightly larger rear-view mirror is visible and this car has the optional radio set fitted. Although the horn push is correct, the steering wheel is an aftermarket item.

The main switch panel on the Mark III dashboard moved to the centre of the car and is shown here. The ignition switch, which now operated the starter motor as well, is in the centre. The heater controls are the same as before, although now inset into the dashboard itself rather than fitted below it.

The lockable glovebox fitted to the Mark III cars was a welcome improvement. On this car the owner has added a neat period map reading lamp.

THE MARK III DASHBOARD

When the Mark III cars entered production in late 1963, a completely revised and modernised dashboard and set of instruments arrived. As only around 7% of these cars were made with RHD, the descriptions that follow focus on the LHD majority. However, the layout of the dashboard, instruments and switches on RHD cars was a mirror image of that for LHD types.

On the passenger's side there was now a lockable glovebox, with a drop-down lid supported by a sliding chromed stay. The interior of the glovebox was made of black, shaped fibreboard which was not particularly durable, especially if it became damp; nor did it offer as much space as the old parcels tray, which was deleted from under the dash. A consequence of this was that the screenwash bottle had to be relocated under the bonnet, as detailed elsewhere.

Both driver and passenger were treated to the luxury of wooden veneer panels in burr walnut, the glovebox and surround for the passenger and the instrument panel for the driver. The wooden veneer panels had a chromed flat "ribbon" style trim fitted around their edges. The padded top section of the dashboard, formed by the rearmost part of the front shroud, was now finished in black vinyl irrespective of the cockpit trim colour, and the two windscreen demisting vents were always painted black. The central upright part of the dashboard was trimmed in vinyl to match the upholstery and now extended downwards to mate with a centre console that incorporated the gear lever with its black rubber boot. Around the outer edge of this boot was a chromed trim ring, and similar chrome trim was used around both edges of the centre console itself. A chromed ashtray was set at the rear

end of the console.

On the Phase I Mark III 3000s, a padded centre armrest incorporating a rear-hinged lift-up oddments box with a magnetic catch covered the prop-shaft tunnel. This box was deleted for Phase II cars from number 26705, giving way to a plain padded armrest which extended almost to the front of the rear seats. Quite why this useful oddments box was dropped after so short a time is unclear – possibly because of cost, or because the driver's elbow could hit it when changing gear.

Provision for a built-in radio set was at last provided, the set itself being positioned in the console forward of the gear

As befitted the car's new found extra performance, the speedometer now read to 140mph. The high-beam warning light was still inset towards the bottom of the speedometer, but was now blue rather than red.

dash on a small separate panel. Below them was a new, shaped and chromed switch panel. Reading from left to right on a LHD car, this panel carried controls for the overdrive, wipers, ignition, panel lights and main lights. The combined ignition and starter switch was surrounded by a deep bezel, and the ignition key number was no longer stamped on the face of the switch.

The actual switches were all similar toggle types, and that often caused confusion, particularly in the dark when it was all too easy to put on the wipers instead of selecting over-drive! This attracted criticism both at the time and over the years. All had black toggles and screwed chromed bezels; "Wiper", "Panel" and "Lights" was embossed in white above the appropriate switches, but the overdrive switch was embossed in red. It was also wired to operate the other way from the earlier cars, so that overdrive was engaged with the switch down and direct drive with it up. On the few cars supplied without overdrive, there was no blanking plate but rather a spare flick switch to fill the hole. The lighting switch had a two-stage action, giving first sidelights and then headlights.

INTERIOR MIRROR

On Mark III cars, the rear-view mirror mounted on the dash top was broadly similar to the earlier type but was a little larger and its shape was a little more oval. It had a black crackle paint finish on its reverse side. The mirror granted a wider field of view than before and, on some later cars at least, was mounted on a black wooden spacer block. This may have been intended to allow a better view over the folded convertible hood, which intruded more into the rear view than had the earlier hoods.

The gear change lever sprouted from the centre console on the Mark III car and was sealed by this substantial rubber boot. The correct type of windscreen wiper can be seen through the windscreen. This was the normal position for a radio to be mounted, a blanking plate being provided if no radio was specified. Also on view is a correct rear-view mirror.

lever. If no radio was fitted, a polished aluminium blanking plate embossed with the 3000 "flash" motif was fitted. Above the radio was a trapezoid-shaped mesh grille behind which a single radio speaker could be mounted – there was no provision for stereo in those days!

The heater controls were located at the top centre of the new-style dashboard. The actual controls were the same as before, but were now built-in rather than hanging below the

The two main instruments on the Mark III dashboard are visible here, together with the two direction indicator warning lights situated above them. The choke control is at top left.

INSTRUMENTS

On LHD cars, and reading from left to right, the main instruments were the fuel gauge, combined oil pressure and water temperature gauge, speedometer (which now read to 140mph as befitted the Mark III's increased top speed) and finally revolution counter. All the instruments, still made by Smiths Industries, were modernised compared with the earlier cars and all had deeper chromed bezels. All also now had matt black faces with white figures, letters and needles.

The new fuel gauge was electrically damped and gave a steady reading rather than the violent fluctuations of the past. The top of the hanging needle was shrouded and the gauge was simply marked E (empty), ½ (half-full) and F (full), irrespective of the car's destination market. The combined oil pressure and water temperature gauge was much as before, with the oil pressure resolutely given in pounds per square inch – although a metric centigrade temperature gauge was offered where appropriate.

As before, the speedometer carried both a three-digit resettable trip recorder and a five-digit cumulative mileage recorder, and inset towards the bottom was the small blue tell-tale light for headlight main beam. A metric speedometer was provided where appropriate, reading to a lofty 240kph. The rev counter no longer had a specific red line but was now marked with coloured segments. It read to 7000rpm in 500rpm units. The first warning colour shade was orange, which ran from 5000rpm to 5500rpm, and there was then a red segment right up to the 7000rpm top reading. (In fact, it would be most unwise to rev any of the Austin-Healey six-cylinder engines in standard form beyond 5000rpm for any length of time or ever to go beyond 5500rpm.) This new rev-counter was electrically driven rather than cable-operated as previously, but it still retained the small inset red ignition tell-tale light towards the bottom of its face.

There were two more controls located towards the inner edge of the instrument panel. At the top was the manual choke control, which sported a new black knob with the word "choke" picked out in white and with a white circle around the rim of the knob. Towards the bottom was the screenwash plunger knob, still manually operated. This was usually plain, but other styles bearing manufacturer's names seem to have appeared at times as well.

The auxiliary instruments were now grouped together outboard of the two main instruments. The fuel gauge was on the outside and its revised design gave a much steadier reading. The combined oil pressure and water temperature gauge had an updated face, as did all the other instruments used on the Mark III dashboard.

The former cable-driven rev counter had given way to this electronic instrument, still with the red ignition warning light. The screenwash plunger button is on show, and to the top right of the rev counter is one of the direction indicator warning lights. At top left, though out of focus, is the choke control. An additional flick switch has been added to the dashboard to the right of the overdrive switch. Also visible around the walnut panel is the chromed "ribbon type" trim referred to in the text.

CONTROLS

On the Mark III 3000, the steering wheel was almost always the adjustable type, but otherwise remained unchanged. Indicators were still operated by the same lever above the steering wheel boss, although two green warning lights now informed the driver whether he was indicating left or right. These were illuminated arrows set in small chromed bezels just above the two main instruments.

There were no changes to the pedals on the Mark III 3000, but a different style of Lucas foot-operated dip switch was

used. This was smaller than the earlier type, and the attachment bracket was altered to suit.

STEERING LOCK

In Europe, local legislation in some countries required a steering lock. This was generally combined with the ignition switch, as on many cars produced from the late 1960s onwards. A number of different types of locks were used and details are hard to come by, but when such a lock was fitted, a chromed blanking plate covered the normal ignition switch position.

INTERIOR TRIM AND BOOT INTERIOR

This Austin publicity picture is well known but nevertheless useful because it shows an original BT7 interior from above, with a BN7 two-seater as well. The BN7 appears to be in no colour that was publicly offered at the time, incidentally. The BT7 2/4-seater has its tonneau support bar erected and the hood concealed behind the rear seat back rest. Very surprisingly, in spite of official disapproval, this car appears to have chromed wire wheels.
(By courtesy of John Wheatley)

T here were two very distinct six-cylinder Austin-Healey interiors. First came that of the sidescreen-equipped roadsters built from 1956 to 1962 (the BN4, BN6, BT7 and BN7), which was essentially the same as that of the Mark II Convertible BJ7s of 1962-63. The second type was the interior found on the modernised and more luxurious Mark III BJ8 Convertibles of 1964-67.

THE 1956-1963 CARS

These cars had the "traditional" Austin-Healey dashboard with sweeping curves, as described in the Dashboard and Instruments section. Front seats on these cars always had leather facings, which included the sides of the seat cushions, while the seat backs were finished in matching vinyl. Contrasting vinyl piping was used, as listed in the Paint and

An accurately restored 100/6 interior demonstrates black seats with white piping. Although partially hidden under the rubber mats, the carpeting is also black, as of course is the dashboard covering.

This Florida Green 100/6 has the interior officially described as grey although it is more of a mushroom or beige colour. The seats are piped in dark green and green carpets are fitted. (Author)

Colour Schemes section, the only exception being when black seats were fitted to British Racing Green Mark II Convertibles, for these had matching black piping.

There were four basic interior colours; these were red, black, dark blue and grey – which was in truth more of a creamy-beige colour. The vinyl material used on all these interiors was known as Vynide or leathercloth, and was a combination of thin vinyl with a cloth backing, the vinyl having a fine-grain "leather look" finish.

FRONT SEATS

Although the seats on all these 1956-63 cars looked superficially similar, in fact there were detail differences, particularly in construction. The first-series BN4s, built up to the temporary cessation of production in April 1958, had seats almost identical to the BN2 four-cylinder cars. These had wooden frames for the seat cushions, which fitted snugly into the metal seat base trays on which the back rests pivoted. The seat cushion facings were drawn tight over the horsehair stuffing and then tacked and pinned underneath to the wooden base. Backrests on all cars hinged forwards for rear access, this being so even on the two-seaters. In addition, both seats had sliding mechanisms for fore and aft adjustment.

Details of the seats in a 100/6 fitted with a blue interior piped in white. The seat pivot bolt can just be seen in the right-hand picture and there is a good view of the ashtray. The central armrest here also has white piping, but not all cars had it; either can be correct.

When the BN6 two-seaters arrived in April 1958, the seat cushion base became metal rather than wood and the cushion sat in a shallower but thicker metal seat frame. This type of cushion was then used for all models up to and including the BJ7. The cushion on all cars had a pleated central portion, with five pleats running fore and aft, and a plain outer section. Contrasting piping surrounded both the pleated centre and the outer edge of the plain part of the cushion facing. The cushion itself was padded with a combination of foam material and traditional horsehair stuffing.

On cars with the metal seat cushion bases, the leather seat cushion face was pulled taut backwards over the stuffing and hooked over "teeth" in the seat cushion base. The sides and front portion of the seat facings were clipped to the seat cushion base with black metal spring clips. When first introduced, the metal bases of the seat cushions were open in the centre, but later the openings were filled in by a perforated metal plate. By the introduction of the 3000 Mark II cars, the seat cushion base became a solid metal plate with neither opening nor perforations.

The seat backrests again had leather faces with vinyl leathercloth for their backs and for the sides of the backrests where they curved around and were pivoted to the seat bases. These side pieces of the backrest were trimmed with vinyl pockets that were separate from the vinyl covering the back of the backrest itself. The seat backrests were formed of shaped steel "shells", the rear of the backrest being padded with several layers of wadding topped with leathercloth.

The front was given thick foam padding, shaped with horsehair stuffing and held in place with a layer of cotton cloth over which the leather facing was fitted. Like the cushion, the face of the backrest had fine pleats in the centre, running vertically. Around the periphery was a plain, horse-shoe-shaped outer panel separated from the pleated area by piping. Piping also surrounded the outer edge of the backrest. The upholstery of the seat back was pulled into place over the shell from the top and fixed to the base of the shell with a

The central armrest on this black-trimmed 100/6 with contrasting white piping is not itself piped the same way. The armrest is fixed with Tenax fasteners but the position of these seems to vary from car to car; they were positioned lower down on some cars.

The original interior on this black and red BN7 Mark II is also red with black piping. This car has the later type of sewn-in armrest and also displays original red carpeting. Note the carpet binding round the gear lever opening. Also visible are seat belts and one of the mounting points on the inner wheel arch, as well as the battery access trap door.

combination of glue and spring-on clips.

To provide for the pivoting action of both seat backs, bolts were welded to the seat bottom frames which engaged with acorn-shaped chromed nuts. On each side of the bolted fixings were one chrome and one brass washer. The seat bottom frames themselves were trimmed on their exposed edges with narrow strips of matching vinyl. The bottom frames bolted to threaded studs welded to the seat slider rails, these being mounted on ⁵⁄₁₆in thick wooden packing strips. These in turn sat on black metal strips resting on the jute padding and tar paper floor covering. The carpet itself and jute underfelt were cut to go around these seat mounting strips. Finally, the seat runners themselves were fixed to the floor by threaded studs attached to their undersides. The studs passed through the floor and were bolted firmly from underneath the car using shouldered nuts and both flat and lock washers.

Between the front seats was a padded and pleated armrest, of which there were two types. The first series of BN4 cars had the larger type, not unlike that used on the four-cylinder cars. Trimmed in leather, it was attached by four Tenax studs and fasteners mounted on the transmission tunnel. The

A well-restored LHD Mark II 3000 displays its interior in blue with white piping. (Author)

This red Mark II Convertible displays its black interior with red piping. The Austin-Healey badged rubber floor mats are an aftermarket addition, as is the wood-rim steering wheel.

A detail of the seat runner and wooden mounting strip with the carpet and underlay removed. Note the press stud screwed to the floor to help locate the carpet.

A pair of nicely patinated original seats is seen here in a 3000 Mark II with central gear change. Note that the central armrest is sewn to the carpet. The steering wheel is not original, of course, in either this or the top picture.

These are the rear seating arrangements on a 3000 Mark I fitted with hardtop. The hood and frame can remain on the car behind the rear seat backrest even when the hard top is in place. A pair of early type seat belts is fitted; note also their mounting points.

Viewed from above, these are the rear seat arrangements in a 100/6. Note the receiving sockets for the hood sticks and the neat way that the trim covers the folded hood.

BN6s, second-series BN4s and 3000 Mark I and II cars all had a smaller central armrest pad, again leather-faced with pleats but with Vynide sides. This was fixed by being sewn directly to the carpet covering the transmission tunnel.

REAR SEATS

All the BN4, BT7 and BJ7 2/4-seaters had the two extra rear seats fitted, always trimmed in Vynide rather than the leather used for the front seats. They were really seat pans only, rather than true seats, shaped something like the basic seats that adorn older agricultural tractors of the Ferguson variety. Space had been found for these seats by adding nearly two inches to the car's wheelbase and by moving the rear bulkhead backwards. The seats were positioned where the battery access trapdoor had been on the BN1 and BN2 cars, so the battery moved to the boot. The change also demanded revised storage for the spare wheel.

The shaped cushions of these occasional seats were pleated, each one having four longitudinal pleats with piping around the edge and a raised horseshoe-shaped rear section. Padding provided some comfort, and the seat pans were secured front and rear by trim screws to the tonneau area floor. The BN4s and BT7s had a single backrest, and this had 10 vertical pleats, piped round the edge, trimmed in Vynide and topped

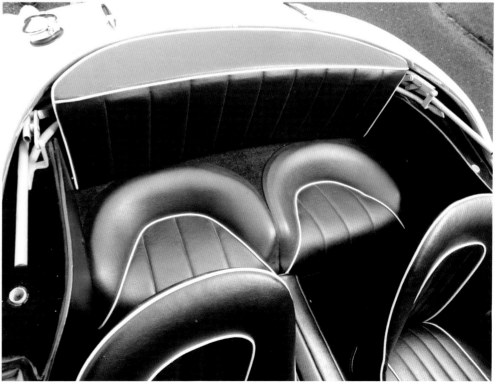

off by a curved top panel which covered the hood and hood frame when it was lowered. To gain access to the hood, this backrest and panel lifted up and folded forwards.

On the BJ7s with the full convertible hood, there was still a one-piece backrest but of a different and flatter type. The 10 vertical pleats were retained. This backrest did not need to fold forward fully because of the fixed hood frame, but it did tip forwards slightly to make neat hood stowage easier. The backrest was held in place by metal loops that clipped into rubber holders, one each side, the holders being attached by brackets which were screwed to the side panels.

REAR TRIM

The rear side trim differed between the first and second series of BN4 cars. On the first-series BN4s, up to April 1958, the hood frame was fixed to the car, and the rear quarter-panels allowed for this, leaving part of the hood frame visible behind the end of the piped Vynide quarter-panel trim. On the second-series BN4s and all subsequent cars without a permanently fixed hood frame, the rear quarter-panels were simplified because they did not need to fit around the hood mechanism's attachment points. On the BJ7s, the attached convertible hood made minor changes necessary to the rear quarter-panel area.

Rear quarter-panels on all the 1956-63 cars were made of fibreboard covered in Vynide. On the 2/4-seaters, the area around the rear of the seat pans forward of the backrest was carpeted, the carpet being glued to the tonneau shelf on which the seat pans rested.

The rear cockpit area of the two-seater BN6s and BN7s was quite different and not unlike that of the earlier BN1 and BN2 cars. The spare wheel lay flat on its shelf, half in the boot and half in the cockpit; it was now mounted centrally in the car rather than offset to the right as in the four-cylinder models. Where the wheel intruded into the cockpit tonneau area, it was covered by a tailored "pocket" attached to a rectangular metal frame on the boot side of the rear bulkhead. The pocket was made of vinyl to match the cockpit, with piping around its circumference on the earlier BN6 cars. On the later BN6s and all BN7s, however, the sides and top of the pocket were of carpet, and vinyl was used only for the pocket base. The carpet, vinyl and piping all accorded with the car's interior colour scheme.

The spare wheel was fastened down by a black leather strap that ran from an anchor point near the battery trapdoor to a buckled anchor point in the boot. The trapdoor was

The battery access trap door on this 1961 3000 Mark II BN7 two-seater has a leather finger pull and, like the surrounding area, is correctly covered with Hardura matting with bound edges. The spare wheel cover fashioned from carpet is correct on this model. On the BN6 and BN7 cars, it was possible to open the battery door with the spare wheel in place; on the 100s, the spare wheel had to be moved back slightly first.

fastened down by two leather straps approximately an inch wide and dyed to match the interior. These straps were riveted to the trapdoor under the vinyl edging, and clipped onto the rear bulkhead using "lift-a-dot" fasteners. A leather finger-pull attached to a metal loop was added to the top of the trapdoor, but not on all cars.

The battery access door itself and the surrounding flat tonneau panel area were both covered with Armacord, a hard-wearing jute and vinyl material. The area was also edged with vinyl, with all materials matching the trim colour. This Armacord was glued down and also had pop rivets visible along the front edge and also on either side of the battery door hinges. The ribbed pattern of the Armacord ran from front to back. It appears that cars fitted originally with the Grey interior trim had Hardura rather than Armacord covering; perhaps Armacord was not available in that colour.

The sides of the area behind the seats on the BN6 and BN7 two-seaters were trimmed with vinyl-covered quarter-panels, secured by trim-screws. The panels were fashioned from either plywood or fibreboard, and there were two of them on each side, the rear one extending under the rear shroud. Together with additional stitched vinyl trim, these panels made a neat cover for the inner wheel arches.

CARPETS

Carpeting on cars up to and including the BJ7 was, in Roger Moment's words, a "dull finish, wool/nylon coarse 'hogshair' material, with some threads of a lighter colour in the blend, with a cut-pile nap about ³⁄₁₆in thick". A hessian backing was provided and the carpet went under the trade name of Karvel. It either matched or toned with the main trim colour, carpet colours being listed in the Colours section of this book. The carpeting was neither bound nor edged, except on the section covering the transmission tunnel.

On the floor under the carpets was a material known as "tar-paper", a kind of lightweight roofing felt which provided both noise and heat insulation. An underfelt of woven jute sat between this and the carpet to provide further insulation. Sadly, however, this also acted as a very effective sponge if the interior got damp, which it usually did sooner or later, and it retained water for long periods. Unsurprisingly, this caused rust to attack the floors and so it is essential to dry this area out in the event of water penetration.

The carpet sections in front of the seats and also under and behind the seats could be removed for drying and cleaning. However, the sections at the front of the footwells, around the gearbox tunnel bulkhead, on the inner sills and on the

This is the interior trim of a 100/6 door, with an arrangement that remained very similar on the 3000 BN7 and BT7 cars. Around the door pocket will be seen a line of stitching. The door was opened by the forward mounted handle; the chromed bracket and lever at the top rear of the door clamped the side screen.

rear bulkhead were glued down, which does not seem to have been very sensible. On the driver's side, the carpet had a black rubber heel-mat let into it, carrying the Austin name in script. The removable carpets were fixed down with brass poppers, the female part being attached to the carpet with small spikes on black wire rings while the male part was screwed directly to the floor, the screws passing through the underfelt. The carpet over the gearbox cover and prop-shaft tunnel was also removable, the underlay being glued directly to it. It was fixed down using the same type of poppers as the

floor carpets. Around the openings for the gear lever and handbrake lever, the carpet edge was bound with vinyl strip which matched the trim colour. Vinyl edge strips were also finished off the front edge of the gearbox tunnel carpet and the rear edge of the prop-shaft tunnel carpet.

TRANSMISSION TUNNEL

The base of the gear lever passed through a black rubber boot that sealed the hole in the gearbox cover. There were two different types of rubber boot. Cars built before November 1961 with the side change gear lever had a smaller and flatter type, while later cars with the centre gear change had a larger bellows type of boot.

Behind the gear lever and forward of the central armrest, all cars had a chromed ashtray with a forward-hinged lid. The carpet had a cut-out around this, and the ashtray base was secured to the gearbox cover by two cross-headed screws. These were covered by the removable inner section of the ashtray. A further cut-out at the forward end of this carpet matched one in the gearbox cover itself to provide access to the gearbox oil filler plug. The gearbox cover aperture had a black rubber moulded cover with a recessed finger grip. There was also an access hole for the front prop-shaft grease nipple near the rear end of the cover, again with a rubber cover.

FOOTWELL AND DOOR PANELS

The footwell side panels were made of vinyl-covered fibre-board attached by trim screws and cup washers. The trim on the doors was more complicated. All cars prior to the BJ7 Convertible had outer and inner door panels, the space between them forming a deep door pocket. However, on the BJ7 with its winding windows, the space was largely consumed by the winding mechanism and the lowered glass.

On the cars with sidescreens, the outer panel was of plywood covered with a thin layer of wadding and finished in vinyl to match the general trim colour. The vinyl wrapped round the edges of the door pocket aperture and was both glued and stitched in place, with the stitching remaining visible. The panel was fixed to the door by trim screws and cup washers. At the top rear of this trim panel was a polished plate in the shape of an arrow head, screwed in place to protect the cut-out notch in the trim panel where it passed over the door striker plate head.

The inner door pocket lining panel was made in two parts,

This is the interior of the Mark II Convertible door, showing the folding pull handle at the top, the door release handle towards the front and the window winder on the inset part of the door. A slim map pocket remained possible even though the lowered window glass and winding mechanism took up most of the space. The inner trim of the door carried four horizontal pleats, which were absent from the later Mark III door.

an upper and a lower. Both were of vinyl-covered fibreboard, unpadded. The top panel overlapped the lower, the horizontal overlap running across the door pocket roughly half way down. The panels were held together by a strip of wood fastened behind them and glued to the inside of the door to which they were secured. The bottom of the door pocket was formed by a further piece of shaped, vinyl-trimmed fibreboard. This simply dropped into place, being held by the inner and outer parts of the door.

On those cars where the colour of the metal visible on the inside of the doors was at noticeable odds with the main trim colour, these visible metal areas were overpainted by hand to match the main colour. For instance, where a black interior was found on a white car, the visible metal on the door interior would be painted black, rather than left white.

Door trim details for the Mark II Convertible cars with winding windows are discussed together with those of the Mark III cars to which they were similar, later in this section.

DOOR SEALS
Draught excluding seals were fitted around the door openings on the first series of BN4s up to April 1958. This seal was a rounded rubber type that fitted hard against the door when closed. It was fitted around the opening in a metal channel screwed to the body. Separate inner Furflex seals were also fitted, fastened under the vinyl trim panels. There was no inner aluminium sill cover on these early cars.

On the later cars, both two-seaters and 2/4-seaters, the rubber seal and Furflex were combined into a single seal, which was secured over the steel door opening lip by the continuous sprung steel strip integral with the Furflex part of the seal. The Furflex trim is visible in the top photograph on page 103. The Furflex matched the main trim colour except on the 100/6 cars trimmed in yellow, which had black Furflex because no yellow Furflex was available. All the later models did have the aluminium inner sill cover, which was screwed along the bottom of the door opening.

BOOT INTERIOR
The boot interior was trimmed with ribbed Armacord material. On the first series of BN4s, this matched the colour of the cockpit carpet, but on all later cars the Armacord was black. It was bound both at the seams and along its edges with black vinyl stripping, secured by double stitching turned inside out so that the stitching did not show. On the BT7s and later BN4s, Armacord was glued in place, both to the inside of the rear inner wings and to the boot front wall. In this latter case, it was riveted in place as well.

Armacord also covered the area either side of the petrol tank and to the rear of the tank inside the lower lip of the boot opening. In these places, it was simply laid loosely in position. The top of the petrol tank, which formed the boot floor, was also covered with Armacord, tailored to fit snugly

This view of the inside of the rear of the boot shows the boot catch engaging hook and the leather strap which was part of the spare wheel securing arrangement. Black Hardura matting covers the petrol tank and forms what is in effect the boot floor. The number-plate lamp is visible on its bracket attached to the inside of the rear bumper.

in place. On these 2/4-seaters the fuel tank filler pipe at the front right of the boot was covered by a fibreboard box given a black grained finish. This box was screwed both to the bulkhead and to the inner wing wall.

The battery and its fixings are discussed in the Electrical Equipment section, but the spare wheel also found a home in the boot on the 2/4-seater cars, so further reducing the luggage carrying capacity. The wheel lay flat on the left-hand side of the boot, largely on top of the petrol tank. It rested against and was located by two wooden blocks trimmed in black vinyl; one block was bolted to the left-hand inner wing and the other to the boot front wall. The bolts which held the second block also secured a black-painted metal bracket. Pivoted from this bracket was a black-painted metal rod with a D-shaped loop at its outer end. The rod was arranged to pass over the spare wheel to secure it, and a leather strap passed through the loop of the D. This buckled strap also

The spare wheel is in place in a 2/4-seater here; the leather strap, black holding rod and its pivot block can all be seen. On the right is the 12-volt battery under the correct type of loose plastic cover, which could have been fitted rather more neatly. Just inside the lower boot opening lip on the right is the battery master switch. These arrangements did not allow for much luggage space, and it is surprising that no flexible cover was provided for what could have been a dirty spare wheel.

formed the hinge for the lift-up section, which also had a little leather finger tab.

The Armacord boot floor covering was laid with the ribbing running laterally, and it was edged with stitched strips of black vinyl. Trim screws fastened the main plywood floor covering down, the lifting hatch remaining loose so that the jack and sundry tools could be stored underneath it. This storage area also had an Armacord lining. The boot sides and front wall around the spare wheel slot had fibreboard trim panels covered in black vinyl and secured by black-painted metal clips. However, the fuel filler pipe was left exposed and unpainted without the boxing-in used on the 2/4-seater. This seems strange in view of the extra trim elsewhere in the two-seater boot. A short rubber hose secured with wire hose clips connected the filler pipe to the inlet at the top of the fuel tank.

THE 3000 MARK II & MARK III CONVERTIBLE

The 3000 Mark III Convertible had a completely revised and modernised interior; its instruments, dashboard and new centre console area are discussed under Dashboard and Instruments. The seating and door trims were also changed significantly.

The revised door trim introduced for the BJ7 Convertible was carried over to the BJ8 Mark III with a few minor changes. The BJ7's interior had been a curious combination of features from the earlier and late cars. The wraparound windscreen adopted for these convertible models led to changes in the dashboard top and outer edges, but the main change was the loss of the deep door pockets to the window mechanisms.

The outer door trim panel was very much the same as on those earlier cars, but the inner trim panel on the BJ7 cars was brought out so that the mechanism could sit behind it. This panel was vinyl covered and carried four rows of horizontal stitching to form pleats. It was located so that there was still a very slim door pocket between it and the outer panel, just deep enough to take a map. The window winder projected through this inner panel towards its forward end.

Just above it was fitted the chromed door opening handle, and near the top in the centre of the door was a chromed folding loop handle intended as a door pull now that the old door pockets could not be used for this purpose. A foam padded top cushion in vinyl to match the trim ran along the top of the door interior, and the loop handle was just below this. Interestingly, the winders and handles used on these Convertible doors were borrowed from the standard BMC parts bin, also being used on the Farina-styled Austin saloons of the period.

When the BJ8 Mark III cars took over from the BJ7, the door furniture and layout remained unchanged, but the door panels were formed of a single built-up piece of vinyl covered fibreboard, and were no longer in two parts. The four hori-

With the wheel removed, the same boot has approximately twice as much space. The prop rod can be seen on the left-hand side, and so can the steel cable that prevented the boot lid from opening too far and so breaking the hinges. The petrol filler pipe is boxed in on the right-hand side.

passed through a chromed metal loop fixed to the boot floor near the edge of the petrol tank; tightening the strap and buckling it clamped the spare wheel securely.

The two-seater BN6 and BN7 cars had the spare wheel fitted differently, as already explained. The boot on these cars was better trimmed than that of the four-seaters, with a plywood floor that sat on top of the petrol tank; the well area on the left of the tank had a separate lift-up section of plywood. Black Armacord glued to the top of the plywood formed the boot floor surface, and the Armacord itself

Compare the boot of this BN7 two-seater with that of the 2/4-seater with spare wheel in place as shown in the bottom picture on the previous page. The spare wheel sits neatly strapped in on its shelf and the twin batteries are hidden at the back of the cockpit under a cover. The petrol filler pipe is not boxed in on this model. There is considerably more luggage space available, even if some bags were stowed on the rear seats of the 2/4-seater as well. The boot lock mechanism is on show, as is the whole of the boot prop rod.

The great majority of Mark III 3000s had Ambla seat coverings; leather was a rarely specified option. The silvered piping discoloured over the years, and the covering on the seat cushion material was always perforated, as shown above.

These two general views of a 3000 Mark III interior show the new type of seats both front and rear, the Ambla seat facings and the centre console that extends right to the forward edge of the rear seats. On the Phase I versions of the Mark III, a lift-up storage box was incorporated into the centre console above the propeller shaft tunnel, but this was deleted on later cars. The revised dashboard and radio mounting arrangements are also shown here.

FRONT SEATS

The BJ8 front seats still had the same construction as on earlier cars, but their coverings were substantially different. Leather seat facings now became an extra-cost option, although one that was evidently not officially available in the USA, and the new Ambla material became the standard covering. This was a man-made "leather look" soft vinyl with a slight grain. The Ambla used for the pleated sections of the seat cushions and backrests was given a "breathable" pattern of tiny squares.

Each cushion had six patterned pleats running front to back, with the outer horse-shoe section in plain Ambla. Likewise, on the wearing face of the backrest, the vertical pleats were of breathable Ambla, and the horse-shoe surround of plain Ambla. Seat piping also differed on the BJ8s in that it no longer contrasted with the main interior colour. All seat piping was now made of a clear plastic material over a silver metal core. With time this piping discolours and takes on a gold rather than a silver appearance. Contrasing piping was not even used with the optional leather seat facings, which had piping to match the main interior colour.

REAR SEATS AND LUGGAGE PLATFORM

Another major change on the BJ8 was the addition of a luggage platform at the rear of the cockpit, formed by folding the rear seat backrest. The rear seat pans were broadly similar to the previous type but were upholstered in Ambla, breathable for the shaped, sitting surface. Again they had pleats running front to rear, but now there were 10 narrow pleats on each seat rather than four wide ones. The

The Mark III cockpit shows the seat backs with the seats tilted forwards. On the right, details of the quarter-light window frame and seal are visible.

zontal pleats of the BJ7 doors had disappeared, the door panel now being plain but still incorporating the slim map pocket (see photograph on page 111). The panel was secured to the door by hidden push-in metal clips. Although the vinyl covering on this panel matched the main trim colour, the top cushion of the door on BJ8s was now always in black vinyl irrespective of trim colour; on the BJ7 Convertibles it had matched the main trim.

Quilted material was used for the rear seat backrest on Mark III cars. Again, this was edged with the silver piping.

This centre console and seats are original un-restored items, as is the carpet. The carpet has been worn by the driver's hand operating the handbrake lever over the course of 50 years.

surrounding horse-shoe outers were, as expected, trimmed in plain Ambla. The rear seat backrest was now trimmed with a vinyl which had an embossed, square quilted pattern, and which was also used to trim the rear quarter panels.

The backrest panel on the BJ8 was made in two pieces, hinged together horizontally across the car. This enabled it to do a double-fold and lie flat right across the rear cockpit area to form a substantial platform. It was secured in its "down" position by two chromed sliding bolts, which engaged with locating holes in the rear quarter panels. The back of the backrest was covered in carpet to match the main floor carpets, and there were press-stud poppers on vinyl tabs at each outer end to hold it in place when upright. To give clearance for the sliding bolts when the backrest was upright, there was a small opening trimmed with a metal ring in each side of the rear bulkhead panel behind the backrest. The whole arrangement was both useful and neat, and many owners who rarely used the rear seats left the luggage platform permanently in place. It could also be used in its half-folded position, leaving just the forward end of the rear seat pans visible.

DOOR SEALS

The Convertibles had the same type of door opening seals as earlier cars –rounded rubber seals held over the steel lip of the door aperture by the continuous spring steel clip within the Furflex, which was coloured to match the trim. A further rubber seal was used to seal the gap between the windscreen pillar and the quarter-light. It was fitted to the screen pillar and on the BJ7s was faced with black fabric and made in two pieces, one fitted to the screen and the other to the trailing edge of the front wing. On the BJ8s, this seal was a single-piece item extending right down the screen pillar and along the front wing edge. This one-piece seal was faced with grey fabric, and was held in place with pop rivets.

These two photographs show the "double folding" rear seat backrest of the Mark III 3000. This was cleverly arranged to form a luggage platform when required. In the first photograph, the backrest is lowered and then pulled over to form the platform in the second photograph. The sliding bolts lock in to the sockets on the quarter-panel side trim. The backrest is held up by the two tabs with press studs than can be seen in the top picture. The two recesses visible in the cockpit back panel take the heads of the sliding bolts when the backrest is upright. The carpet and trim on this car are all known to be original, as is the load cover. Again, original BMC seatbelts are in evidence.

The interior of the Mark III 3000 door: the horizontal pleats found on the Mark II Convertible have now been deleted and the central trim panel is plain. The map pocket has now shrunk almost to nothing. The correct rubber seal is visible on the trailing edge of the front wing against which the door closes.

BODY AND BODY FITTINGS

There were a considerable number of detail differences between the bodies of the six-cylinder cars and the previous four-cylinder versions, even though they looked very similar to the untrained eye. Unlike the earliest Austin-Healey 100s, the body of the six-cylinder cars was always built of steel with the exception of the front and rear shroud panels, which were made from aluminium alloy pressings welded up to form a cohesive whole. BMC, incidentally, always referred to the rear shroud as the "tonneau assembly".

A major difference was of course the extra two inches in the wheelbase that gave more room in the cockpit for the two (very) occasional rear seats. The two inches were added to the length of the doors, so that the length of both front and rear wings remained the same as on the 100s. The dishes pressed into the door panels behind the handles to allow for hand access and the handles themselves are an immediate recognition feature of the later body.

The four-cylinder cars also had a double-X cross-bracing and shroud support in front of the radiator, but the radiator was moved forwards on the six-cylinder cars and the bracing was reduced to a single X and moved correspondingly forwards.

BODY PANELS

As already noted, both shrouds were always of aluminium alloy and all four wings of steel; like the bonnet, the boot lid was always made from steel.

The forward end of the rear shroud on the BN6 and BN7 two-seater cars differed from that on the 2/4 seaters and was very similar to that on the BN1s and BN2s. The tonneau shelf panel had a battery trapdoor on the two-seaters. As well as a battery access door, the two-seater rear bulkhead had a central slot through which the spare wheel protruded from the boot, together with a rail reinforcement assembly which gave support to the leading edge of the rear shroud.

On the 2/4-seaters, the forward end of the rear shroud was cut away to allow for the seats, and the whole body area behind the seats was modified. The battery access door of the two seater was deleted and the tonneau shelf panel was reshaped to allow for the rear seat pans. The rear bulkhead panel, heel-board panel (either side of the propshaft tunnel) and tonneau shelf panel were all modified to allow for rear seat space. The propshaft tunnel was lengthened and the rear cockpit bulkhead was moved rearwards. The rear wheel arches also had to be modified.

Polished wing beading separated the steel wings from the aluminium shrouds, in an attempt to prevent corrosive interaction between the two metals. The later, wider and flatter, type of headlight rim is in evidence.

The side flashes on the front wings were carried over from the 100 models, and although they were the same as the earlier ones there was no actual vent in the wing behind them. These flashes are handed, and are often fitted on the wrong sides of the car so that they end up pointing the wrong way. The swage line by the front wheel arch can just be seen at the bottom right of the picture.

The two-tone paint finish (where used) followed the body swage line pressed into the wings and doors. As seen here, it stopped about one inch short of the front wheel arch and turned downwards to the base of the wing.

WINGS

The rear wings were virtually identical to those of the four-cylinder cars, but the front wing swage line no longer faded away forward of the chromed side flash; instead, it continued towards the front wheel arch and then made a hooked turn downwards to follow the line of the arch towards the base of the wing, always about an inch from it. This revised pressing was used as the break line on cars with two-tone paint; the top colour now continued downwards next to the wheel arch, and the lower colour was used only behind this new pressing line. This produced a pleasing colour contrast effect.

The chromed side flash continued on the 100/6 and 3000s, but the air vent that it had previously covered was no longer fitted to the wings, which were solid behind the flash. Rubber buffers mounted on angled support brackets painted in the body colour were riveted to each front inner wing edge, arranged so that they touched and supported the inside face of the outer front wings.

BEADING

As steel and aluminium interact to cause corrosion over the long term, they were prevented from making direct contact by a polished stainless steel beading interposed between the wings and the shrouds. This was attached by means of tabs pinched between wing and shroud flanges as they were bolted up. The tabs were then bent over from underneath as an additional retainer. There were also sections of beading between headlights and side lights, and between side lights and the bases of the front wing-to-shroud joins. However, these were not of stainless steel, but rather of a silver-coloured vinyl material. This was again pinch fixed by the action of bolting the panels together..

BONNET

The six-cylinder car bonnet was quite different to that on the 100s. Firstly, it was hinged at the rear rather than the front, and secondly, its forward end had a raised pressing fitted with a subsidiary air intake grille. This was to clear the top of the radiator, which had been moved forward because of the longer engine. The bonnet panel was also longer, its leading edge being nearer to the front grille than before. This and its being rear-hinged made engine access somewhat better than on the four-cylinder cars.

One peculiarity of most 100/6 cars was that they had a central longitudinal crease pressed into the bonnet; however, not all 100/6s had this feature and no 3000 cars ever did. The Longbridge-built 100/6s all appear to have had the crease, but on Abingdon-built 100/6s of both types it seems almost to have been fitted at random. No differentiating part numbers nor other changes are recorded in any of the official literature. Bracing on the underside of the 100/6 bonnet also changed during production; early BN4 bonnets had only a brace at the rear across the hinge attachment points, whereas later bonnets had a front brace added as well. It appears that there were bonnets with a central crease and only a rear brace, some with a central crease and both braces, and some with no central crease and both braces, and all of them could be found on the 100/6! This last type of bonnet, with both braces but no central crease, was the style that was used throughout the Healey 3000 production run.

Bonnet props were always manual, but changed sides on the 100/6 after production transferred from Longbridge to Abingdon, although there is some doubt about the exact change point. On the early cars, the prop was fitted to the left-hand side of the bonnet, but all later Healeys had it on

This 1958 100/6 BN4 has the central crease line to the bonnet; as a later 100/6 type, the bonnet also has the forward cross-brace. The bonnet securing pin and spring are visible as are the twin safety catches and the bonnet prop.

This is the underside of a late 3000 Mark III bonnet. The rubber push clip with its split-pin fixing is on the bonnet at bottom left. The bonnet prop rod is secured into this when not in use.

the right-hand side. It pivoted from a bracket towards the front of the bonnet and was held in place by a split pin and washer. A rubber push clip retained by a large split pin held the other end of the prop to the bonnet when it was not in use. When the bonnet was raised, the free end of the prop rod engaged with a bracket fitted to the underside of the front shroud.

When closed, the bonnet sat on rubber buffers riveted around the bonnet opening. On early BN4 cars there were three of these buffers on each side, but on Abingdon cars the rear left-hand buffer was replaced by a strip of rubber seal about 18 inches long that was fixed over the shroud

This is the central crease line that was used on most but not all 100/6 bonnets. Note the Austin-Healey "winged" front badge.

edge. This was an attempt to stop water entering the carburettors and when the tri-carb Mark II 3000 appeared, the rubber strip was lengthened to 26 inches.

The bonnet was held shut by a central pin surrounded by a heavy-duty spring and mounted on a double right-angled bracket. The receiving latch for this pin was attached to the body by a braced bracket and two cross-head screws. The latch was released through a pull-rod and bell crank arrangement that ran under the bonnet opening lip of the front shroud, on the right-hand side. This rod passed through the bulkhead and terminated in an oval pull loop sited above the parcels tray under the dashboard on left hand drive cars. It remained in the same position on right hand drive cars..

There were also two safety catches, one at each side towards the forward end of the bonnet. Both were in effect spring-loaded hooks with a finger tab attached.

The bonnet hinges, front latch bracket and safety catches were all painted body colour. The securing pin bracket, prop rod, pull rod and springs were black, and the securing pin was generally zinc plated, as were most of the mechanism's fasteners.

The 100/6 and Mark I 3000 had this standard Austin-style "crinkled" front grille with horizontal slats. The top and bottom finishers were chromed. Visible just below the badge bar is the so-called "splash shield", a valance panel that closed the area between the front bumper and the lower front shroud. It was not fitted to early examples of the BN6 model, but was present on all the other six-cylinder cars.

This is the subsidiary air intake grille on the 100/6 and 3000 Mark I. The pressing on the top of the bonnet also gave clearance to the top of the radiator. The Austin-Healey "winged" badge was used on both these models.

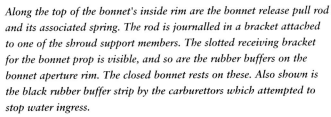

Along the top of the bonnet's inside rim are the bonnet release pull rod and its associated spring. The rod is journalled in a bracket attached to one of the shroud support members. The slotted receiving bracket for the bonnet prop is visible, and so are the rubber buffers on the bonnet aperture rim. The closed bonnet rests on these. Also shown is the black rubber buffer strip by the carburettors which attempted to stop water ingress.

DOORS

Doors were always of steel with a braced inner framework. Their outer skins had a pressed swage-line that continued the line found on both front and rear wings. They were attached to the A-posts by cast aluminium hinges, each of which was secured to the body by four large countersunk cross-headed set screws. Hinges were painted body colour.

Door check mechanisms that doubled as a means of holding the door open – quite sophisticated for a sports road-ster – were provided. When in good condition, these friction devices could hold the door open at 45° even against a slope. The flat-bladed part of the stay mechanism disappeared into a slot in the door when the door was shut, a fibre friction disc providing the means to hold the door open. The door stay

components were generally zinc-plated, but on some cars seem to have been painted body colour.

The door aperture was finished along its sill edge and B-post face with polished aluminium trim plates with a mottled, dotted pattern. These were secured by self-tapping screws, and the sill edge plates were arranged to trap the bottom of the B-post plates. The door latch was bolted to the inside of the door frame, and the door striker was fixed towards the top of the B-post by four screws. A chromed door bolt with an angled end and spring loading slid from the door to engage with a receiver hole in the striker plate, so securing the door shut. There was also a "half-shut" position when a hooked end on the striker plate connected with the door bolt. This provided a measure of safety in the event of the door bolt not fully engaging. The striker plate incorporated some measure of adjustment so that the door could be made to close fully.

Longbridge-built 100/6 models had a key lock on the left-hand door handle only, which was the driver's side on cars which were bound for the USA – and these formed the great majority. It was deleted when production moved to Abingdon. At the forward end of the handle, it is just possible to see the tiny rubber buffer that stopped the handle damaging the bodywork.

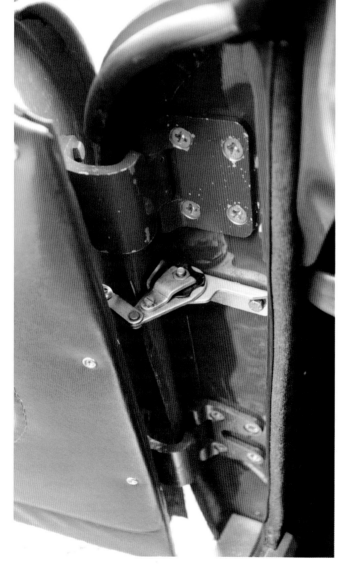

Here we see the substantial door hinges and the rather complex door stay mechanism. The Furflex edging and seal around the door aperture is noticeable, as is the rubber seal on the trailing edge of the front wing.

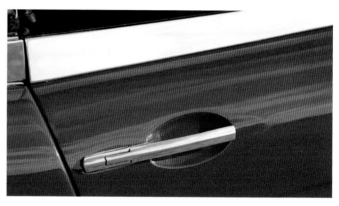

This is the driver's door handle on a Mark II Convertible. Even as late as 1964, key locks were not being fitted, and they only arrived with the Phase II Mark III Convertibles. The deep chromed finisher at the top of the door is very visible.

Finally, a different style of door handle with a push-button lock was fitted from car number 26704 in 1964.

Doors were opened from the inside by a chromed lever mounted at their forward ends. This was connected to the latch by a metal bar hidden behind the door trim. External door pull handles were provided for the first time on an Austin-Healey. On the Longbridge-built BN4s, these had a key-operated lock in the left side (the driver's side on US-bound cars) with a plain handle on the right side. Both were chrome plated. The right side door could also be locked from the inside by means of a lock lever on the latch.

When production moved to Abingdon, the lock was deleted and plain pull handles were fitted on both sides of the car. The reason is unknown, but may have been associated with cost. These handles were then used on all cars until the Phase II Mark III Convertible arrived in 1964 at car number 26704. Under the free end of the exterior pull handle, a tiny rubber buffer was fitted to prevent the handle damaging the paintwork as it snapped back into position.

Major changes took place to the door area when the Convertible Mark II BJ7 cars were introduced in 1962. Detachable sidescreens were at last consigned to history and winding glass windows arrived, with swivelling quarter lights in a fixed frame on both sides. These had chromed locking levers at their lower trailing edges. A deep chromed finishing piece was added to the top of the door, getting deeper as it ran towards the rear of the car. This made the door appear to be almost horizontal across its top edge. A matching chrome finisher was added on each side to the top front of the rear shroud.

The internal framework of the doors had to be altered to allow for the installation of the window winding mechanism and the door pockets became very much shallower. The window winding handles, chromed with black plastic knobs, were situated towards the forward end of the door roughly half-way down. When the Phase II Mark III 3000s were introduced, proper locking door handles with a push button operation were finally provided on each side. One key operated both locks, the ignition switch and also the boot lock. These later doors were opened from the inside by chromed handles situated towards the front of the door. These operated the latches by a link rod hidden behind the door trim. The door latches themselves were modified for the Convertible Mark IIs and Mark IIIs, when a new style of latch with a rotating catch was fixed to the door internally. A lock plate was fitted to the door shut face and this engaged with a new type of striker plate on the B-post. Tongues on the striker plates top and bottom slid into guide pieces on the lock plate and a central pin on the striker plate engaged with the rotating lock catch. When the vehicle was locked, the rotating catch was prevented from moving and this held the pin tight and the door shut. The striker plate was held to the B-post by two large countersunk cross-headed screws which passed through the post to thread into a packing plate behind it. A folding chromed handle at the top of the interior panel allowed the doors to be pulled shut from inside the car.

HOOD WELL

The body behind the cockpit had to be modified on the Mark II convertibles and the Mark III cars to take the bulkier convertible hood. The leading edge of the rear shroud was given a slightly more pronounced lip with a chromed finishing strip instead of the previous polished aluminium cockpit capping. This strip ran right around the top of the hood well to meet the chromed finishers situated just behind the door tops. Although the front quarter-lights on the convertible were framed, the actual door glasses were not; they relied for location when raised on the channelling at the trailing edge of the quarter-light frames, plus the rubber seal channels on the hood frame.

BOOT LID

The boot lid was the same on both two-seater and 2/4-seater cars, although it had a slightly different curvature from its equivalent on the BN1 and BN2 models. The lid fitted into its lipped aperture in the rear shroud, and along the base of the boot opening were three small dome-headed black rubber buffers, one central and one at each edge, to ensure an even panel gap. Twin external chromed hinges attached the lid at its front edge, mounted through the shroud by threaded studs and nuts.

A black boot lid prop was attached to a bracket welded to the left-hand underside of the boot lid. The prop was a bent wire rod, much cheapened from the automatic sliding boot lid prop found on the four-cylinder cars. It engaged at its lower end with a hole in a bracket that was welded inside the lower left lip of the boot opening. Also screwed to this

This photograph of a rare BN6 two-seater shows the extended rear shroud area ahead of the boot lid. This was where the model differed substantially from the 2/4-seaters. The cockpit capping rails surrounding the cockpit opening can be seen, as can the two chromed hooks which engaged the rear of the tonneau cover or hood. (By courtesy of Brightwells of Leominster)

The rear Austin-Healey badging was attached to the lower right-hand corner of the boot lid. That used on the 100/6 is shown here.

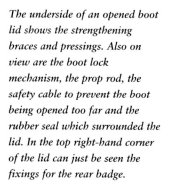

The underside of an opened boot lid shows the strengthening braces and pressings. Also on view are the boot lock mechanism, the prop rod, the safety cable to prevent the boot being opened too far and the rubber seal which surrounded the lid. In the top right-hand corner of the lid can just be seen the fixings for the rear badge.

A detail of one of the boot hinges. This car is fitted with a locking petrol cap.

An item that remained unchanged from 1953 to 1967 was the locking boot handle with its associated chromed plinth. Here it is on a 100/6.

bracket was one end of a steel cable with eyelet ends, the other end of which was attached to the rearmost stud of the left-hand hinge. This cable prevented the boot from opening too far if caught by wind and thereby breaking the hinges. When the boot prop was not in use, it fastened into a rubber clip that was attached by a large split pin to a bracket welded to the inside of the boot lid.

The boot had a chromed locking handle, set on a flared chromed plinth that was carried over from the BN1 and BN2 cars and was one item that never changed throughout the Big Healey's run. The handle had a square rod that connected with the unpainted catch mechanism; this was fixed by countersunk cross-headed screws to the underside of the boot lid, on a large double-angled bracket that was painted in the body colour. The catch on the boot lid engaged with a large chromed hook bolted to the central shroud support member on the body and located at the lower rear of the boot.

BODY FITTINGS
Bumpers, over-riders and valance panel
Rather surprisingly, bumpers and overriders continued unchanged throughout the six-cylinder Healey's 11-year production run. Not only that, but the front and rear bumpers were similar, at least externally. Both of them had a small semi-circular cut-out centrally at the edge. This should be facing downwards when fitted correctly. Bumpers were chrome plated externally, with their reverse sides being finished in silver paint.

Mounting brackets were painted black and attached with zinc-plated fixing bolts. At the rear, the four brackets (in two pairs) actually passed through the rear shroud panel, where the holes were sealed with shaped rubber grommets. The

This is how the forward end of the commonly fitted boot rack was attached to the boot hinge.

brackets were bolted to the two rear chassis extension pieces. Mounting brackets at the front, four in number, passed under the lower edge of the front shroud and were bolted direct to the chassis rails. The brackets had slotted bolt holes that gave some measure of alignment adjustment when the bumpers were being mounted. The inner front brackets were straight, culminating in a right angle where they reached the rear of the bumper to which they were bolted. The outer front brackets curved outwards to line up with the outer front bumper bolts. Chromed dome headed bumper bolts were used.

Over-riders were fitted to both front and rear bumpers, spaced from the bumper faces by shaped black plastic piping. Although basically similar in design to those on the 100s, they had a different rear profile to mate to the differently shaped bumper. They were attached by a bolt inserted from inside the bumper which engaged with a captive nut inside the over rider itself.

The great majority of six-cylinder cars had a shaped metal valance panel fitted between the front bumper and the lower front shroud. Officially called a "splash shield", this was painted in the body colour. It appears to have been purely decorative and did not quite touch the front shroud, a constant gap of roughly ½ inch being left between the rear of this panel and the shroud. For some unexplained reason, the splash shield did not appear on the early BN6 100/6 two-seaters up to chassis 4022, although it was present on the later ones and on all 3000 and BN4 100/6 models. It was attached at its front to the inside of the front bumper by the bumper bolts and its position could be adjusted along with the bumper by using the slotted holes in the bumper brackets where they were bolted to the chassis.

Radiator grille

The radiator grille on the six-cylinder cars was both wider and lower than the old 100 grille, and any echo of the old Healey cars' diamond-shaped grille had now been obliterated. The grille was oval in shape, somewhat akin to that of the 100 S racing cars. It had the Austin corporate style of crinkled horizontal chromed bars, as used on the mid-1950s Austin Cambridge and Westminster, and this type of grille sufficed for both the 100/6 and the Mark I 3000.

A two-piece finisher surrounded the horizontal bars. The top section was polished stainless steel and was much deeper than the lower section, which was chrome-plated. The top section was bolted to the grille itself and also fixed at its outer ends with screws, and the lower section was pressed over the bottom edge of the grille opening in the front shroud. The horizontal bars were fastened to three vertical supports by small copper rivets. The outer edges of the grille section were bolted to the body out of sight, by the same bolts that fixed the forward end of the air deflectors behind the grille.

The big change came with the introduction in 1961 of the Mark II 3000s, when a grille with vertical chromed bars fashioned from anodised aluminium was introduced. The bars had a noticeable change of angle just short of half-way down their length, which created a horizontal crease line across the grille. They were attached by rivets to horizontal upper and lower support rails. The Mark II grille again had separate upper and lower finisher sections, but these were different, being somewhat wider and deeper in section than those of earlier cars. Both sections were chrome plated on the Mark II grille, which was carried forward unchanged to the Mark II

The rear bumper and over-riders, like their equivalents at the front, did not change. From this angle, the number plate light up behind the bumper is invisible.

This is the standard-issue non-locking petrol cap, mounted on the right-hand side of the rear shroud. The filler was in the same place on both LHD and RHD cars.

The traditional Austin-Healey lightning flash motif was mounted in this position on the front grille. On the 100/6 the badge was as shown in the upper photograph, whereas on the 3000 Mark I the badge was as shown in the lower one. The numbers in both cases were picked out in red enamel.

Along with the new grille came a revised subsidiary grille at the front of the bonnet; this also now had vertical bars. The model designation badge was now fixed to the shroud rather than to the radiator grille and had a new design. The wing motif was still used for the main badge, but below the words Austin-Healey was a subsidiary badge stating "3000 Mark II" or "3000 Mark III" as appropriate. The hyphen between Austin and Healey, which was present on the earlier cars, had now been removed.

This is the front grille area of a 3000 Mark III. This badge bar is certainly working for its living...

The Mark II and Mark III 3000s carried this entirely different front grille which had vertical chromed bars. The grille surrounds were also somewhat wider and had a different profile. As can be seen, the grille bars were angled slightly roughly half-way down their length. This photograph also gives an excellent view of the front bumper and over-riders. These remained unchanged throughout the production run of the six-cylinder Austin-Healey.

Convertible and Mark III cars. Fixing methods also differed and involved studs, nuts and bolts.

Bonnet air intake

All six-cylinder cars had an air-intake pressing in their bonnets that gave clearance above the radiator, and this was finished at the front by a small grille made of chrome-plated brass.

Again there were two different types. On the 100/6 and Mark I 3000, the intake grille had three vertical bars linked by a single horizontal bar, whereas the Mark II and III cars had all-vertical bars in an echo of the later type of main grille. Both types had a broad chromed band running laterally across the front of the bonnet bulge pressing, just above the intake grille. This was fastened on the underside of the bonnet by studs bolted through the grille.

Body cappings

As with the 100s, shaped anodised aluminium capping rails were screwed along the tops of the doors and around the rear of the cockpit on pre-BJ7 cars. However, the capping rail above the dashboard that was found on the BN1 and BN2 cars was not retained, and the top of the dashboard was trimmed in Vynide instead.

There were two types of cockpit rear capping rail. The BN6 and BN7 two-seaters had a single-piece rail, while the 2/4-seater cars had a three-piece rail consisting of two long sections and a very short joining piece in the centre. All these rails were secured by cross-headed screws of various types.

The polished aluminium capping rail which surrounded the cockpit on the pre-Convertible cars is shown here. Also visible are a Tenax post and turn button fixing that served both the hood and the tonneau cover. The socket just behind the door edge took one of the hardtop locating pegs, and the larger socket hole with its associated polished finisher was for the hood frame. The top of one of the side screen fixing wing nuts can also be seen on the extreme right

The practice, used on the BN1/2 cars, of stamping the underside of these capping rails with the car's body number continued for the 100/6s, but seems to have died out with the arrival of the 3000s. The BJ7 and BJ8 convertibles were more fully trimmed, and needed no capping rails.

Number-plate brackets

All cars were supplied with rear number-plate backings. Home market cars also had a black front backing plate which hung below the bumper, to which it was attached by two black painted metal straps.

The rear backing plate was fixed below the bumper to the lower rear shroud area by a bracket which bolted to the shroud and spaced the plate slightly away from the body. A similar arrangement was used on North American cars. A slightly different rear arrangement was provided for cars for parts of Continental Europe and for other areas of the world, depending on local regulations.

Rear arrangements were changed for the Mark II and III convertibles, again for some markets only. On these cars, an adjustable U-shaped metal bracket positioned the rear plate and the number-plate lamp above the bumper rather than below it. This type of fitting was adopted for US-market cars in February 1966.

Badges

Badges were always fitted to the Austin-Healey's front grille. The 100/6 had the well-known Healey "lightning flash" motif, with the figure 6 added in a round medallion at the point where the flash formed a Z-shape. Both the 100 figures and the 6 medallion had red enamel detailing and background. This lightning flash badge was on the right-hand side

All Healey 3000s carried this type of rear badging. Although the hyphen in Austin-Healey had been deleted from the front badge of the Mark II and Mark III cars, at the rear it was still in use; maybe BMC simply had a large stock of rear badges to use up? This is a 1966 Mark III car.

This was the final Austin-Healey 3000 badge. On the earlier Mark III cars, the red background was properly enamelled, but on later vehicles it was apparently merely painted.

There were also several different types of screen washer jet. This is a typical example that is correct for the period.

of the grille when viewed from the front of the car.

A second badge sat above the centre of the front grille, mounted on the shroud forward of the bonnet's leading edge. This was the winged Austin-Healey badge from the 100s that Gerry Coker had reputedly designed and had made overnight after the first day of the 1952 London Motor Show. It was chromed, with the words Austin-Healey (with the hyphen) picked out in red enamel. This badge continued on the 3000 Mark I cars, but they carried a different grille badge. This used the familiar lightning flash but with the number 3000 superimposed upon it and picked out in red enamel. Grille badges were fixed by two studs projecting from their rear side, fitting into corresponding holes in the grille bars and retained by two small clips.

Badgework had to be altered to reflect the arrival of the Mark II 3000s with the new grille. The grille badge was deleted altogether, and the car was now identified at the front solely by a revised version of the winged motif badge; this had the words "Austin Healey", now without a hyphen and on a red vitreous enamel background, on a chrome plinth. Below this was a slightly smaller trapezium-shaped badge that carried the legend "3000 Mk II", again with the red

enamel background. This badge was carried onto the Mark III cars with the obvious amendment. Late in the Mark III production run, in what seems a penny-pinching move, the red vitreous enamel was deleted in favour of simple red paint.

Identification at the rear of the 100/6 cars was confined to an Austin-Healey badge fixed to the lower right-hand side of the bootlid. On all 3000s, below this was added a "lightning flash" similar to that found on the front grille of the Mark I 3000s. Again, the number 3000 was superimposed on the flash and was picked out in red. This rear badge continued along with the Austin-Healey badge right through to the end of production in December 1967. These new badges were fixed using two integral studs, each pressed through holes drilled in the bootlid and retained with push-on clips.

WINDSCREEN AND WIPERS
Windscreen
Windscreens on six-cylinder Healeys came in two types: the largely flat screen found on the BN4, BN6, BN7 and BT7 cars and the more modern, semi-wraparound type used on the convertibles. This was particularly curved at its outer ends where it bent round to meet the new quarter-lights. The somewhat eccentric folding windscreen of the 100s had gone; in truth it was of little practical use and often led to cracked glass.

Though not identical to the folding type, the screen used for the 100/6 Mark I and Mark II cars was similar, but it was supported by fixed stanchions which were painted body colour. These were cast aluminium items, and their bases were interposed between the rear edges of the front wings and shroud. They were fastened to the A-post by three heavy-duty set screws. At the base of the exposed part of the stanchions were rubber sealing pads which passed over the rearmost portion of the wing beading. At the top of each stanchion was a chromed stud which engaged with the soft top catches.

The screen frame itself was of chromed brass, screwed together at the corners with small set screws. Along its lower edge was a black rubber weather seal which pressed down onto the rear of the front shroud and which was notorious for leaking once the rubber had aged. The frame was attached to the stanchions by four screws each side.

The convertible's wraparound windscreen dispensed with separate stanchions and had a much thicker chromed surround, again with a full-width rubber seal at its base. It was attached to the A-posts by frame extensions each side that projected downwards between wing and front shroud. The outer top ends of the screen had locating pegs for the soft top catches.

Various different types of windscreen wiper arm and blade were fitted over the years, and this is a typical example. The angled spacer and hexagonal nut through which the drive spindle passed are on view. A rubber seal was fitted at the base. The rubber seal fitted at the base of the windscreen can also be seen, as can the reverse of a correct interior mirror.

All windscreens were originally laminated and were made by Triplex. Original windscreens will have a Triplex trade mark etched into their lower left-hand corner. Late Mark III cars sent to the USA were sometimes fitted with an improved "high impact" safety glass. All screen glasses were mounted to their frames using black rubber seals.

Windscreen wipers
Windscreen wipers were made by Trico, and were originally of the Rainbow type, with rubber blades in polished stainless steel holders and stainless steel arms. They were generally arranged to park on the driver's side of the vehicle. Wiper arms were mounted by push-fit onto the splined spindles that passed through the shroud to engage with the wiper rack mechanism.

To provide the required angle for the blades, the spindles passed through angled spacers mounted on the shroud. These were chromed, had a rubber seal at their bases, and were retained by a large chromed nut at their tops. Blades were generally 9in long, although both slightly longer and slightly shorter items are also found. Blades were fitted to the wiper arms on pre BJ7 cars by a hook arrangement, whereas those on BJ7s and BJ8s had a clip-in fitting.

Several details are apparent in this photograph: the windscreen frame and its rubber seal, the original type of rear view mirror, screen wash jets, wipers and arms, and through the screen can also be seen the demister vents painted to match the trim and the aluminium cockpit capping piece along the top of the door.

The distinct curve of the 3000 Convertible's windscreen shows here, in its substantial and deep chromed windscreen frame, again with a rubber seal at its base. Note the Lift-a-Dot fastening post that is fitted on the chromed finisher above the door. This engages with the front outer end of the tonneau cover. The sealing arrangements of the Convertible hood are also on view – and note the correct tiny metal finisher above the windscreen on the front corner of the hood.

The front quarter-light with its rubber seal and frame was a useful feature of the Convertible 3000. This period type of mirror, which clamps into place is a most useful addition for modern traffic conditions. As in the above picture, the screen frame, hood finisher and Lift-a-Dot post are all visible.

The windscreen stanchions on the 100/6 are properly painted to match the car's colour, as here. The stanchion was mounted on a substantial rubber sealing boot.

This side view of an Austin-Healey body shell under restoration shows the front and rear inner wing structure, and the sill and bulkhead area.

This rear three-quarter view of the same body shell shows the A- and B-posts by the door aperture, and the way the rear structure is built up. Note the rear chassis extension pieces where they pass through the boot floor. This car is a two-seater, and the spare wheel slot is visible in the rear bulkhead. Note that there is no forward end to the boot floor, as this is the point where the underside of the petrol tank performs this function. This also allows access to the tank drain plug from under the car.

This view illustrates the rear structure of the car and the boot floor. The open area at the forward end of the boot will be closed by the installation of the petrol tank. The rear chassis extension pieces can be seen projecting rearwards at eithe side of the boot floor.

WEATHER EQUIPMENT

There were four distinct types of hood used on the six-cylinder Big Healeys. The "build it yourself" hoods of the BN4, BN6, BN7 and BT7 "sidescreen" cars were of three types, one for the two-seater cars and a somewhat different one for the 2/4-seaters that came in both early and late versions. The fourth type was the civilised full convertible hood, as used on the Mark II and Mark III BJ7 and BJ8 cars with glass winding side windows.

Hood material was cloth fabric with an outer covering of Everflex vinyl as weatherproofing, and it came in three colours – black, blue or grey to tone with various paint colours as set out in the Colours section of this book. Hood rear windows were made of transparent flexible vinyl by either Vyback or Tri-lite, the maker's name being visible on the window itself. The window was seam-welded to its opening in the hood.

THE EARLY BN4 HOOD

The first series of 1956-58 BN4 cars had a complicated hood frame with three bows. These were attached to the car body on either side by short sliding channels located just to the rear of the door shut faces below the cockpit surround. The bows were connected by two flat black or grey webbing strips secured to the top of the rear two bows and to the front stretcher rail. On each side, a short "leg" clipped into a rubber receiver piece not unlike those used to retain the boot and bonnet props.

The hood material was attached to a wooden stretcher across its front edge, but this was not directly attached to the metal hood frame. The stretcher was covered with a separate piece of hood material which was tacked to it, as was the leading edge of the hood material itself. Across the outside of the stretcher at the front was attached a metal finishing strip, which had a lip that extended over the top of the windscreen frame. A foam rubber seal was glued to the underside of the stretcher, and rested on the top of the screen frame with the aim of forming a rain-proof seal when the hood front stretcher was clamped to either side of the screen frame. This clamping was achieved by a chromed over-centre catch on cither side; the catches were screwed to the stretcher and engaged with a peg on the screen stanchion. These catches

were identical to those used to secure the hood front on the BN1 and BN2 cars, although on those cars the catches were fitted externally and on the BN4 they were internal.

The rear of this first type hood was clipped to the top of the rear wing on each side with a turn-button fastener. Around the cockpit opening it was secured by a number of Tenax fasteners, which were attached to the lower edge of the hood and engaged with Tenax posts located across the rear shroud. The hood frame, painted grey like all Big Healey hood frames, dropped when folded into openings between the cockpit cappings and the inner rear quarter trim panels. The cross-bows, stretcher and hood itself folded into the space just in front of the rear cockpit capping, and the whole assembly was hidden from view by the backrest cushion of the rear seats, which folded forwards to allow the hood to drop into its well.

This photograph shows the hood of the BN4 and BT7 2/4-seater cars with its row of Tenax fasteners all around the rear edge. Although it is almost certainly a replacement hood, it is similar in style to the original with a relatively small rear window area.
(Author)

This photograph shows one of the pegs at the top of the windscreen stanchion that engage with the hooks on either side of the hood front rail.

The three transverse bows of the later BN4 and BT7 hood frame are seen here in a semi-erected position. It was not difficult to trap one's fingers whilst performing this operation.

The hood frame is seen here folded down behind the rear seat backrest. The backrest pulls forward to enable both the frame and the hood fabric itself to be stowed behind. It is rather difficult to do this neatly, as is obvious here.

THE LATER BN4 HOOD

The first hood arrangement was used on all Longbridge-built 100/6s and on those Abingdon cars built before the temporary suspension of production in April 1958. However, when the BN4 came back into production in September 1958, it had the second type of 2/4-seater hood, which was also used on the 3000 Mark I and Mark II BT7 cars.

This later hood and its associated frame were removable. The cranked side legs were now located into sockets positioned on the body at the very top of the door shut face. At car BT7-1528, the side leg frame supports were modified to be straight rather than cranked and were mounted further back into the holes on the inner wing well that also held the tonneau cover support (see later) when this was in use. To lower this hood, the frame needed to be lifted clear of the sockets and the hood material pulled clear of the frame and bows. The folded hood and frame were stored as before in the hood well behind the rear seat backrest, which again pulled forward to ease access. The toggle-type catches that latched the front of the hood to the screen stanchion pegs were different from those used with the first type of hood.

THE BN6 AND BN7 HOOD

The BN6 and BN7 two-seater cars had the third type of hood, an altogether simpler affair which had only two transverse bows rather than three. As on the BN1 and BN2 hoods, there was a collapsible cant rail on each side above the door aperture to provide a positive link between the bows and the front transverse stretcher to which the front of the hood was attached.

The hood and frame were completely removable from the car and when erected, the frame side posts located into sockets in the top of the rear quarter trim panels. Polished aluminium finishers surrounded these sockets. The bottom two inches of the support legs were covered with a cream plastic sleeve designed to protect the trim and finishers. Some adjustment of the hood tension was possible as these support legs bottoms had adjusting screws fitted.

The two-seater hood here has been removed entirely from the car, complete with its frame. The transverse header rail with inset rubber seal is visible, as are the hooks to engage the front of the hood with the pegs on the windscreen frame.

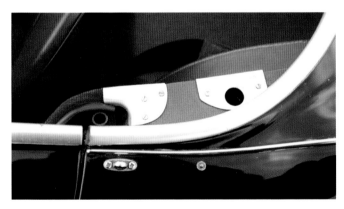

The two-seater hood frame located into these holes on either side of the rear cockpit. The forward hole seen near the door gap was there to locate the pegs from the optional hardtop. A turn button post and a Tenax post are both visible.

A different type of latch was used to secure the front of the hood to the windscreen. These latches were internally mounted and included threaded hooks at their bases which engaged with the windscreen stanchion pegs. The threaded hooks provided some measure of adjustment, which was useful for when the seal at the front of the hood grew less efficient with time. The rear fixing method for the BN6 and BN7 hoods was different again, and reverted to an arrangement similar to that used on the four-cylinder cars. A flat bar of steel, slightly curved and with tapered ends, was sewn into a pocket at the rear bottom of the hood. This pocket had two openings along its length where the steel bar was visible, and at these two points, the bar was designed to catch under two flat chromed hooks bolted to the rear shroud deck. The bolt holes allowed for a certain measure of adjustment in the positioning of the hooks so that the hood could be properly tensioned. The hood was also fixed at each rear side by a turn-button and two Tenax fasteners.

Two grey or black webbing straps connected the hood bows to the front transverse stretcher, and were held in position on the rear bow by two plates. Screws passed through the plates and webbing and into the metal bow itself. A novel idea was a looped piece of webbing fitted in the centre of the rear bow; this formed a finger-pull for use when erecting and tensioning the hood frame.

When stowed, this type of hood and its frame sat behind the seats, with the support legs fitting through holders on the rear bulkhead known as "stirrups"; they were in fact straps of trimmed metal screwed through the side and rear trim. The bases of the hood frame support legs slotted into trimmed pockets mounted on the floor outboard and to the rear of each seat.

This is one of the two chromed hooks into which the concealed steel bar at the rear of the two-seater hood engaged.

This is an original hood rear window, which carried instructions for its care in one corner.

At the centre of the front transverse header rail on this BJ8 Convertible hood is the chromed folding handle used to draw the hood over one's head.

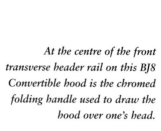

THE CONVERTIBLE HOOD

The fourth and final style of hood was the so-called Convertible type fitted to the BJ7 and BJ8 cars. This was very much improved, both in terms of weather sealing and ease of erection and stowage. Indeed, it could be raised in a few seconds by a single person sitting inside the car – a far cry from the earlier hood designs. These were best erected by two people, both outside the vehicle, and took at least two minutes to erect – a long time when a sudden thunderstorm had arrived!

This new hood had one disadvantage, which was that it no longer stowed flush with the rear deck of the car, but sat higher by several inches when folded. This did not look as

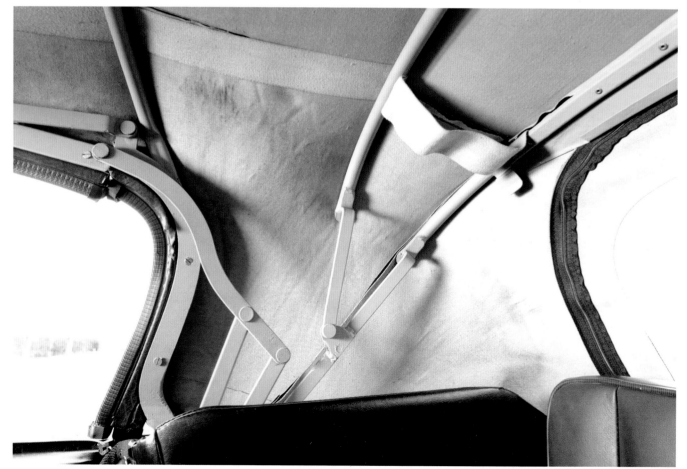

Part of the hood frame mechanism of the Convertible hood is seen here fitted to a BJ7 Mark II car. As it is a late model, the removable rear window fastened with a zip rather than toggles is correct. Note the seal and trim arrangement around the window opening.

The substantial over-centre hook that clamped the front of the Convertible hood to the windscreen frame is seen here. This hook engaged with the second hook mounted on the screen frame; the main hook was threaded and had a lock nut to allow adjustment.

neat and also restricted the rear view, particularly for shorter drivers. There is no doubt, though, that it was a timely improvement and one demanded by a mid-1960s market that was no longer prepared to endure fiddly and rattling side screens and leaky and awkward hoods. The Big Healey was almost becoming civilised!

The Convertible hood was more complex than any of the earlier types and was also permanently attached to the car. It would normally be removed only for repair, renewal or to allow a hardtop to be attached. The frame again had three transverse bows and a front stretcher, and again clipped to the windscreen stanchion pegs by chromed hook and toggle catches. In the centre of the stretcher was a chromed, loop-type handle to be used when pulling the hood over from inside the car.

The grey-painted frame itself was bolted at either side to steel pieces welded to the top front of the inner rear wheel arches behind the B-posts. Meanwhile, the rear of the hood material was permanently fixed to a rain gutter that sat under the trim which ran around the whole rear of the cockpit. Side-pieces, made of laminated wood, formed the rear part of the side window opening on each side, and a single U-shaped wooden section passed over the top of the side windows and also formed the front transverse stretcher. Rubber seals which bore on the raised side window glasses were fitted to the wooden sections around the window openings, and rubber buffers on the ends of the wood both added to the seal and prevented rattles. Again, two strips of webbing were used to ensure that the top bows retained their correct spacings.

As before, the hood material was the Everflex cloth-and-vinyl composite in black, grey or blue as appropriate, and the

When fully tensioned, the webbing of the Mark III Convertible hood is tight and the fabric fits neatly. Note the rubber and Furflex type trim around the window aperture.

This view depicts the Convertible hood in its fully folded state and shows clearly the rubber seals that were designed to keep the weather out. The hood looked rather untidy when folded, so every car was provided with a neat hood bag to cover it.

Here the hood bag is seen in position over the folded hood. It was tricky to fit neatly but it was worth the trouble, as it tidied up the appearance of the open car considerably and also stopped the folded hood frame from rattling and creaking.

This Mark III Convertible has a nicely tensioned hood which is here seen erected. The three transverse bows are quite obvious.

The hood on Peter Healey's car is known to be an original item and carries its 50 years remarkably well.

rear window was made of Vyback or Tri-lite clear plastic. An innovation was that the rear window could be dropped down and folded while the hood was still erected, to give ventilation in hot weather. On BJ7 cars up to April 1963 (body 59372), the window was secured to the hood at the top corners by toggles, but thereafter until the end of BJ8 production, it had two zip fasteners to secure it more positively.

When the BJ8 model arrived, a separate vinyl "gutter" was added with stitching to each side of the hood. This ran along the top of the window, down the rear edge of the join between window and hood, and then along the top of the chromed finisher on the top of the wing behind each door. It was fairly successful in keeping rain from penetrating into the car when stationary.

All cars came with a matching tailored vinyl hood cover which clipped over the folded hood and was secured by Tenax fasteners. This tidied the appearance of the folded hood and its mechanism, which sat somewhat proud of the rear deck. The hood cover was itself provided with a storage bag.

TONNEAU COVERS

All tonneau covers were of the same Everflex material as the hoods and, when factory supplied with a new car, matched the hood colour.

Almost all the pre-Convertible cars were supplied as standard with tonneau covers, the only exception being the very rare "standard" Mark I and Mark II 3000s. On all Convertibles the tonneau cover was an extra, as it was considered not to be as

This is the tonneau cover for the BN4 and BT7 two-seater cars. At the rear, it used the same Tenax fasteners as the hood itself. Just visible to the rear of the door is the flap with turn button that was part of the securing mechanism. The stitching for the pockets that carried the five longitudinal strengthening bars is also obvious. The tonneau support bar is in place.

necessary as before in view of the ease of raising the new hood. All Convertibles from car number 20392 had tonneau cover fittings built in, even where the optional tonneau cover had not been ordered. Before that, however, such fittings had only been supplied where the tonneau cover had been specified.

To prevent the tonneau cover flapping when it covered only the rear area, all cars had fasteners fixed to the heel-board, to which the furled cover could be clipped. Tonneau covers came with a protective bag, and a further bag was provided for stowage of the two-piece tonneau support rail if there was one.

The two-seater tonneau cover

Tonneau covers for the pre-Convertible cars were of two types, differing in length. The cover for the two-seater cars was shorter, although the forward part of both covers was the same. The two halves of the factory tonneau cover were held together by a brass zip fastener, although most later replacements had plastic zips. This allowed the passenger area to be covered when the driver drove alone, useful in winter weather when the heat from the heater was conserved under the passenger side of the cover.

Front fixings consisted of a turn-button ring at each front corner which fitted over turn-button posts attached to each side of the scuttle. A Tenax post and popper at the inner front end of the passenger's half of the cover held it in place when the driver's side was open. Near the rear of the doors, at the front end of each wing, was a further turn-button post. These engaged with turn-button rings fixed to small vinyl flaps sewn to the underside of the cover.

The two-seater cover, like its associated hood, clipped to the two flat chromed hooks described above in the section on the BN6 and BN7 hood, and mounted on the rear deck. Two short sections of flat bar were sewn into the rear of the cover in two pockets, where small gaps were left. The chromed hooks engaged with the sections of bar visible through the gaps in the underside of the fabric. Two Tenax fasteners each side attached the rear outer parts of the cover.

The 2/4-seater tonneau cover

The longer cover of the 2/4-seater cars fixed at the rear to the row of Tenax fasteners just outside the rear capping rail which doubled as rear hood securing points. The Tenax posts had tiny leather washers fitted under them to protect the paintwork.

The tonneau cover for the 2/4-seater covered a larger area unsupported, and so it had stiffeners – five metal bars sewn into pockets in the rear portion of the cover. These bars ran longitudinally, parallel to each other and are frequently omitted on cheaper, aftermarket tonneau covers. Turn buttons and flaps on the underside of the cover held the bars in place. Further support came from a transverse two-piece tube, just behind the seats, which located into holes in the tops of the rear trim quarter panels.

In this picture of the Abingdon-built BN4 2/4-seater, the hood and the back of its frame are stowed behind the rear seat backrest. Dropped into position is the transverse tonneau cover support bar.

The tonneau cover on the BN6 and BN7 two-seaters was a much simpler affair. As the rear shroud extended further forwards, no support bar was thought necessary. The cover was fastened at the rear in the same way as the two-seater hood, except that two short pieces of bar rather than one long one were used to engage the hooks on the rear shroud.

The Convertible tonneau cover was an elaborate tailored affair, shown here. A support bar was used, and when the cover was fitted correctly it looked particularly neat.

in it, roughly level with the rear line of the doors. These were to allow the seat belts to pass through the rear of the cover when they were in use if the rear half of the tonneau cover was erected. Two further, larger flaps were also sewn to the top of the cover further forward; these clipped onto lift-a-dot posts fitted below the front of the rear seats to secure the tonneau when it was folded to cover only the rear seats.

As the rear of the hood was fixed to the car and had no separate fasteners, four Tenax posts for tonneau cover fixing were added. There was one each side at the rear, and one each side just behind the chromed finishing piece just aft of the door opening. Further fasteners were added at the front. There was one each side just behind the quarter-lights, usually with lift-a-dot type fasteners, and a central one on the dash top to the passenger side of the rear view mirror. Again, a bag was supplied in which to stow what was a rather bulky item when folded. In fact, with spare wheel, battery, tonneau support rail and bag, tonneau cover and bag and wheel-changing tools, it is surprising that there was any room left in the boot for luggage!

The Convertible tonneau cover

The tonneau cover for the Convertible models covered not only the cockpit but was also tailored to include the folded hood and frame. Again covering quite a wide area, this type of tonneau cover was considered to need support. Accordingly, a two-piece tubular metal support bow was provided, which sat just behind the seats when in use. When folded, it was provided with an Armacord L-shaped storage bag with a flap and cotton ties. In practice, many owners found that the tonneau cover held up sufficiently well without the support bow and did not bother to fit it.

The cover for the Convertibles had two press-studded flaps

SIDESCREENS

The winding windows on the Convertible are covered in the Bodywork section, but the pre-Convertible cars of course had to rely on somewhat primitive sidescreens to keep the weather at bay. Of these, there are four types, although the first three types were used only on the 100/6 cars. All of them had an aluminium frame and Perspex windows.

First type of sidescreen

The first type, which quickly proved to be inadequate, were used only on the first 50 or so 100/6 cars, and probably very few examples survive today. Detailed research by Roger Moment in the USA has revealed what these sidescreens were like; I have never seen a pair myself.

They had very thin section frames and the overlap between the two side Perspex panels sloped backwards from bottom to top. Only the front panel could slide open. A stud at the forward end engaged with a chromed socket in the door and was fixed by an unusual four pointed, star-shaped chromed nut. The bracket at the rear of the sidescreen fitted over a stud on a chromed plate attached to the door panel by three countersunk chrome-plated cross-headed screws. The bracket was attached by a large, single-eared wing nut.

Second type of sidescreen

Within a matter of weeks, these thin-framed sidescreens were replaced by the second type. These are instantly recognisable by the overlap between the two side panes, which slopes forward, from bottom to top.

These sidescreens had much more substantial aluminium frames with a thicker cross-section, and the frames were

The later Convertible BJ8 tonneau cover had flaps to allow seat belts to pass through. The larger flaps shown at the forward end of the tonneau were for clipping the partially open tonneau cover down to the rear heelboard, below the rear seats, to stop the cover flapping.

made in separate sections held together with corner brackets. Again, the front Perspex panel slid open, with the back panel held firm by small separate alloy pieces attached with small cross-head screws. A bracing strut of polished alloy was added at the sidescreen's lower front corner, this being part of the front fixing bracket.

These sidescreens were attached to the doors using the same fasteners as the first type. There was also a black rubber seal which ran all along the bottom of the sidescreen, bearing onto the door top, and then ran up the leading edge to seal against the screen stanchion. This seal was fitted into a groove in the frame itself.

Third type of sidescreen

In September 1957 the third type of sidescreen arrived, used from car number 47704. The frames were altered slightly and now the front Perspex panel was fixed and the rear Perspex panel was able to slide. The overlap on the Perspex now reverted to the original design and sloped rearwards from bottom to top. Clear plastic finger-grip blocks were glued to the Perspex sliding panel, one at the inside front and the other at the outside rear.

The earlier type of brackets were replaced by a separate flat bracket at the rear and a separate bracket with a peg at the front. These brackets were bolted to the frame by chrome-plated "acorn" nuts; the nuts faced the inside on the front bracket and the outside on the rear one. The rear bracket had a rubber cushion on the inside to prevent it from rubbing the cockpit cappings. These sidescreens were attached to the car by the star-shaped nut at the front and wing nut at the rear. The rubber weather seal was the same as on the second type of sidescreen, but the inside front corner of each screen had a rubber buffer to prevent the frame rubbing against the windscreen frame.

Fourth type of sidescreen

The third type of 100/6 sidescreen was used for only eight months until the break in production in April 1958. Then yet another type of sidescreen arrived with the introduction of the BN6 two-seater. This fourth type was also used on the BN4 2/4-seater when production recommenced in September 1958. It was sufficiently satisfactory to be retained for all BN6s and also all 3000 Mark I and Mark II cars until the winding glass windows arrived in 1962.

This final design had a frame of even width all the way around, with welded rather than bracketed corners. The front Perspex panel was fixed and the rear panel could slide, the overlap again sloping rearwards from bottom to top. Mounting brackets and rubber seals were unaltered, but the same large chromed wing nuts were now used both front and rear to attach the sidescreen brackets to the doors, and the star-shaped nut had gone. These sidescreens carried the maker's name of Weathershields stamped on the inside surface of the frame.

After April 1958, this became the standard type of sidescreen for both the two-seater and the 2/4-seater. The Perspex block to assist with sliding the back part of the screen can be seen. This is an original sidescreen and there is some deterioration of the black rubber seal at its base.

The same sidescreen is seen from the other side and the fixing wing nuts are also visible. The brackets are fixed to the sidescreen frame by means of small "acorn" nuts.

Sidescreen bag

Pre-Convertible models were all supplied with a black vinyl sidescreen bag. This was unsurprisingly sidescreen-shaped, just large enough to accept both screens. There was a folding closing flap with two press studs to fasten it. The interior of the bag had a vinyl central divider to prevent the two sidescreens from scratching each other.

TOOLS AND HANDBOOK

This badge is clearly a rarity, but it is an original piece supplied with some cars purchased new from the Donald Healey Motor Company.

Here we see the majority of the tool kit supplied with the 100/6 and 3000 Mark I cars that had the wire wheel option, which explains the presence of a copper-faced wheel nut hammer. The threaded stud with the nut attached is the device to remove the front hub dust cap. Both feeler gauges are shown, as is the small valve removal tool. The jack is not present but it would have been similar to that shown in the photograph on the next page, although probably painted black. The black plastic bag is correct. (By courtesy of Roger Moment)

All six-cylinder Healeys were provided with a toolkit. As production progressed, this became increasingly basic, reflecting perhaps the sadly dwindling number of owners either prepared to do or capable of performing home maintenance.

100/6 AND 3000 MARK I

All 100/6s and Mark I 3000s were provided with a toolkit contained in a black plastic envelope-shaped bag with two plastic tie straps. The bag contained:

• A crude black screwdriver made from a single piece of bent steel rod; this doubled as a tommy-bar.

• A sparking plug spanner. This was a black tube with a plug-sized hexagon at one end, the other end being plain but for a hole through which the screwdriver was passed to act as a tommy-bar.

• A device to extract the front hub dust cap so that the bearings could be greased. It consisted of a threaded shaft, two large steel disc washers, and a nut that threaded onto the shaft.

• A zinc-grey grease gun of the plunger type, approximately 8½in long. It was almost always of Tecalemit manufacture,

although other designs may have been supplied in times of shortage.

• A combination feeler gauge comprising two blades, one sized .025in for the plugs and the other for the tappet clearance of .012in. These blades retracted into a holder to which they were pivoted.

• A further feeler gauge which doubled as a small flat screwdriver. This had pivoted to it a .015in feeler gauge for ignition contact points setting.

• A tyre valve removing tool, consisting of a small, knurled brass rod slotted at one end to fit over the tyre valve.

• For wire-wheeled cars only, there was also a Thor brand copper-faced wheel nut hammer with a wooden shaft. For cars supplied to markets where octagonal hub nuts were required, an octagonal hub nut spanner was also included. Disc-wheeled cars were provided with a bent lever to spring off the chromed hubcaps, plus a wheel nut spanner.

All cars were of course also dispatched with a lifting jack. The 100/6s and early 3000s had a screw-type jack, driven by bevel gears. The metal two-piece operating handle had a square drive peg at one end and a loop at the other end through which a tommy-bar was inserted to provide leverage. The jack was painted black and was either of Shelly or King Dick manufacture. After cars numbered BT7-10565 and BN7-10610, a ratchet-type jack was substituted, made by Shelly and painted a bright orange-red. This jack had a round handle about 18in long and came in both early and late types with detail differences. On earlier cars, the jack was stowed loose in the boot, but on Mark II cars a black webbing fixing strap was provided. This buckled the jack to one of the rear bumper fixing irons on the inside of the boot.

3000 MARK II

By the time of the Mark II 3000 in 1961 the toolkit was still supplied in the same bag but was somewhat reduced in size. Included now were only the sparking plug box spanner, a tommy-bar to operate it, and either the knock-off wheel nut hammer for wire-wheeled cars or the hubcap removing tool and wheel nut spanner for disc-wheeled cars. All other items had evaporated! These cars had the same jack and wheel-changing tools as the later Mark I 3000s.

This was the smaller tool kit found on later 3000s. This one comes from a car fitted with octagonal wire wheel hub caps, which needed the large spanner. (By courtesy of Roger Moment)

3000 MARK II CONVERTIBLE AND MARK III

The Convertible Mark II and Mark III cars were provided with a Shelly ratchet-type jack similar to that already described. Again it was finished in orange-red paint and again there were two slightly differing types. This jack was stored in the boot on the left-hand side of the fuel tank and was secured to the bumper iron with a black webbing buckled strap.

The same tool bag was still provided and now contained just the box-type plug spanner and associated tommy-bar, the two-piece jack handle and a Thor copper-faced hammer, replaced in 1964 by a Simmons lead-headed type. Again, as before, the rare disc-wheeled cars had a wheel nut spanner and a hub cap removal lever, and the cars with octagonal wheel nuts also had the appropriate octagonal spanner.

HANDBOOK

Each of the six-cylinder Big Healeys was equipped with a hard-cover "Owner's Handbook". This was given a red cover for the 100/6 models and a blue cover for the 3000s. The book was also available in several continental European languages for overseas markets.

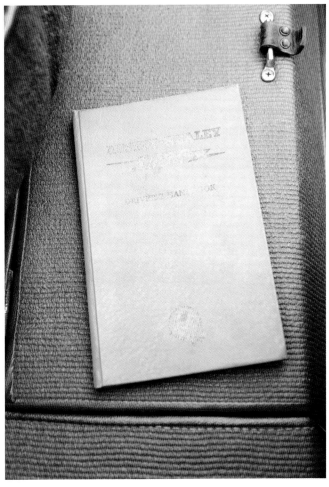

The original Drivers' Handbook supplied with each car was a hard-covered item, coloured blue in the case of 3000s and red for the 100/6s. Reproductions are available today.

An original suppliers' plate is a nice touch and only generally found on un-rebuilt cars. It could be attached to the dashboard or to the front face of the parcel shelf or, as here, to the aluminium sill finisher inside the door shut face.

OPTIONS, EXTRAS AND ACCESSORIES

A removable hard-top instantly gives to the " 100 Six " the appearance and convenience of a sports saloon.

For extremely cold climates, a fresh air heater with demisters can be neatly installed.

OPTIONAL EXTRAS

A fully comprehensive range of optional extras and alternative equipment is available for the Austin Healey " 100 Six."
Heater and demisters, radio, overdrive, hardtop, wire-spoke knock-on wheels and " Road Speed " tyres can all be fitted to order, at extra cost.

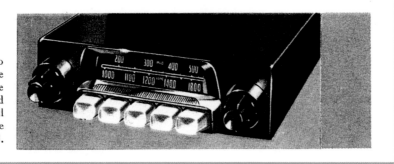

If you like a radio in your car, there is a set available which gives good reception in all countries of the world.

This section from a rare 100/6 brochure dealt somewhat cursorily with the factory-fitted options that were then available. It is interesting that the heater was said to be for "extremely cold climates"....did that include the UK, one wonders?

These items fall into three categories. The first is those options and extras that could be ordered and added to a new car at the factory; the second is "dealer fit" items added to the new car once it arrived at the selling dealership; and the third is items fitted later, either by dealers or owners, to a used example.

As a rule, the factory offerings were items that would be harder to fit to a car after it had been built, such as a heater, overdrive or wire wheels. There were exceptions, of course, such as the locking petrol cap that was a factory-fit option. Certain easily fitted items, such as boot-racks, wing mirrors and badge bars, were more usually dealer-fitted.

What follows is an alphabetical list of the factory-fitted options and extras, with comments about their availability for individual models and whether dealer fitment was available.

ACE MERCURY WHEEL DISCS
These bizarre period items were of course only available for steel disc wheels, over which they clipped. Each one had a chromed, fake knock-on hub nut superimposed on a polished aluminium wheel disc that covered the whole wheel. I have only ever seen one set, though contemporary advertisements do depict them. Amazingly, they remained on the options list until the end of production in 1967, although they must have been exceedingly rarely specified.

ADDITIONAL LIGHTS
Both fog and spot lamps appeared in the list of factory fitted options for the convertible models, although in practice they were very often dealer fitted. Lucas lights of types S700 and S576 were the most common, controlled by an auxiliary switch panel fitted just below the heater controls. It may have been possible to order extra lamps ex-factory on earlier cars too – the source material is not clear. Such lamps were usually mounted either on brackets attached via the front over-rider bolts or else directly to the valance panel between the bumper and front shroud.

ADJUSTABLE STEERING
This was a standard fitting on 100/6 cars in the first year of production. It then became an extra-cost option, although

This type of full-width badge bar was a frequently fitted accessory. It made a convenient mount for auxiliary lights as well as for badges. The lights here are a matched pair of Lucas 5½in fog and driving lamps.

The earlier type of Lucas auxiliary lights seen here had a 7in diameter; later ones had a 5½in diameter. Note the Austin-Healey club badge with its Union flag and stylised image of Warwick Castle.

towards the end of production it seems to have been fitted more often than not. Two different types of steering wheel are found, depending on whether adjustable or non-adjustable steering was fitted.

BRAKE SERVO

This became a factory option in August 1961 at car number 15104, but might have been available earlier as a dealer-fitted option. From the introduction of the Mark III model, the brake servo became a standard fitting.

CIGAR LIGHTER

This was listed as being available ex-factory, but it is very rare and not something I have ever seen. No details are available about its type or its location on the car.

HARDTOP

No factory hardtop had ever been produced for the four-cylinder BN1 and BN2 cars, but a very smart factory item was designed for the 100/6 and was available almost from the start of production, from around February 1957. It featured a wraparound panoramic rear window in Perspex, with two internal strengthening bars visible from the rear that made the window look like a three-piece affair, which it was not.

This style of hardtop featured on the well-known and successful works rally Healeys, and it is consequently always referred to as the "Works Hardtop". A new car could be ordered from the factory with this hardtop and it could of

The shorter type of badge bar is fitted to a Mark 1 3000 here. The headlights have been given stoneguards, a period accessory that carried certain "boy-racer" overtones !

The classic Works style hardtop was used on countless Big Healeys over the years, and was probably never bettered for looks and style. Designed and supplied by BMC, it was weatherproof, rigid, easy to fit and long lasting....no wonder that examples in good order are sought after and fetch large sums today.

The Donald Healey hardtops sported this neat badge, one on each side quarter.

BMC declined to supply a hardtop for the Convertible models because, they believed, the new hood gave such good weather protection that nobody would want one. Nevertheless, a moderate demand did exist, for which the Donald Healey Motor Co(and others) decided to cater. Here is the DMH Co hardtop in place on a Mark III car, complete with a Mini-van style roof vent. Note that the two rear strengthening struts are absent on this hardtop.

The front fixings of the Works hardtop engaged with the same screen pegs that the hood used, by means of this type of over-centre clip.

At the rear, this clamp held the hardtop down firmly to the edge of the cockpit surround.

course be retro-fitted. It was easily removable, although two people were needed.

The hardtop was made of fibreglass and had polished aluminium gutter rails and edging strips around the rear windows and along the base of the rear. The window was fitted using a deep rubber seal. A headlining was provided in an off-white plasticised material with an embossed pattern. The hardtop could be had ex-factory already sprayed Ivory White, Black, Colorado Red, Florida Green or Healey Blue. It was also available in primer for local finishing. The top fixed at its forward end to the screen stanchions using the same catches as the soft top. Pins also located into sockets at the top of the B-posts, while two large threaded hooks clipped under the lip of the rear shroud. Out-sized aluminium wing nuts clamped these hooks down and the whole fitted very snugly – in fact, it tightened up the feel of the car on the road quite noticeably.

Although looking superficially similar, the hardtop for the two-seater and 2/4-seater did in fact vary to take account of differing curvature of the two cars' rear shrouds, and the rear window area also differed. The two types were thus not immediately interchangeable.

These hardtops remained available for the 3000 Mark I and Mark II cars, both fitted to new cars and for later fitting. There were also several aftermarket hardtops available, the most notable of which was the fully transparent Plexidome variety. This was, in effect, a plastic bubble, and although it kept the water out, it tended to fry the occupants if the sun appeared! These tops discoloured over the years and very few of them have survived.

When the Convertible Mark II and Mark III cars arrived, no Abingdon factory hardtop was offered. This was principally because the entire soft-top and its mechanism needed removal to fit one, but in any event, there was less need for it now that the new convertible hood sealed so much better. However, a small demand did still exist, so hardtops that resembled the factory-supplied item for the 100/6 and 3000 Mark I became available from aftermarket manufacturers. Principal among these was the "works-style" hardtop offered by the Donald Healey Motor Co. Ltd itself. This looked very like the tops on the earlier cars and can be identified by a small badge set on each rear quarter-panel, carrying the Union flag and the maker's name. Interestingly, the 3000 Mark III works rally cars used these hardtops, looking very like their earlier brethren.

This was the authentic style of locking petrol cap. When ordered with a new car, it might have used the same key as the ignition, which was handy. Note the neat, retractable radio aerial positioned on the rear shroud.

HEATER

Again, the great majority of cars had this factory fitted, although it came at extra cost because it was officially an "extra". Usually, only cars supplied to consistently hot countries did not have the heater fitted, but there are instances known of even home market cars being supplied with no heater. It was probably not long before those misguided first owners were visiting their local parts department to order the retro-fit heater kit that the factory made available.

LEATHER UPHOLSTERY

Leather was standard on all cars up to and including the Mark II Convertible in 1962-63. However, the then-new Ambla upholstery became standard when the Mark III cars arrived; this was a man-made pseudo-leather.

Genuine leather upholstery remained available to order, but as an extra-cost option. However, the option was not available on North American market cars, which all had Ambla trim. So, in practice, well over 90% of deliveries had Ambla trim and leather is therefore very rarely found on Mark III cars.

LOCKING FUEL FILLER CAP

This was frequently dealer fitted, but it was available as a factory order too. It is not known definitely whether factory fitment always meant that the key to open the cap was the same as that for the ignition.

LUGGAGE RACK

A luggage rack could be mounted on the boot lid hinge pins and clamped to the trailing edge of the boot lid. The most common type of rack was arranged to hold the luggage away from the boot lid itself and level rather than at an angle, as was the case with racks of other designs. If the rack was ordered ex-factory, then a driver's side door or wing mirror (see below) was always fitted as well, because otherwise luggage on the rack would have obscured the rear view. As shown in the adjacent photograph, there was also a second type of luggage rack.

OVERDRIVE

Although the large majority of 100/6s and 3000s were ordered new with overdrive, a small percentage were not. So the factory made available a kit to enable overdrive to be retro-fitted – quite an undertaking and much more expensive than ordering it initially. It is not clear whether the kit included a change of axle

This type of boot rack carried the load level and swung up with the boot lid when it was opened. It was supplied for Healeys for many years. It had non-damaging attachment points, using the boot hinge pins and clamps on the lower edge of the bootlid. Also seen here is one of the more dramatic two-tone colour schemes that were a factory option, in this case Black over Colorado Red.

This was the other style of boot rack supplied, which carried the load on the slope. Again, it did not demand any drilling of the lid but was attached by the hinge pins and clipped over the bottom edge of the boot lid.

This was the correct position for the radio in a Mark III 3000, with the speaker above. This would be a typical "push-button" set from the mid-1960s. The wood-rim steering wheel is a nice period touch and was commonly fitted. With this wheel, the horn push and indicator switch have been able to remain as original. What appears to be a battery condition meter appears on the right-hand side of the centre console.

An extending radio aerial is here mounted on the front wing; also clear here is the polished beading between the aluminium front shroud and the steel wing.

ratio; however, the car had sufficient power to pull the higher non-overdrive axle ratio even when overdrive was added.

As mentioned earlier, there existed a "standard" model of 100/6 and early 3000 which had no overdrive, no heater, steel disc wheels and tubeless tyres. This was probably offered in order to keep the headline price down for comparison purposes, and it seems likely that few such cars were actually sold. Indeed, customers were almost certainly strongly discouraged from ordering one! However, a larger number of cars were sold with one or more of these options deleted, for all four could be ordered or deleted individually rather than as a package. Customers who took all four were presented with what was called the De Luxe model, and two-tone paint was added as well if required.

RADIO AND AERIAL

A radio could be ordered as a factory fitting on a new Healey and the factory usually supplied a Radiomobile set. Many more radios were dealer-fitted, which gave the customer a wider choice of set. On North American cars it was normal not to supply a radio ex-factory, this being left to the supplying dealership so that local conditions could be taken into account. The aerial was usually mounted either on a front wing or the rear tonneau panel.

SEAT BELTS

It was only from car number 13757 in 1961 that seat belt mountings were built in at manufacture. Belts were not supplied, but a car could be specially ordered with them fitted, although it was much more common for belts to be a dealer fitment. Mountings and belts could of course be retro-fitted to earlier cars by dealerships, and a mounting kit was

The BMC-supplied seat belts were lap-and-diagonal types, and came complete with a BMC rosette.

available from BMC.

Seat belts did not become compulsory on new cars in the UK until 1 January 1965, and in the UK it remains true that cars built prior to that date do not need belts. If they *have* been fitted, however, they must be worn. On the home market, belts were still listed and charged for as an "extra" even when their presence was obliged by law – a kind of compulsory option!

The approved seat belts were of Kangol manufacture and carried the BMC rosette. They were of the three-point mounted Magnet type. Belt mounting points were on the rear wheel arches, on each side of the prop-shaft tunnel and on the floor by the rear edge of the doors. The wheel arch mountings consisted of ⁵⁄₁₆in studs extending through the trim panels and covered with chromed dome nuts. The other mountings were eye bolts which threaded into reinforcing plates welded below the floor or prop-shaft tunnel as appropriate.

SPORTING ACCESSORIES

Other accessories could also be added by dealers, such as thicker anti-roll bars, badge bars, headlight stoneguards and wood-rimmed steering wheels. There was also a more comprehensive tool kit; as already explained, by the time of the Mark III cars the standard tool kit provided had shrunk considerably.

Interestingly, in view of the Big Healey's success both in racing and rallying, no performance-enhancing extras were offered ex-factory on new cars. There was of course the dedicated Special Tuning department based at Abingdon who were only too pleased to sell Big Healey owners some performance extras, up to and including triple Weber carburettors and racing camshafts. Indeed, even in period the 3000 could be tuned to produce almost 200bhp with reasonable reliability, albeit at a cost of terrifying fuel consumption. Special Tuning would also convert your 3000 into a replica of one of their international rally winning cars if your wallet was deep enough.

On the question of braking upgrades, the four-wheel Dunlop disc braking system available in late 1957 is described in the Brakes section. Strictly, of course, this was less an optional extra than part of what would today be called a limited edition. However, it is well established that a number of Healey 3000s also had rear disc brakes fitted, possibly from new. Whether this was an Abingdon Special Tuning modification or was done at the Donald Healey Motor Company's Warwick works is not entirely clear. Nor is it clear whether the modification could be ordered on a new car; I have not seen any evidence either way.

TONNEAU COVER

A tonneau cover was supplied as standard with all 100/6 cars even, it is thought, with those that left the factory with hardtops fitted. However, on the basic "standard" 3000 Mark I

and Mark II cars, it was not supplied and had to be ordered at extra cost. It did however come as standard on cars ordered with overdrive and/or wire wheels. The Mark II and Mark III Convertibles did not have a tonneau cover as standard equipment; it was always an extra option on these cars.

The various types of tonneau cover are described in the section on Weather Equipment.

TWO-TONE PAINT FINISH

This was usually factory applied, but there are many known instances of dealers adding a second colour to a customer's order on a new single-tone car. Two-tone paint was always at extra cost and where a car was factory ordered with a hardtop and two-tone paint, the hardtop colour usually always matched the lower body colour.

TYRE OPTIONS

The basic car was fitted with normal Dunlop tubeless cross-ply tyres, size 5.90x15. Cars ordered with either overdrive and/or wire wheels automatically got the higher speed rated Dunlop Road Speed tyres; these were still cross-ply types, however and used inner tubes.

By the early 1960s, radial tyres were becoming more popular and it became possible to order a new Healey so fitted. The factory usually supplied Dunlop SP41 tyres sized and rated 165x15HR. Some cars for France and other parts of Continental Europe may have had Michelin X radial tyres from new of similar size.

Whitewall tyres were very popular in the 1950s and 1960s, particularly in the USA. The Mark II and Mark III Convertibles could be ordered new with these fitted, but it is not clear if this is true of earlier cars. Certainly, very many 100/6 and Mark I 3000s delivered in the USA did sport whitewall tyres, but these may well have been fitted by dealers after the cars had reached their destination.

WING MIRRORS

Wing mirrors of either round or trapezoidal shape could be ordered from the factory for one or both sides.

The conventional type of wing mirror, mounted well forward on the front wings, was in truth of limited use. Mirrors mounted on the screen stanchions are a lot more effective, but nobody seems to have thought of those in the 1950s.

The other type of mirror was the so-called racing mirror of the 1960s, with the bullet shape seen here. It was rather better than the earlier style, but still not perfect for actually informing the driver about what was happening behind him.

Through the spokes of this non-original chromed wire wheel can be seen the rare Dunlop disc brake that was fitted to around 50 of the 100/6 cars in late 1957. This is a rear wheel, and part of the handbrake mechanism can also be seen.

Wire wheels were a perennially popular option. They came with the great majority of cars, especially in later years. Here is the aftermarket strengthened 72-spoke type, not available to order in period.

WIRE WHEELS

These were always an optional extra and always came with tubed tyres. The tyres were generally Dunlop Road Speeds, originally RS4 but later RS5.

The wheels themselves were also of Dunlop manufacture. Up until June 1963, they had a 48-spoke design, barely adequate for the weight of the Healey, but thereafter the stronger 60-spoked variety was supplied. The 60-spoked wheels could be had prior to this date at extra cost as a factory fitment, but it is not known when this option became available; it may have been around the time of the 3000's introduction. Certainly, for Triumph's lighter TR3A, 60-spoked wire wheels were optionally available as early as 1958.

Although Triumphs built with wire wheels were in a distinct minority, the majority of six-cylinder Healeys were built with them. As with the Triumphs, a large proportion of cars originally built with disc wheels have later had these changed for the more troublesome but racier spoked variety.

The question of chromed wire wheels is controversial. The factory was disinclined to supply chromed wire wheels because chroming the spokes weakens them, and it is thought that they never did so – not even for North American cars when such items were popular. However, there is no doubt that a number of Healeys, and particularly US deliveries, did have chromed wire wheels from new and that these were dealer fitted before the car was delivered to the customer.

Again, wire wheels could be retro-fitted and a kit was available, but it was a more involved and expensive job than on Triumph's TR.

PAINT AND COLOUR SCHEMES

The Austin-Healey lent itself particularly well to the use of Duotone colour schemes, a popular trend in the late 1950s and early 1960s. These dual-colour schemes had first become available on the 1955-56 BN2 models, and many of their attractive combinations were carried over to the six-cylinder cars.

An interesting aside is that generally the later the car, the less likely it is to have been specified in Duotone. By the time of the later Mark III 3000s in the mid-1960s, Duotone cars were fairly rare – with a single exception. This exception was the perennially popular combination of Healey Metallic Blue over Ivory White. This was such an attractive colour scheme that it remained popular even when Duotone schemes were falling out of fashion generally.

Factory-supplied hardtops introduced a further complication. As a hardtop could be requested in primer, it could be painted in any colour, which in theory could have led to some unlikely and possibly garish and/or clashing combinations.

Primrose Yellow was never a very common finish, and even rarer was the dramatic Primrose over Black... no such car could be found in the UK for photography. Primrose was deleted before the end of 1961 and not replaced by any other yellow.

The long-term favourite colour combination for the Big Healey has to be Healey Blue over Ivory White, a colour scheme available from the 1955 BN2 to the end of production in 1967.

BN4, BN6, BN7 AND BT7 COLOUR AND TRIM COMBINATIONS

Single-colour paint combinations

Paint colour	Upholstery	Seat piping	Carpet	Hood and Tonneau	Hardtop
Black	Red	Black	Red or Black	Black	Black, White or Red
Colorado Red (6)	Red	Black	Red	Black (1)	Black, white or red
	Black	Red	Black	Black	Black or Red
	Grey	Red	Red	Grey	Black, White or Red
Florida Green	Grey (2)	Green	Green	Grey or Black	White
Healey Metallic Blue	Blue	White	Blue	Blue	Black, White or Blue
Ivory White	Red	White	Red	Black	Black or White
	Black	White	Black	Black	Black or White
Pacific Green (5)	Grey	Green	Green	Grey	White or Florida Green
Primrose Yellow (5)	Black	Yellow or White	Black	Black	Black
	Yellow	Black	Black	Black	Black

Duotone paint combinations

Colours (upper colour first)	Upholstery	Seat piping	Carpet	Hood and Tonneau	Hardtop
Black/Colorado Red	Red	Black	Red or Black	Black	Black, White or Red
Black/Ivory White	Red	Black	Black	Black	Black or White
	Grey	Red	Red	Grey	Black or White
Colorado Red/Black	Red	Black	Black	Black	Black or Red
	Black	Red	Black	Black	Black or Red
	Grey	Red	Red	Black	Black or Red
Florida Green/Ivory White	Grey	Green	Green	Grey	White or Florida Green
Healey Metallic Blue/ Ivory White	Blue	White	Blue	Blue	White or Blue
Ivory White/Black	Red	White	Red	Black or Grey	Black or White
	Black	White	Black	Black	Black or White
Pacific Green/Florida Green (3) (5)	Grey	Green	Green	Grey	Black or Florida Green
Pacific Green/Ivory White (5)	Grey	Green	Green	Grey	White or Florida Green
Primrose Yellow/Black (4) (5)	Black	White	Black	Black	Black or Primrose
	Yellow	Black or Yellow	Black	Black	Black or Primrose

Notes
(1) Grey hood available as an alternative, but only on 100/6s.

(2) A few early 100/6s in Florida Green had Black trim and hoods.

(3) Not found on 3000 Mark II cars (it is believed).

(4) When this combination was used, some pieces of trim that would normally have been expected to be yellow were in fact black.

(5) Both Pacific Green and Primrose were deleted before the end of BN7 and BT7 production.

(6) Some very early BN4 Longbridge-built 100/6s were finished in the Reno Red used on BN2 models, rather than in Colorado Red.

Strangely, as it is a pleasing combination, Colorado Red over Ivory White was never an official colour scheme, although a number of cars are known to have been painted this way. (Author)

This Californian-registered 100/6 visited the UK in 2013 and displays its Florida Green over Ivory White colour scheme. Opinions about the merits of this combination are divided. (Author)

Florida Green over Ivory White was always an extremely rare combination on home market cars. However, the author caught this Mark II 3000 in the car park at Shelsley Walsh Hillclimb. (Author)

An equally rare combination on home market cars is Pacific Green over Ivory White; however, here is a very nice 3000 Mark I complete with Works-style hardtop. (Author)

BJ7 AND BJ8 CONVERTIBLE COLOUR AND TRIM COMBINATIONS

Single-colour paint combinations

Paint colour	Upholstery	Seat piping (Mark II only)	Carpet	Hood and Tonneau
Black	Red	Black	Red	Black
	Black	Red	Black	Black
British Racing Green (3)	Black	White	Black	Black
	Grey	Green	Green	Grey
Colorado Red	Red	Black	Red	Black
	Grey	Red	Red	Grey
	Black	Red	Black	Black
Dark British Racing Green (3)	Black	–	Black	Black
Florida Green (1)	Grey	Green	Green	Grey
	Grey	Green	Green	Black
Healey Metallic Blue	Blue	White	Blue	Blue
Ivory White	Red	White	Red	Black
	Black	White	Black	Black
Metallic Golden Beige (2)	Red	–	Red	Black
	Black	–	Black	Black

Duotone paint combinations

Colours (upper colour first)	Upholstery	Seat piping (Mark II only)	Carpet	Hood and Tonneau
Black/ Colorado Red	Red	Black	Red	Black
	Red	Black	Black	Black
Colorado Red/ Black	Red	Black	Black	Black
	Black	Red	Black	Black
	Grey	Red	Red	Black
	Grey	Red	Red	Grey
Florida Green/Ivory White (4)	Grey	Green	Green	Grey
	Grey	Green	Green	Black
Healey Metallic Blue/Ivory White	Blue	White	Blue	Blue
Ivory White/ Black	Red	White	Red	Black
	Red	White	Red	Grey
	Black	White	Black	Black

Notes

(1) Florida Green was discontinued sometime between September 1966 and mid-1967.

(2) Metallic Golden Beige was introduced in June 1967 and was only used on 553 cars in total.

(3) British Racing Green (Code GN25) was used only on Mark II Convertible BJ7s.
Dark British Racing Green (Code GN29) was a new and much darker shade used only on Mark III BJ8s.

(4) The rare combination of Florida Green over Ivory White was discontinued along with Florida Green at some point between September 1966 and mid-1967.

Although this Mark I 3000 is finished in very dark blue it appears black, and gives a good idea as to what a Big Healey looked like finished in the very rare black single tone finish.

This Austin publicity picture of an early Mark I 3000 BN7 two-seater shows a car in Pacific Green, a colour which in certain lights looks almost blue and which does not reproduce well photographically. Although a demonstrator car, this one had disc wheels. (By courtesy of John Wheatley)

Black over Colorado Red was much more often specified than plain black and looks a particularly dramatic combination.

Another car (or could it be the same one?) finished in Pacific Green, demonstrating how this colour can change in different lights.

PAINT COLOUR CODES

Colour name	BMC code	ICI code
Black	BK1	122
British Racing Green	GN25	8120
Colorado Red	RD2	3742
Dark British Racing Green	GN29	(Not known)
Florida Green	GN1	2997
Healey Blue	BU2	2697/2301M
Ivory (Old English) White	WT3	2379/2122
Metallic Golden Beige	BG19	3006M/2496M
Pacific Green	GN9	2659
Primrose Yellow	YL3	3011

British Racing Green over Ivory White is a further combination that was never listed as available, and yet some cars were definitely produced in this colour scheme. It is surprising that buyers were not officiallty offered this particularly pleasing arrangement.

This 1967 Phase III Mark III car carries the only new colour to be introduced during the last few years of production, named Metallic Golden Beige. It is said that only 553 cars had it, the great majority going to North America.

This late home market Mark III 3000 wears another unusual paint combination, Ivory White over Black. Although rarely specified, this combination was in fact available throughout six-cylinder Austin-Healey production.

"You can't go far wrong with a red sports car....." as they used to say, and this very nice example of the BJ7 Mark II Convertible demonstrates the fact. The photograph was taken in Devon, but it looks to the author like African Savannah in the background, albeit without any lions!

The classic Colorado Red bodywork with White works hardtop is perennially popular with its echoes of the works team rally cars, although these were usually finished in signal red.

GENERAL NOTES ABOUT COLOURS

These notes apply to all Healey 100/6s and 3000s.

(a) Ivory White was in fact the same shade as Old English White on the BN1 and BN2 cars.

(b) Colorado Red had a more orange tinge to it than the old Carmine Red on BN1s and BN2s (although the previous Reno Red had had this tinge too). As a result, the Works Rally Cars were usually finished instead in Signal Red. As a consequence of this, some production BN7s also appeared in Signal Red, presumably to special order.

(c) Duotone cars ordered as such new were first painted at Jensen's all over in the main colour, and the lower contrasting colour was then added over the main colour. The lower colour was not continued on the inside faces of the doors or across the lower part of the rear shroud, which remained in the main colour.

(d) British Racing Green was surprisingly not available officially on the any of the BN4, BN6, BN7 or BT7 cars. However, when the "works" Sebring race cars appeared in this shade in the early 1960s, some customers ordered it. It thus became a semi-official colour until it was made a regular option in 1963 on the BJ7 convertible. Quite a number of the earlier cars in fact appeared in British Racing Green, usually with black trim.

(e) The Grey upholstery, trim and hood colour referred to in the table was not a true grey, but rather a light beige colour.

(f) In these tables, any special-order "one-off" colours have been ignored. It was possible, at a cost, to order a car in an unlisted colour or colour combination. For instance, records prove that one car was supplied in Black over Pink with Pink trim! Indeed, a car could be ordered simply in primer, although this was very rare. Hardtops again could be supplied in primer, and this led to some bizarre colour combinations.

(g) Some cars were supplied as CKD (Completely Knocked Down, or kit form) vehicles to be assembled locally. These were often finished in locally supplied and therefore non-standard paint finishes.

(h) Both disc wheels and wire wheels were always finished in silver paint, sometimes called Aluminium.

(i) All cars had black boot lining material with the exception of Longbridge-built BN4 100/6s, where the material was colour coded to match the carpet colour.

(j) On Duotone cars, the colour break line was very similar, but not quite identical to that used on the Duotone BN2 100s. The lower colour was added below the swage line pressed into the wings and doors; the swage point bevel itself remained finished in the upper colour.

(k) It appears that all cars received a brown coloured metal primer at Jensen's, which covered both the body and chassis units. The primer was applied to the individual panels and shrouds separately, which were then fitted up into a car. Once this operation was complete, the assembly received the primary colour all over. No other form of rust proofing was added in manufacture, as became painfully obvious to many owners over the years.

(l) Hardtops were not officially available for the BJ7 and BJ8 convertibles, so there is no column for these in the table in this section.

(m) Mark III BJ8s did not have contrasting seat piping. Ambla-trimmed cars had piping in "imitation chrome", whereas leather-trimmed cars had piping the same colour as the trim.

IDENTIFICATION AND DATING

This section relies heavily on the work of Anders Clausager, the former archivist of the British Motor Industry Heritage Trust at Gaydon, Warwickshire. He was in a unique position during his tenure there to peruse and research the original Austin-Healey factory build records, and what follows is therefore very much thanks to him. It has not in the subsequent 25 years proved possible for any further or better work to be done on this subject and we therefore take Anders Clausager's work to be definitive.

THE 100/6 MODELS

The principal difficulty concerns those BN4 100/6 cars built at Longbridge in 1956 and 1957, because Austin's record keeping was not as good as it might have been and certainly not as good as that for the Abingdon-built cars. For instance it is impossible to tell how many 100/6 BN4s built at Longbridge had left or right hand drive (unless thousands of individual records were to be examined).

This is compounded by the fact that Austin insisted on using the same series of car or chassis numbers, albeit with a different prefix, for both Austin-Healeys and other Austin models. This makes extrapolation from the records of numbers built more difficult. Austin's habit was to use the same number for both car and engine at this time (the so-called "unified" numbering system), so all Longbridge-built 100/6s would originally have had an engine carrying the same serial number as the car. The first car or chassis number

This BN4 chassis number plate dates from 1958. The Abingdon works' serial or allocation number can just be seen stamped below the words "Made in England". Above the number plate is the separate body number plate with the batch number at top left and the individual body number at lower centre.

known to have been issued to a 100/6 was 22598, and the last number for a Longbridge car was 54285. However, this does not mean that 31687 100/6s were built there, because this number series also included other Austin products, principally Austin Westminster saloons.

Nevertheless, Austin-Healeys are always identified in the Longbridge records by their prefix of BN4, with the letter L being added to this for a left-hand-drive car and O for an overdrive car; S was used for a standard or non-overdrive car. The four-cylinder Austin-Healeys had carried the prefixes BN1 and BN2, but BN3 was allocated to a single prototype car, as was the prefix BN5. For this reason, the two-seater when it arrived became prefix BN6.

Engine numbers

Engine serial numbers were the same as the car serial numbers. They carried the prefix of 1C-H in the case of the Longbridge-only galleried-head engine; C denoted a Morris-built C-series engine and the H stood either for "high compression" or possibly for "Healey specification". It has not proved possible to decide which.

When the six-port engine arrived in late 1957, it carried the prefix of 26D, followed by the letter U on non-overdrive cars or letter R (sometimes RU) for overdrive cars. A final H was added usually before, but sometimes after, the actual serial number to denote either "high compression" or possibly "Healey specification". So a random 100/6 engine number might read 26D-R-H 60000, denoting a 2.6 litre, six-port engine with overdrive transmission and built with either "high compression" or to "Healey specification". No 100/6 engines are known to been low-compression types, but they would logically have had the letter L instead of the H, as was usual BMC practice.

Body numbers

There is more logic when it comes to numbers on the Jensen-built bodies. As they did for the BN1 and BN2 types, Jensen allocated each body two numbers. The first was a single batch number which covered a number of bodies, and the second was an individual number for each body. Fortunately this latter series number started at 1 and proceeded logically without gaps so far as is known. There are no known records

This is the original identification plate from a 3000 Mark II BN7 car built in late 1961. By this time the "unified" engine number scheme had been abandoned, and so the engine number does not appear on the plate.

The body number plate from the same BN7 car shows the body number itself; the batch number is hidden behind the pipe.

of batch numbers, but it seems that they always consisted of four figures and had numbers higher than 3000. So an example Jensen 100/6 body number could be 3456-1510, denoting that the body was part of batch number 3456 and was the 1510th 100/6 body to be built.

It appears that individual body numbers on Longbridge-built 100/6s ran to about 7100, but it is believed that only 7053 such cars were built. The 47 or so extra bodies seem to have been used on early Abingdon built 100/6s, although it is also possible that a few bodies were built as spares to be used on damaged cars. We can say therefore that the first batch of Abingdon-built cars had bodies numbered from somewhere just below 7100, and that the highest number of that batch seems to have been 8819. The second batch of Abingdon cars had bodies numbered 9001 to 11301.

The body number, with batch number, was stamped on a plate fixed to the engine side of the front bulkhead, and was also stamped on the edge of the bonnet, as it had been on the 100s. This remained true until the end of Big Healey production. On 100/6s only, it was also found stamped on the reverse of the cockpit capping rails, and on most cars it was additionally on the prop rod bracket on the bootlid and the bonnet release catch bracket.

ABINGDON-BUILT BN4 CARS

Assembly of the Healey moved to Abingdon in late 1957, and the lowest car number traced for an Abingdon-assembled car is 50759. As already noted, the highest Longbridge number was 54285, but this was because there was a considerable overlap of some weeks during which cars were being produced at both plants and also because of the saloons being produced within the same numbering series. Abingdon cars continued with the Austin unified car and engine numbering, and thus continued to be intermixed with cars of other models produced elsewhere by BMC. However, Abingdon decided to give each BN4 car what they called an allocation or serial number and these commenced at 501 and ran, it is thought, consecutively without a break.

The first of the two distinct Abingdon batches comprised cars with allocation numbers from 501 to 2441, which covered car and engine numbers 50759 to 62190 approxi-

mately. The second series, from allocation numbers 2442 to 4741, comprised cars drawn from the series of car and engine numbers between 67273 (approximately) and 77766 (approximately). Bear in mind that these series of numbers included several other types of Austin cars as well, and that the car and engine numbers were not necessarily issued in strict order – all very confusing! Anders Clausager managed to compile approximate details of the BN4 car and engine numbers issued in each calendar year, together with the approximate allocation numbers where appropriate. His findings were as follows:

| 1956 | 22598 – 32000 approx |
| 1957 | 32000 approx – 54520 approx |

(allocation numbers 501 to 829 but for Abingdon-built cars only)

1958	54500 approx – 74400 approx
	(allocation numbers 830 to 3623)
1959	74400 approx – 77766
	(allocation numbers 3624 to 4741).

As Anders remarked, the sequence of allocation numbers and/or body numbers is a more reliable guide than the car and engine numbers to the actual order in which cars were built, intermingled as they were with other Austin products. The total number of BN4 2/4-seaters built from 1956 to 1959 at both plants was 11294 cars. This includes an unknown number of CKD cars from Longbridge and 3 CKD cars from Abingdon.

Engine numbers were found low down on the left-hand side of the block, stamped on an oblong aluminium plate, rivetted to a cast-iron plinth. They were positioned near the left-hand engine mounting, seen here, and below the exhaust manifold, making them somewhat difficult to spot. This is the number from a six-port 100/6, hence the "26D" prefix. Also showing on the right is the block drain tap. (Author)

THE BN6 CARS

The Abingdon-only BN6 two-seaters again carried Austin engine numbers from the same series as the BN4s. These ran from 60044 (or possibly 60949) up to 77765, but did not share that serial number with the car identifier, so breaking with the Austin "unified number" principle. Instead, Abingdon gave BN6s a new car number series commencing at 501 and running without a break to 4650, accounting exactly for the 4150 BN6 cars built between March 1958 and March 1959. This number includes 114 CKD BN6s.

As the body was a new style, being neither a 2/4-seater BN4 type nor quite the same as the old BN1 and BN2 two-seaters, a new series of body numbers was introduced. This started from 2 and ran to 4151; body number 1 was presumably a prototype. These new body numbers were preceded by a Jensen four-figure batch number, for all Big Healey bodies emanated from that same source. Clausager gives the following calendar "year splits" for BN6 production:

1958	cars numbered 501 - 4321
1959	cars numbered 4322 – 4650

(4150 cars in total)

For Longbridge BN4 production, he gives:

1956-57 model year	5521 cars
1957-58 model year	1512 cars

(7053 cars in total).

Because of Austin's lack of detail in the records, a calendar-year, rather than a model year, split for Longbridge-built BN4s cannot be made, and nor can any split between LHD and RHD production. However, it is reasonable to assume that, as with BN1 and BN2 models before and 3000s afterwards, somewhere around 90% would have been LHD export cars.

Abingdon-built cars were better recorded and a split between LHD and RHD types is possible. There is nevertheless no differentiation in the records between LHD North American export cars and LHD cars for other export markets until the start of Mark II convertible production. Diligent research by Clausager from individual car build records has allowed this missing statistic to be calculated both for Abingdon-built BN4s and BN6s and for the pre-convertible 3000s. Tables showing these breakdowns and also numbers built for all six-cylinder Healeys will be found in this book from pages 154 onwards.

Identification plates

Identification plates carrying the car number for all 100/6s are found on the bulkhead behind the engine. The plates differ slightly between BN4s and BN6s. The body number plate (including the batch number) is usually fixed to the bulkhead very near to the car number plate. The numbers were stamped into both plates. Note that some German market cars had different plates showing also weight limits as required in that country.

Visible just below the car number plate is the allocation number plate (see photograph on page 150). The number is stamped on this and is preceded by the stamped legend "serial number". Engine numbers are stamped on a small aluminium tag with rounded ends that is riveted to a plinth low down on the left-hand side of the cylinder block.

THE 3000 MODELS

Matters took a further turn towards clarity when BMC revised their intermingled, unified numbering system. This occurred at about the same time as the 3000 was introduced. The 3000s carried car numbers in a new series commencing at 101, with the two-seaters and 2/4-seaters numbered in the same series. A letter H was put in front of the usual prefixes to denote Healey, and L was still added on LHD cars. The type numbers of the two 3000 Mark I variants were BN7 for the two-seater and BT7 for the 2/4-seater, this type numbering continuing on to the Mark II cars in 1961.

Both these and the Mark I 3000s had car number plates, body number plates and engine number plates located and styled like those on the 100/6 cars. However, the body number was now usually followed by the model code, such as BN7, BT7 and so on.

Engine numbers

3000 engine numbers had prefixes commencing with the number 29, as outlined in the Engine section, followed by one or two letters denoting the actual type of engine. These letters were RU for an overdrive equipped car or U for a non-overdrive one, followed by H for high compression or L for the very rare low-compression engine. To take a random example,

The identification plate from a 1963 BJ7 Mark II Convertible. Note the choke cable and its bracket positioned just above the plate.

Both the batch number and body number are visible on the body number plate from the same car. The car's type code, here BJ7, is anow added to the batch number as can be seen.

engine number 29E/RU/H/1234 would indicate engine number 1234 to tri-carb Mark II specification, with high compression and fitted originally to an overdrive equipped car; the E indicates the triple carburettor specification.

Each engine number series, 29D, 29E, 29F and 29K commenced at number 101 and (it is believed) ran consistently except in the case of the 29D engine fitted to Mark I 3000s. Here, confusingly, the engines were still intermixed with 29D engines fitted to Austin Westminsters, so although the series still commenced at 101, it ran to 26212; quite obviously, a good many of the engines were not fitted to Healeys, for only 12650 Mark I 3000s were built in total.

Body numbers

Body numbers commencing at 101 ran in a single series for the Mark I and Mark II cars, but the Mark II and III convertibles had a new series of body numbers commencing at 55000. It is important to realise that bodies were made in batches and were not used on cars in strict numerical order. The Convertibles were given new type codes, BJ7 and BJ8, the J indicating the Convertible body style as opposed to the N and T used for the earlier roadsters. Towards the end of the Mark III Convertible production, around June 1967, the letter U replaced L on LHD cars for North America only. Quite why this was done is unclear. Confusion with the U indicating a non-overdrive car was avoided, as that was part of the engine number rather than the car number. Finally, those same late North American export 3000s had a further letter added as a suffix to the car number, in this case a G to indicate build in the Abingdon MG factory.

Another identification plate, this time from a late BJ8 Mark III 3000 built in 1966.

Both batch and body numbers are again visible on the body number plate from the same 1966 BJ8.

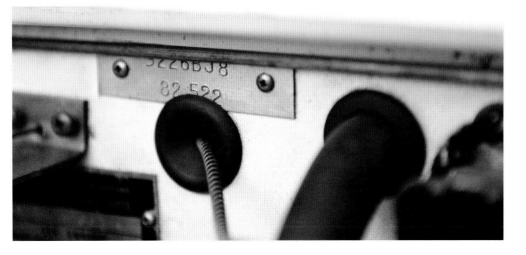

CAR NUMBERS

All Austin-Healey 3000s, irrespective of mark or body type, had their car numbers in a single series that commenced at 101 in March 1959. Anders Clausager provided a table dealing with all 3000 models, which helps to clarify matters and is reproduced here.

	Mark I 2 seater	Mark I 2/4 seater	Mark II 2 seater	Mark II 2/4 seater	Mark II convertible	Mark III convertible
Chassis no prefix	H-BN7	H-BT7	H-BN7	H-BT7	H-BJ7	H-BJ8
Car nos, first and last	186 -13734	101 -13750	13991 - 18888	13751 - 19853	17551 - 25314 (a)	25315 - 43026
Production period	Mar 59 to May 61	Mar 59 to May 61	May 61 to Mar 62	May 61 to Jun 62	May 62 to Nov 63	Oct 63 to Dec 67 (d)
Engine no prefix	29D (b)	29D (b)	29E	29E	29F 29FF	29K 29KF (c) 29KFA
Engine nos, start and finish	101 - 26212	101 - 26212	101 - 5799	101 - 5799	101 - 6188	101 - 17631
Body nos, start and finish	701 - 12763	101 - 13787	12764 - 19129	13788 - 19239	55000 – 60999 and 70000 - 70166	70200 - 87903

Notes

(a) There was an overlap between the end of Mark II (BN7 and BT7) production and the start of Mark II Convertible production. The first Mark II Convertible was built as early as January 1962 at number 17551, but series production of these cars only started in May 1962. All cars are Convertibles from number 19854 on.

(b) The 29D engine number series included a large number of Austin Westminster saloon engines as well as the Austin-Healey engines.

(c) 29FF and 29 KF engines had a special 2860cc size for export to France. Their engine number series were 29FF 101–157 and 29KF 101–399. 29 KFA engines hade the normal 2912cc size though still exported to France; this engine number series began at 29KFA 224, but the highest number is unknown.

(d) Plus the one car assembled from parts in March 1968

CAR NUMBERS BY YEARS

Anders Clausager produced a table linking Healey 3000 car numbers to calendar years, and this is reproduced below.

	BT7	BN7	BJ7	BJ8
1959	101 - 6520	186 - 6686		
1960	6521 - 13561	6831 - 13538		
1961	13562 - 17126	13539 - 17051		
1962	17127 - 19853	17052 - 18888	17551 - 21782	
1963			21783 - 25314	25315 - 25658
1964				25659 - 30532
1965				30533 - 34479
1966				34480 - 39974
1967				39975 - 43025
1968				43026

Note: The 1968 car was built up from parts after series production ceased in December 1967.

THE NUMBERS BUILT
THE AUSTIN-HEALEY 100/6

TOTALS OF 100/6 CARS BUILT

BN4s from Longbridge (including CKD cars)	7053
BN4s from Abingdon	4238
BN6s from Abingdon	4042
CKD cars from Abingdon	111

Grand total
100/6s of all types built.   **15,444**

LONGBRIDGE-BUILT CARS
All these cars were BN4 2/4-seaters.

1956-57 model year	5541
1957-58 model year	1512
Total	**7053**

Note Poor detail in the Longbridge build records makes it impossible to break down Longbridge-built 100/6s into LHD and RHD numbers, or to ascertain how many cars were delivered to which markets.

ABINGDON-BUILT CARS

Type BN4	Year	RHD home	RHD export	LHD export	LHD North American Export	Total
	1957	14	0	26	289	329
	1958	121	81	399	2190	2791
	1959	21	6	110	981	1118
Totals		156	87	535	3460	4238

Type BN6	Year	RHD home	RHD export	LHD export	LHD North American Export	Total
	1958	118	40	324	3237	3719
	1959	15	5	18	285	323
Totals		133	45	342	3522	4042

THE CKD CARS

A small number of 100/6s of both types were produced in Completely Knocked Down (CKD) form, as kits of parts for final assembly in various markets. The lack of figures available for Longbridge production makes it impossible to say how many Longbridge CKD 100/6s there were, but Anders Clausager estimates that there may have been around 175. Whatever the exact figure, the Longbridge CKD cars are included in the 7053 total above.

As records for Abingdon-built cars are much more comprehensive, we can say for certain that 111 examples were built in CKD form, all but three of which were BN6 two-seaters. Of these 111 cars, 85 RHD examples were sent to South Africa, 18 LHD examples to Mexico and 8 LHD examples to Cuba. Of the Cuban cars, five were BN6s and the other three were the only BN4 2/4-seater CKD cars from Abingdon.

This late 1957 BN4 was one of the last 100/6s built at Longbridge, and was fitted from new with Dunlop 4-wheel disc brakes. It was also one of the first cars to be built with the six-port cylinder head.

A 1958 BN4 2/4-seater, one of 4238 such cars built at the Abingdon plant. Only 156 of them were for the home market.

THE AUSTIN-HEALEY 3000

ALL ABINGDON-BUILT CARS

Type Mark I 2/4-seater (BT7)	Year	RHD home	RHD export	LHD export	LHD North America	CKD RHD	CKD LHD	Total
	1959	212	54	301	4184	5	6	4762
	1960	386	67	904	4517	30	16	5920
	1961	74	9	19	31	10	0	143
Totals		**672**	**130**	**1224**	**8732**	**45**	**22**	**10825**

Mark I 2-seater (BN7)		home	export	export	North America	RHD	LHD	
	1959	68	22	168	1422	5	6	1691
	1960	72	4	122	852	35	0	1085
	1961	17	5	12	10	5	0	49
Totals		**157**	**31**	**302**	**2284**	**45**	**6**	**2825**

Mark II 2/4-seater (BT7)		home	export	export	North America	RHD	LHD	
	1961	171	30	518	2431	5	0	3155
	1962	90	8	83	1759	0	1	1941
Totals		**261**	**38**	**601**	**4190**	**5**	**1**	**5096**

Mark II 2-seater (BN7)		home	export	export	North America	RHD	LHD	
	1961	25	2	53	134	0	0	214
	1962	9	3	4	125	0	0	141
Totals		**34**	**5**	**57**	**259**	**0**	**0**	**355**

Mark II Convertible (BJ7)		home	export	export	North America	RHD	LHD	
	1962	126	15	277	2163	0	0	2581
	1963	329	29	318	2856	0	0	3532
Totals		**455**	**44**	**595**	**5019**	**0**	**0**	**6113**

Mark III (BJ8)		home	export	export	North America	Others*		
Phase I	1963	0	0	1	343	0		344
Phase I	1964	108	7	81	850	0		1046
Phase II	1964	314	23	287	3200	4		3828
	1965	310	28	325	3281	3		3947
	1966	237	19	238	5000	1		5495
	1967	176	14	128	2733	0		3051
	1968	1	0	0	0	0		1
Totals		**1146**	**91**	**1060**	**15407**	**8**		**17712**

Note: There were no 3000 Mark III CKD cars.

* "Others" comprises seven cars built as works rally cars and one chassis allocated to the Abingdon Development Department.

122 MKM is a 1960 Mark I 3000 BT7, one of 386 such cars built that year for the home market.

The BJ7 Mark II Convertible was short-lived. There were 6113 of these "crossovers" made in 1962-63, and they are now much sought after for their combination of some of the best features from the earlier and later 3000 models.

Here is an extreme rarity – an original RHD Mark II 3000 BN7 two-seater. Only 39 were ever constructed, and even in LHD form there were only 316 more.

OVERALL PRODUCTION TOTALS

Total production of the Austin-Healey 3000
was therefore as follows:

Mark I	BT7	10825
Mark II	BT7	5096
Mark I	BN7	2825
Mark II	BN7	355
Mark II	Convertible	6113
Mark III		17,712
Grand total		**42,926**

This rare 3000 Mark I BN7 two-seater was built in late 1960, one of only 111 RHD examples built that year. There were a further 974 LHD examples.

Abingdon built the lion's share of the Big Healeys, and the figures are as follows:

	BN4	BN6	BN7 Mark I	BT 7 Mark I	BN7 Mark II	BT7 Mark II	BJ7	BJ8	Total
1957	329								329
1958	2794	3821							6615
1959	1118	329	1691	4762					7900
1960			1085	5920					7005
1961			49	143	214	3155			3561
1962				141	1941		2581		4663
1963							3532	344	3876
1964								4874	4874
1965								3947	3947
1966								5495	5495
1967								3051	3051
1968								1	1
Total	4241	4150	2825	10825	355	5096	6113	17712	51317

OVERALL PRODUCTION FOR THE BIG HEALEYS, 1953-1967

Total production of the Austin-Healey over the 15 years from the start of four-cylinder
production in mid-1953 to the end of 1967 was as follows:

Abingdon production (above)	51,317
Longbridge production of BN4s	7053
Longbridge production of BN1 and BN2 four-cylinder cars	14,614
Warwick production of very early cars, 100 S racing cars and special test cars	75
Total number of Big Healeys produced	**73,059**

More than 73,000 cars was quite an achievement for what was essentially a relatively
expensive vehicle, both to buy and to run. The Healey also proved to be an excellent
dollar earner for the UK at a time when the message was "export or die!" Survival rates
worldwide are notoriously hard to estimate, but the general opinion among the experts is
that certainly more than 20%, possibly 25% and conceivably 30% of all the cars
produced survive today in some form or other, from concours to derelict.

*A LHD 3000 Mark I which has been given the full
rally car treatment, this car has even received one of
the Abingdon type RX registration numbers.*

A total of 1146 Mark III 3000s were built for the home market, and this must be one of the most original survivors, having been cherished from new. It is owned by Donald Healey's grandson, Peter Healey.

This is a 1966 Phase III 3000 Mark III, one of 237 cars built that year for the home market. Probably no more than a handful of these were finished in this colour combination.

PRODUCTION CHANGES

The bulk of this list was compiled by Anders Clausager during his time as archivist of the British Motor Industry Heritage Trust; however, it has been augmented by research carried out in the USA by Roger Moment and in the light of additional facts which have come to light over the last 20 years or so. The number prefixes in brackets used below are:

B body number (not including the body batch number)
C car/chassis number
C/E unified car/chassis/engine number
E engine number (with appropriate prefix)
(Note that "L" prefixes for LHD cars have been omitted in most cases for clarity)

100/6

May 1956	(C) BN4-L 22598 First Longbridge-built car, LHD
June 1956	(C) BN4-22880 First Longbridge-built RHD car (B) 50 Improved sidescreens with separate brackets and sliding front panel
February 1957	(C) 35707 (LHD) and (C) 35827 (RHD) Longer front coil springs fitted to raise ride height at the front
April 1957	(E) 40501 Fully-floating gudgeon pins fitted to pistons
May 1957	(C) 41124 (RHD) and (C) 41135 (LHD) Right-hand seat and carpet modified to give more clearance to handbrake
August 1957	(C) 47184 (RHD) and (C) 47191 (LHD) Air deflector plates added behind front grille to direct air through radiator
September 1957	(C) 47703 (LHD) and (C) 47865 (RHD) Sidescreens revised; rear Perspex panel now slides instead of front one (C) 48114 (RHD) and (C) 48387 (LHD) Left-hand external locking door handle replaced with non-locking plain type as used on right-hand side
October/ November 1957	(E) 48863 on for some cars, (E) 52602 for all cars Introduction of "six-port" cylinder head with separate inlet manifold; larger valves, larger HD6 1¾in SU carburettors, higher compression ratio, solid skirt pistons (E) 48863 for all cars Clutch and brake master cylinders containing integral fluid reservoirs replaced by new (non-reservoir) cylinders with a single remotely mounted reservoir serving both brake and clutch systems
November 1957	(C/E) 50759 First Abingdon-built Austin-Healey off production line 20 November 1957 Snap-lock instead of spring-loaded ball joints to accelerator linkage rods
December 1957	(C) 52704, (B) 7320 Bulkhead panel strengthened around gearbox aperture in an attempt to eradicate scuttle shake (C/E) 54285 Last Longbridge-produced BN4 car
January 1958	(C) 54755 Windscreen assembly altered in an attempt to reduce cracking
March 1958	(C) 60413 HP type fuel pump replaced by high-capacity LCS type pump (C) BN6-501 First BN6 produced
April 1958	(C) 62190 BN4 production suspended at Abingdon temporarily
May 1958	(C) BN6-1183 Trafalgar glass screen washer bottle replaced by Tudor plastic bottle
July 1958	(C) BN6-1995 Steering gear ratio changed from 14:1 to 15:1 (C) BN6-2030 Water temperature gauge sensor moved from radiator header tank to thermostat housing
August 1958	(C) BN6-2878 Modified clutch slave cylinder Cars for Switzerland and Germany fitted with wire wheels now have octagonal rather than knock-off hub nuts

September 1958   (C) BN4-68960

BN4 production reintroduced incorporating May to August modifications outlined above; adjustable steering column now optional whereas it was formerly standard; bonnet prop moved from left-hand side to right-hand; Furflex door seals now colour coded; all boot mats now black; new hood frame introduced; re-introduced BN4s had the same sidescreens as the BN6 model

Note that although BN4-68960 was the first car actually built in this series, 16 BN4s built after it actually had lower C/E numbers from 67273 upwards

November 1958   (C) BN6-4022

Valance panel between front bumper and front shroud added to BN6 cars (this had always been fitted on BN4s)

December 1958   (C) BN4-74421, (C) BN6-4319

Locating ring added to petrol filter pipe to combat air locks

March 1959   (C) BN4-77766 and (C) BN6-4650

Last 100/6 cars made

3000

March 1959   (C) 101, (E) 29D-101

3000 model introduced, with 2912cc engine, 9.0:1 compression ratio, 10in clutch plate, revised gear ratios and uprated gears, disc brakes on front wheels, changes in badging

April 1959   (E) 29D-663

White metal engine bearings replaced by lead-indium bearings
(E) 29D-895
Hobourn-Eaton rotary vane oil pump replaced by gear-type pump

July 1959   (E) 29D-2864

Electric starting carburettor introduced instead of manual choke
(C) BN7-2276, (C) BT7-2194
Cars for North America now built with sealed beam headlights
(E) 29D-3079
Thermostat opening point lowered from 70°C (158°F) to 68°C (154°F)

November 1959   (C) BN7-5234, (C) BT7-5310

Electric starting carburettor deleted and manual choke substituted

December 1959   (C) BN7-6487, (C) BT7-6320

New radiator introduced, with 12 gills per inch instead of 10; screenwash bottle fitted with larger filler neck

February 1960   (C) 8222

Improved type of battery fixing rods (BT7 only)
(E) 29D-10544
Uprated gearbox mainshaft assembly
(E) 10897 (overdrive cars), (E) 11342 (non-overdrive cars)
Gear ratios raised, plain bushes instead of needle rollers on gearbox layshaft

March 1960   (C) BN7-9450, (C) BT7-9088

Dust covers fitted to front disc brakes of cars with disc wheels
(C) BN7-9453, (C) BT7-9090
Dust covers added to wire-wheeled cars

April 1960   (C) 9239

Swedish-market cars now fitted with asymmetrical dipping headlights

May 1960   (C) BT7-9389, (C) BN7-9453

"Bullet" type rear reflector lenses deleted on cars for the USA to comply with new legislation

June 1960   (E) 14566 (overdrive cars), (E) 14910 (non-overdrive cars)

Needle roller bearings reintroduced for gearbox layshaft
(C) BT7-10299, (C) BN7-10309
Dunlop Road Speed Tyres changed from type RS4 to RS5
(C) BT7-10303, (C) BN7-10329
Front coil spring rates revised to improve road holding
(C) BT7-10876, (C) BN7-10842
Rubber sleeve added to fuel pump to improve water-proofing

July 1960   (E) 29D-18656

Improved fast-idle mechanism for carburettors

August 1960   (E) 29D-20598

Gear lever now cranked to facilitate easier changing

December 1960   (C) 13488

Export cars (except for North America) have rear reflectors fitted on bracket attached to rear bumper
(C) 13531
Rear number plate lamp now fitted with two bulbs

January 1961   (C) 13601

Six-bladed fan now available as an option on export cars. Cars exported to Continental Europe now usually built with an extra transversely mounted rear exhaust silencer with tailpipes on the right-hand side

March 1961 (C) 13751
Introduction of 3000 Mark II models in both BT7 2/4-seater and BN7 two-seater forms; new engine number series prefixed 29E commencing at 29E-101, this engine having triple SU HS4 carburettors and re-designed camshaft; vibration damper now added to timing chain; seat belt mounting points now built into body, which has a new front grille and an air intake grille, both with vertical bars
(C) 13831
Fuel pump type changed from SU AUA72 to AUA172

May 1961 (C) 14171
Main headlight beam warning light colour changed from red to blue, but at this stage only for cars with metric speedometers
(C) 14240
Cars with metric km/h speedometers now always fitted with Centigrade temperature gauges – previously by special order

June 1961 (C) 14378
Accelerator relay shaft and lever now welded together instead of bolted

August 1961 (C) 14922
Valve spring specification improved
(C) 15104
Brake servo becomes available as an optional extra; accelerator pedal shaft lever and pedal strengthened

September 1961 (C) 15163
Cars bound for Germany and Sweden modified to meet local legislation with combined steering and ignition lock which incorporates starter switch, plus separate amber lenses front and rear for direction indicators, with body modifications to suit

November 1961 (C) BT7-15881, (C) BN7-16039
Redesigned gearbox with central rather than side gear change mechanism; new fibreglass gearbox cover, shorter speedometer cable, new brake and clutch pedal levers; carpet changed accordingly
(E) 29E-2246
New design of water pump
(E) 29E-2995
Carburettor floats now made from nylon rather than metal

January 1962 (C) BT7-17129, (C) BN7-17236
Front shock absorbers uprated
(C) BT7-17352, (C) BN7-17547
Fuel pump moved from left-hand to right-hand side at rear of car to avoid fuel vaporisation caused by exhaust heat; fuel pump now type AUA 173
(C) BJ7-17551, (B) 55000, (E) 29F-101
First Convertible built, with two HS6 SU carburettors, revised body with convertible hood, wraparound windscreen, winding glass windows, new doors incorporating quarter lights; coil

spring rates raised; 29F series engine number series
Note – production overlaps as BN7 and BT7 cars continue to be built alongside pre-production batch of BJ7 convertibles

March 1962 (C) 18764
North American export cars have new type headlamps
(C) BN7-18888
Last BN7 two-seater car produced

April 1962 (C) 19191
Steering connections now "sealed for life" non-lubricated type without grease nipples

June 1962 (C) BT7-19853
Last BT7 2/4-seater produced, being also the last Big Healey produced with detachable sidescreens
(C) BJ7-20110
One-piece rubber seal for quarter-lights
(C) BJ7-20126
Screen washer tubes increased in diameter from 3/16in to 1/4in; new pump with single outlet and revised tubing layout

August 1962 (C) BJ7-20392
All cars now fitted with tonneau fastenings even when no tonneau cover is specified

September 1962 (C) BJ7-20880
Canadian cars now equipped with towing eyes to comply with local legislation
(E) 29F-2012
New type of main bearings
(E) 29F-2269
Tecalamit oil filter design revised
(E) 29F-2286
New camshaft and outer valve springs fitted

October 1962 (E) 29FF-101, (C) BJ7-21049
Special 2860cc engine introduced for the French market cars only; this engine type also had uprated ignition suppression equipment

December 1962 (E) 29F-2592
Bellows-type thermostat replaced by wax type, set to open at 83°C (182°F)

January 1963 (E) 29F-2724
Standard spark plug fitment now Champion UN12Y which replaces previous N5 type

February 1963 (E) 29F-3563, (C) BJ7-22695
Lucas DM6A distributor replaced by 25D6 type

April 1963 (B) 59372
Toggle-release rear window in hood replaced by a zipped window

May 1963	(E) 29F-4898 9½in diameter diaphragm type clutch introduced
June 1963	(C) BJ7-24367 48-spoked wire wheels finally replaced by 60-spoked variety
August 1963	(B) 60792 Wiper motor type changed from Lucas DR2 to Lucas DR3A
October 1963	(C) BJ8-25315, (B) 70200, (E) 29K-101 Series production of 3000 Mark III commenced; new type wood dashboard with new instruments including 140mph speedometer (240kph) and electronic rev-counter; switchgear and certain controls revised; rear seat squab now hinges down to form a luggage platform; Ambla trim fitted as standard with revised pattern seats; starter switch now combined with ignition switch; screenwash bottle re-sited under bonnet as former parcel shelf deleted and replaced by locking glovebox; hinged oddments box fitted to central armrest; brake servo now standard; new type fuse box, regulator control box and uprated dynamo; longer mainshaft in gearbox and revised gear ratios; 150bhp 29K-series engine introduced, with revised camshaft, twin 2in HD8 SU carburettors, uprated valve springs; fully dualled exhaust system with four silencers and twin tail-pipes that exit on right-hand side
November 1963	(C) BJ8-25400 Brake servo air filter changed (E) 29K-279 Longer dipstick introduced, positioned higher on cylinder block to improve access
May 1964	(C) BJ8-26705 Phase II 3000 Mark III cars introduced, incorporating revised chassis at rear (dipped under axle), six leaf rear springs, addition of twin radius arms to control axle and concomitant deletion of Panhard rod, improved rear ground clearance, modified rear shock absorber arms; disc brakes modified; new "handed" front swivel assemblies; coarser threads (8 per inch) introduced for wire wheel hubs; locking door handles introduced, with push button door release; central oddments box deleted and replaced with longer armrest on central tunnel; front sidelamp lenses increased in size and all sidelamps and indicators given plastic instead of glass lenses; fans changed on cars for some export markets, with six, eight or even 16 blades in an attempt to improve cooling
August 1964	(C) BJ8-28225 Fuel pump changed to type AUF301
October 1964	(E) 29K-4108 Diaphragm clutch diameter reduced to 9in from 9½in

March 1965	(B) 76138, (C) BJ8-31336 All cars now have separate amber front and rear indicators of modernised type, plus minor bodywork changes to accommodate these; rear reflectors on all cars now fitted to rear bumper by brackets
May 1965	(C) BJ8-31931 Modified horns fitted
September 1965	(B) 78042 Headlamps now Mark X type, replacing Mark VI type; two number-plate lamps now fitted on cars for European markets (this change had occurred for German market cars from (B) 75208)
February 1966	(B) 79900 Modified licence plate bracket introduced for North American cars
March 1966	(E) 29K-10272 V-section fan belt introduced, with resulting changes to pulleys; crankshaft pulley now has built-in damper
August 1966	(B) 82776 Shape of trim liner to rear quarter modified; corner of wheel arch and floor liner section cut away
June 1967	(C) BJ8-41930 Transparent brake fluid reservoir fitted to cars for France, Holland, Belgium and Luxembourg; these cars now had a separate clutch fluid reservoir
July 1967	(C) BJ8-42039, (B) 86904 High-impact windscreen fitted to some US export cars
December 1967	(C) BJ8-43025 Last series-production BJ8 Big Healey produced on 21 December 1967
March 1968	(C) BJ8-43026 One final car assembled from parts at Abingdon; this is the last Big Healey of all

Two things that never changed throughout the six-cylinder Healey production run were the rear bumper with its over-riders and the boot handle and escutcheon.

The way for the driver to keep warm on a miserable day is to drive with the tonneau cover in this position, covering the passenger seat. This tends to keep the heater output within the cockpit.

Alternatively one could fit the snug and weatherproof hardtop......

The one disadvantage of the Convertible hood is that when folded it impedes rear view, so a mirror mounted externally on the screen frame has been added to this car. Note that the central dash-top mounted mirror cannot be seen over the folded hood.

This Phase III Mark III 3000 displays its oversize reflectors in their correct position on the outer edges of the rear bumper. With this configuration of lighting there was really nowhere else for them to go. On cars for some markets these reflectors are positioned under rather than above the bumper.

Note the transverse additional rear silencers on the Mark III car. A nice original touch on Peter Healey's Donald Healey Motor Company supplied 3000 is the appropriate Warwickshire "NX" registration.

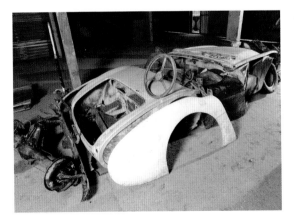

A kit of parts looking for a new chassis and owner..... Lots of work, but even Healeys in this state are well worth restoring now that no more new ones are being made.

Finally we see the ultimate development of the 3000, a "full house" replica of the final Abingdon Mark III rally cars from 1965 to 1967. Note that the exhaust system sits right under the passenger door to improve ground clearance and no doubt produce even more noise and heat than usual.....

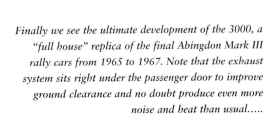